THE DARKER SIDE OF SOCIAL MEDIA

The Darker Side of Social Media: Consumer Psychology and Mental Health takes a research-based, scientific approach to examining problematic issues and outcomes that are related to social media use by consumers. Now in its second edition, it relies on psychological theories to help explain or predict problematic online behavior within the social media landscape through the lens of mental health.

With an aim to provide solutions, the authors spotlight the key issues affecting consumer well-being and mental health due to the omnipresence and overuse of social media. The book dissects the unintended consequences of too much social media use, specifying key problems like disconnection anxiety, eating disorders, online fraud, cyberbullying, the dark web, addiction, depression, self-discrepancies, and serious privacy concerns (especially impacting children or young people). The book provides grapples with mental health disorders such as anxiety, depression, self-harm, and eating disorders that can be intensified by, or correlated with, too much social media use. The authors meticulously review the various facets of the darker side of online presence and propose actionable solutions for each of the problems stated, providing scholars with a conceptual model with propositions for continued research.

This international exploration of social media is a must-read for students of marketing, advertising, and public relations, as well as scholars/managers of business, marketing, psychology, communication, management, and sociology. It will also be of interest to social media users, those navigating new media platforms, parents, policymakers, and practitioners.

Angeline Close Scheinbaum (Ph.D., The University of Georgia) is the Dan Duncan Endowed Professor of Sports Marketing and Associate Professor of Marketing at Clemson University, South Carolina, in the Wilbur O. & Ann Powers College of Business. She is an author of *Advertising & Integrated Brand Promotion* (Cengage 2022), editor of *The Dark Side of Social Media: A Consumer Psychology Perspective* (Routledge 2018), editor of *Online Consumer Behavior: Theory and Research in Social Media, Advertising and E-tail* (Routledge 2012), and co-editor of *Consumer Behavior Knowledge for Effective Sports and Event Marketing* (Routledge 2011).

THE DARKER SIDE OF SOCIAL MEDIA

Consumer Psychology and Mental Health

Second Edition

Edited by Angeline Close Scheinbaum

NEW YORK AND LONDON

Cover image: Created with Adobe Firefly by Angeline Close Scheinbaum

Second edition published 2024
by Routledge
605 Third Avenue, New York, NY 10158

and by Routledge
4 Park Square, Milton Park, Abingdon, Oxon, OX14 4RN

Routledge is an imprint of the Taylor & Francis Group, an informa business

[First edition published by Routledge 2018]

British Library Cataloguing-in-Publication Data
A catalogue record for this book is available from the British Library

Library of Congress Cataloging-in-Publication Data
Names: Scheinbaum, Angeline Close, editor.
Title: The darker side of social media : consumer psychology and mental health / Angeline Close Scheinbaum.
Description: Second edition. | New York, NY : Routledge, 2024. | Includes bibliographical references and index.
Identifiers: LCCN 2023055609 (print) | LCCN 2023055610 (ebook) | ISBN 9781032530680 (hardback) | ISBN 9781032530673 (paperback) | ISBN 9781003410058 (ebook)
Subjects: LCSH: Social media—Psychological aspects. | Branding (Marketing)—Psychological aspects. | Consumers—Psychology. | Consumer behavior.
Classification: LCC HM742 .D37 2024 (print) | LCC HM742 (ebook) | DDC 302.23/1—dc23/eng/20240201
LC record available at https://lccn.loc.gov/2023055609
LC ebook record available at https://lccn.loc.gov/2023055610

ISBN: 978-1-032-53068-0 (hbk)
ISBN: 978-1-032-53067-3 (pbk)
ISBN: 978-1-003-41005-8 (ebk)

DOI: 10.4324/9781003410058

Typeset in Sabon
by Apex CoVantage, LLC

To my children Corbyn, Barrett,
and Wesley Scheinbaum

CONTENTS

FOREWORD

Light begins where darkness ends

The publication of *The Dark Side of Social Media: A Consumer Psychology Perspective* in 2018 (Scheinbaum, 2018) represented an important milestone in understanding how social media involvement can lead to unexpected consumer psychology consequences, both positive and negative. In particular, it focused on the "dark side" outcomes associated with social media usage, providing a more balanced assessment than most contemporary scholarly research of what it means for both consumers and society as a whole.

Fast-forward to 2024. The list of troubling consequences associated with social media misuse (and abuse) has expanded, and their severity has grown. In response, Angeline Close Scheinbaum has assembled this new, and altogether darker, compilation of chapters that aims to identify, understand, illuminate, and address the negative effects of social media, particularly on consumer well-being and mental health. Given the expanding nature of problems (well documented in the introductory chapter with Angeline Close Scheinbaum and Betul Dayan) that are exacerbated through social media presence and usage, the book's focus on finding actionable solutions to these challenges is both valuable and timely.

As Pitt (2018) observed in his preface to the first *Dark Side of Social Media* book, "most of us love technology, and social media is no exception . . . because we feel that it gives us freedom, choice and control." However, this freedom carries with it the responsibility to consider more carefully the consequences of statements and actions. This is true not just for individual social media users but also for firms, marketers, and policymakers. The *Darker* book that you are now reading emphasizes the nature of these consequences and clarifies the burden of responsibility for all of us. In doing so, it provides a powerful lens through which the bifurcated nature of social media can be evaluated. This is useful in pointing to potential solutions at both the individual and institutional levels of society.

The fundamental challenge in undertaking such change is that eliminating the darker consequences can also adversely affect the positive aspects of social exchange. For example, Chapter 4 describes a set of "dark personality traits" that are accentuated in the anonymous confines of the "dark web." The dark web is notorious for its facilitation of illegal transactions (e.g., drugs; see Thomaz, 2020; Martin, 2014), yet it also embraces "a libertarian, hacker ethos" where users can "utilize 'anonymity-granting technologies' to protect their privacy from government agencies, political opponents, trolls, [and] data hungry organizations" (Thomaz et al., 2020).

As such, privacy is an important theme, one explored in this book through a focus on several burgeoning topics, including the recognition that the need for children's privacy is a critical consideration underlying adolescent well-being. Similarly, the explosion of artificial intelligence (AI) within social media has the potential to adversely affect consumer privacy, as described in Chapter 7. However, at the same time, "consumers are frequently willing to exchange their own privacy for personalized offerings." For example, consumers often exchange personal information (e.g., photos, location) to obtain a social media account. This complex trade-off between personalization and privacy is known as the "personalization paradox" (Thomaz et al., 2020).

These two examples point to the dual nature of social media use and underscore the need for meaningful interventions/policies that consider both the benefits and costs related to social media use or overuse. The fact that these benefits (and costs) vary across groups within the market makes the determination of appropriate solutions quite complex. And in some cases, solutions are neither readily available nor enforceable. For example, dark web participants can be physically located anywhere in the world, so local laws are not necessarily enforceable.

On the other hand, we cannot just ignore our growing concerns about social media either. This book provides a valuable framework for recognizing, thinking about, and then responding to its darker aspects. This will likely involve working with collaborators from diverse backgrounds that include criminology, economics, sociology, and computer science. Doing so will help us heed the clarion call to address some of the darker sides of social media voiced in these pages. The proposed solutions encourage more responsible social media use, seeking to minimize its darkest elements while illuminating the more positive aspects.

John Hulland
The University of Georgia

References

Martin, J. (2014). *Drugs on the dark net: How cryptomarkets are transforming the global trade in illicit drugs*. Palgrave Macmillan.

Pitt, L. (2018). Foreword: The dark side of social media. In Angeline Close Scheinbaum (Ed.) *The dark side of social media: A consumer psychology perspective* (pp. 20–22). Routledge.

Scheinbaum, A. C. (2018). *The dark side of social media: A consumer psychology perspective*. Routledge.

Thomaz, F. (2020). The digital and physical footprint of dark net market. *Journal of International Marketing*, *28*(1), 66–80.

Thomaz, F., Salge, C., Karahanna, E., & Hulland, J. (2020). Learning from the dark web: Leveraging conversational agents in the era of hyper-privacy to enhance marketing. *Journal of the Academy of Marketing Science*, *48*(1), 43–63.

ABOUT THE EDITOR

Angeline Close Scheinbaum (Ph.D., The University of Georgia) is the Dan Duncan Endowed Professor in Sports Marketing and Associate Professor of Marketing at Clemson University. She is an expert in the dark side of social media, consumer psychology, integrated brand promotion, and sponsorship/experiential marketing in contexts of sports and social media/online consumer behavior. Her research is often based in 15 plus years of industry and research funding experience working in sports marketing with event sponsors such as Dodge, Ford, Volkswagen, Toyota, College of Southern Nevada, Shell, Lexus, Suzuki, Mazda, USA Cycling, and AT&T. Dr. Scheinbaum has published in *Journal of Academy of Marketing Science*, *Journal of Business Research*, *Journal of Advertising*, *Journal of Advertising Research*, and *European Journal of Marketing*. She is an author or editor of the following books: *Advertising & Integrated Brand Promotion*, *Consumer Behavior Knowledge for Effective Sports and Event Marketing*, *Online Consumer Behavior: Theory and Research in Social Media, Advertising & E-Tail*, and *The Dark Side of Social Media: A Consumer Psychology Perspective*. Dr. Scheinbaum's research has won awards such as the American Marketing Association Sports SIG Paper of the Year and The Academy of Marketing Science's DeLozier Best Conference Paper Award. Professor Scheinbaum integrates research and industry experience in the classroom. She has taught many different courses, ranging from undergraduate to doctoral, and has experience mentoring and publishing with doctoral students. She serves on the Editorial Review Boards for journals such as *Journal of the Academy of Marketing Science*, *Journal of Advertising*, *Journal of Advertising Research*, and *Journal of Business Research*. She also has

a long-standing commitment to service with the American Marketing Association and the Academy of Marketing Science, where she served as VP Membership and Director of Social Media. She is also an active member of the Association for Consumer Research. Prior to Clemson, she served The University of Texas at Austin as Associate Professor at The Stan Richards School of Advertising & Public Relations at The Moody College of Communication at Texas.

ABOUT THE CONTRIBUTORS

Tor Wallin Andreassen (Ph.D., Stockholm University) is a professor of innovation at the Norwegian School of Economics (NHH). He was previously the director for The Center for Service Innovation (CSI) and Digital Innovations for Sustainable Growth (DIG) at NHH. He is the founder of The Norwegian Customer Satisfaction Barometer (BI), the Norwegian Innovation Index (NHH), and The Innovation Index Coalition (IIC). He has published numerous articles in leading journals, received several awards, including H. Paul Root/Marketing Science Institute Award, which recognizes *the Journal of Marketing* article that made the most significant contribution to the advancement of the practice of marketing within the calendar year. Andreassen has published nine books on the topics service, relations, innovations, and value creation.

Laura F. Bright (Ph.D., The University of Texas at Austin) is the Associate Director and Associate Professor of media analytics in the Stan Richards School of Advertising and Public Relations at the University of Texas at Austin. Laura's research focuses on consumer behavior within social media as related to privacy, digital well-being, and analytics. Her work has been published in the *Journal of Advertising*, *Journal of Current Issues in Research and Advertising*, the *Journal of Interactive Advertising*, *Computers in Human Behavior*, the *Journal of Marketing Communication*, *Psychology & Marketing*, and *Internet Research*, among others. She has been Associate Editor for the *Journal of Interactive Advertising* and serves on the editorial review boards for the *Journal of Advertising* and other leading journals.

Madison K. Brown (BS, BA, The University of Texas at Austin) is a recent graduate who is preparing for a career in law. During her time in Texas, Madison was a participant in the honors programs. She studied abroad in Paris, where she participated in the Contemporary Global Challenges in Paris program. Madison served as the vice president of the Texas chapter of the NAACP for two years, Communications Director on the Student Government executive board, and vice president of the Black Honors Student Association. She was also a member of the Texas Sweetheart spirit group as well as a legacy member of the Delta Xi chapter of the Alpha Kappa Alpha sorority incorporated.

Betul Dayan (BS, Koc University) is a master's degree student studying marketing at Clemson University. She holds a bachelor's degree in business administration with a minor in psychology. Her research interests are consumer and brand behavior, consumer and social psychology, social media marketing, and cross-cultural and diversity management. She has experience doing research with a marketing Professor at Koc University on consumer and brand behavior, analyzing consumer reactions to brand decisions.

Alexandra M. Doorey is a Senior Brand Marketing Strategist at Mr. Cooper Group in Dallas, Texas. She holds an M.A. in Advertising from the University of Texas at Austin, where she also received bachelor degrees in Public Relations, B.S. and Plan II Honors, B.A. Her research focuses on investigating consumer behavior and strategic marketing management, with a particular emphasis in exploring digital media, marketing, governmental regulation, and privacy, and has appeared in Computers in Human Behavior and marketing and communication conferences, including the American Marketing Association. Research topics include mobile marketing and the social and psychological antecedents of user engagement, data-driven advertising personalization, consumer information privacy concerns, data regulation, and e-commerce.

Matthew S. Eastin (Ph.D., Michigan State University) is a professor at the Stan Richards School of Advertising and Public Relations, Moody College of Communication, The University of Texas at Austin. He is a Jim and Mary Pat Nelson Chair, B2B analytics, and is the Co-Director for the Nelson Center for Brand & Demand Analytics. His research utilizes information processing as a central mechanism to new media engagement, knowledge acquisition, and persuasion.

Bob M. Fennis (Ph.D., Utrecht University, the Netherlands) is a professor of consumer psychology at the University of Groningen, the Netherlands. His research interests sit at the interface of marketing and psychology and include persuasion, social influence, consumer self-regulation, nudging and heuristics, consumer health and well-being, and food-related decision-making. His research has been published in top journals in the field, including the *Journal of Consumer Research, Journal of Consumer Psychology, Journal of Personality and Social Psychology, International Journal of Research in Marketing, and Journal of Experimental Social Psychology*. His research has received funding from the Dutch Research Council (NWO) and the Netherlands Organisation for Health Research and Development (ZONMW).

Anjala Krishen (Ph.D., Virginia Polytechnic Institute and State University) is the Mel Larson Endowed Chair of Marketing, a professor of marketing and international business (MIB), and Department Chair of MIB at the Lee Business School. Previously, she served as the Director of the MBA program for the college and successfully navigated the MBA program's transition online and into a hybrid format during the pandemic. Anjala has over 75 published journal papers. Her research spans three sub-disciplines of consumer behavior: advertising and retailing, interactive e-marketing and information processing, and marketing pedagogy. She has received research and teaching awards, including the UNLV Foundation Distinguished Teaching award, the Barrick Scholar Award, and the Scholarship of Teaching and Learning Award.

Line Lervik-Olsen (Ph.D., BI Norwegian Business School) is a professor of marketing at BI Norwegian Business School. She is affiliated with the Digital Innovation for Sustainable Growth center at the Norwegian School of Economics and is one of the developers of the Norwegian Innovation Index. Her research interests are within service and strategic marketing with a focus on service innovation, customer satisfaction, customer loyalty, and sustainability.

Jiemin Looi (Ph.D., The University of Texas at Austin) is an assistant professor at Hong Kong Baptist University's School of Communication. Her research evaluates how opinion leaders, media messages, and technological affordances on digital interfaces shape consumers' knowledge, attitudes, and behaviors. Jiemin's work also examines the determinants of public opinion and knowledge gaps regarding novel and controversial technologies, such as artificial intelligence, nanotechnology, and nuclear energy. Jiemin was awarded the Graduate Research Fellowship for early-career researchers from the Social Science Research Council in Singapore. Her papers have also won awards from the International Communication Association (ICA), Association for Education in Journalism & Mass Communication (AEJMC), and American Academy of Advertising (AAA). She has also published extensively in journals such as *Public Understanding of Science*, *Energy Policy*, *Energy Research & Social Science*, and *Environmental Communication*.

Monica Mendini (Ph.D., Università della Svizzera Italiana) is Lecturer-researcher in marketing at the Department of Business Economics, Health and Social Care of the University of Applied Sciences and Arts of Southern Switzerland. Dr. Mendini is the reference person for the marketing, communication, and consumer behavior sector at the competence center for Management and Entrepreneurship. Her research focuses on consumer behavior, with reference to consumer-brand relationships, cause-marketing, design thinking, extended reality technologies, and consumer well-being. Her work has been presented to prestigious international conferences (e.g., ACR, AMA Winter and Summer, EMAC, and EURAM) and published in the *Journal of Business Research*, *Journal of Consumer Behaviour*, *Qualitative Market Research*, *Journal of Consumer Marketing*, and *Marketing Education Review and Organizational Dynamics*.

Prashant Mishra (Ph.D., Devi Ahilya University, Indore) is Professor of marketing and Dean at School of Business Management, NMIMS University. Prior to the current assignment, he was also associated with IIM Calcutta (on leave) as Professor of marketing. His research interests include sales and marketing processes, consumer psychology, digital marketing, and sustainability. His work has been published in journals such as *Journal of Advertising, AMS Review, Journal of Business Ethics, Journal of Business and Industrial Marketing, Marketing Intelligence and Planning, Journal of Strategic Marketing, and Australasian Marketing Journal.*

Ashesh Mukherjee (Ph.D., The University of Texas at Austin) focuses on marketing communications, word-of-mouth, online behavior, and prosocial behavior. In his research on marketing communications, Dr. Mukherjee has studied topics such as the use of humor in advertising, the use of scarcity in advertising, and the advertising of high technology products. In his research on word-of-mouth, Dr. Mukherjee has studied the impact of product advisors on consumer decision-making. Dr. Mukherjee examines methods to increase charitable donations and environmental conscious behaviors among consumers. His research has been published in the *Journal of Consumer Research*, *Journal of Consumer Psychology*, *Journal of Advertising*, *Psychology & Marketing, and Marketing Letters*, and he has presented his work at academic conferences such as the Association for Consumer Research and Society for Consumer Psychology. Dr. Mukherjee's research has been funded by grants from the Social Sciences and

Humanities Research Council of Canada (SSHRC) and has been reported in media outlets such as *The Economist*.

Samveg Patel (Ph.D., Kadi Sarva Vishwavidyalaya, Gujarat, India) is an associate professor and Area Chairperson, Finance, in School of Business Management at Narsee Monjee Institute of Management Studies (NMIMS), Mumbai, India. He serves as a knowledge partner to Vivek Financial Focus Ltd, which is a stock broking firm registered with BSE, NSE, and NSDL. He does provide need-based customized consultancy services to various financial intermediaries (stock brokers, investment advisers, research analyst) across India. He has more than a decade of academic and corporate experience. Prior to joining NIMMS, he had worked at Goa Institute of Management, Sanquelim, Goa and S K Patel Institute of Management and Computer Studies, Gandhinagar, Gujarat. He has taught as visiting faculty at top B-schools across India. He has published and presented several research papers in reputed national and international journals and conferences.

Paula C. Peter (Ph.D., Virginia Polytechnic Institute and State University) is a professor of marketing at San Diego State University (SDSU) where she has taught for the past 15 years at the undergraduate (consumer behavior and integrated marketing communications) and graduate level (product innovation management). Her research interests are on psychological consequences of new technologies as they may facilitate (or not) user experiences (UX). With a particular focus on consumer well-being and sustainability, she explores the role of emotions and cognitions as they contribute to consumer decision making. Her most recent work has looked at positives and negatives of Instagram and how extended realities might contribute to alternative food consumptions. Dr. Peter's research has been published in journals such as *Journal of Service Research*, *Journal of Public Policy and Marketing*, *Journal of Business Research*, *Marketing Theory*, *Journal of Marketing Management*, *Journal of Marketing Education*, *Journal of Consumer Affairs*, *Journal of Consumer Marketing*, *Journal of Research for Consumers*, and *Journal of Applied Social Psychology*.

Kathrynn R. Pounders (Ph.D., Louisiana State University) is an associate professor at The University of Texas at Austin. Her research focuses on consumer behavior at the intersection of persuasion and consumer well-being. She examines how emotions, motivation, and identity interact to influence consumer attitudes, beliefs, and behaviors. Her research investigates information processing as well as social and psychological factors to understand consumer response to media, marketing, and messaging. She also explores gender, identity, and branding. She has been published in top journals in the field, including the *Journal of Marketing, the Journal of Academy of Marketing Science, Journal of Advertising, Journal of Business Research, Journal of Advertising Research, International Journal of Advertising, Journal of Current Issues and Research in Advertising, Psychology & Marketing, Journal of Health Communication*, and *the Journal of Health Psychology*.

Arani Roy (Ph.D., McGill University) is an assistant professor in the Marketing Department at the Indian School of Business. His research interest is in the area of self-discrepancies. Specifically, his research explores how feelings of not having enough resources and control in life affect an individual's decision-making. He is interested in exploring the impact of self-discrepancies on relevant consumption contexts, such as privacy behavior, local consumption likelihood, and subscription choices. His teaching interests are brand management, consumer behavior, principles of marketing, and digital and social media marketing. He has previously taught the Principles of Marketing course at McGill University. At ISB, Professor Roy teaches brand management.

Neha Sadhotra (Fellow Program in Management, Indian Institute of Management Lucknow) is an assistant professor of marketing and Program Chairperson, MBA HealthCare Management in School of Business Management at Narsee Monjee Institute of Management Studies (NMIMS), Mumbai, India. She is a fellow in marketing from IIM Lucknow. She has worked as a consultant for Coir Board, India; Ministry of MSME, Government of India; and Pawan Hans Limited. She is the recipient of the Liam Glynn Research Award by Center for Services Leadership, Arizona State University. Her research is related to understanding different stakeholder's perspectives on implementation of Service Robotics. Her recent engagements have been with Marketing Executives from Dr Reddy's Laboratories Ltd., GSK, Larsen & Toubro, VFS, APOTEX, Elecon, and Everest.

Angeline Close Scheinbaum (Ph.D., The University of Georgia) is the Dan Duncan Endowed Professor in Sports Marketing and Associate Professor of Marketing at Clemson University. Professor Scheinbaum is an expert in the dark side of social media, consumer psychology, integrated brand promotion, and sponsorship/experiential marketing in contexts of sports and social media/online consumer behavior. She is also the editor of this book.

Asma Sifaoui (MA, University of Minnesota) is a Ph.D. student, Stan Richards School of Advertising and Public Relations, Moody College of

Communication, The University of Texas at Austin. Her research looks at the intersection of advertising technology and privacy.

Kristen L. Sussman (Ph.D., University of Texas at Austin) leverages her expertise in native and third-party social media platforms to connect, monitor, and assess consumer behaviors. Her research focuses on the impact of artificial intelligence (AI) and aims to uncover the relationship between advancements in generative AI and media effects, consumer behavior, and social network engagement. She established and successfully operated her own social media marketing agency called Social Distillery from 2011 to 2019. Notable clients include Facebook (now Meta), Dairy Queen, Chuy's Restaurants, Micro Focus (now HPE), Spredfast (now Khoros), Farm Credit Bank of Texas, Jive Software, KVUE-TV, among others. Sussman has been published in the *Journal of Research in Interactive Marketing*, *International Journal of Advertising*, *Journal of Digital & Social Media Marketing*, and *Journal of Marketing Development and Competitiveness*.

Gary B. Wilcox (Ph.D., Michigan State University) is the John A. Beck Centennial Professor in Communication in the Stan Richards School of Advertising & Public Relations, Moody College of Communication, The University of Texas at Austin. His most recent interests include marketing mix modeling, unstructured data analysis, and advertising's impact on alcohol products and brands.

Qin Zeng (BA, San Diego State University) is currently enrolled in the graduate program in applied psychology at New York University. She has a bachelor's degree with a major in psychology and a minor in marketing from San Diego State University (SDSU). During her studies, she focused on understanding consumer behavior and in particular the role of Instagram in influencing Gen-Z consumers.

PART 1

Mental Health and Dire Consequences

Addiction, Cyberbullying, Depression, Self-Harm, and Social Media

Part 1 is the broadest section, as it entails an overview of potentially devastating consequences that could relate to social media use. A first wide-ranging topic to consider with respect to mental health and social media use is the potential dire consequences of unhealthy, toxic, or overuse of social media. Chapter 1 (Scheinbaum and Dayan) offers an overview of the topic of the darker side of social media from a mental health/consumer well-being lens. In this chapter, the authors review literature on the following topics as they relate to social media: addiction to social media, eating disorders, anxiety/depression, suicides, cyberbullying, doomscrolling, negative self-comparisons, privacy for children, and privacy with artificial intelligence.

1. The Darker Side of Social Media for Consumer Psychology and Mental Health: A Framework and Research Directions

   Angeline Close Scheinbaum and Betul Dayan

Chapter 2 (Lervik-Olsen, Fennis, and Andreassen) examines addiction/addictive social media use. As addiction to phones, technology, and/or social media is becoming more prevalent, the authors explain the individual differences and societal or cultural factors that may impact people to compulsively use social media or even become addicted to it, much like other drugs such as caffeine or even alcohol where the person has urges and

DOI: 10.4324/9781003410058-1

needs to fulfill their fix. As the authors note, some unfortunately seem to be always logged on to a social account.

2. Compulsive Social Media Use and Disconnection Anxiety: Predictors and Markers of Compulsive and Addictive Social Media Consumption

   Line Lervik-Olsen, Bob M. Fennis, and Tor Wallin Andreassen

1

THE DARKER SIDE OF SOCIAL MEDIA FOR CONSUMER PSYCHOLOGY AND MENTAL HEALTH

A Framework and Research Directions

Angeline Close Scheinbaum and Betul Dayan

Introduction: The Darker Side of Social Media and Mental Health

Importance of Topic

This chapter and the corresponding book are dire and crucial because the vast majority of scholarly research in the domain of social media features it as a marketing, business, and communication tool for individuals to connect. For example, the future of social media in marketing is often strategic and discussed for brand-building or sales purposes (Appel et al., 2020). Most of the extant research notes the bright side of social media, such as easy communication, staying in touch with prior acquaintances, having readily available information, and efficient engagement with groups. However, it is paramount to also consider the darker side of social media with respect to people's mental health and well-being. Shockingly, 41.5% of people self-report that they have depression and anxiety; this is the highest incidence of all time in the United States according to the Centers for Disease Control (Vahratian et al., 2021).

Motivation to Provide Solutions to the Dark Side of Social Media

Mr. Kumar is someone who knows the dark side of social media all too well, and he, among others, is a motivating force to bring awareness and solutions to the dark side of social media. Mr. Kumar is a father who lost his only son Manav as a consequence of social media–based cybercrime. He shares his story of cyberbullying and suicide in his working book that

DOI: 10.4324/9781003410058-2

is in progress *One Last Jump*. Bravo to Mr. Kumar for being brave and vulnerable to share his family's story, pain, loss, and ideas with the world in his related book. Hopefully, readers will take his story (and the other cases that will be presented in this book) to heart and be part of solutions.

When he finished his book, he contacted me last year because he had read my book *The Dark Side of Social Media: A Consumer Psychology Perspective*. He asked that I share some research-based perspectives and offer some solutions to the issues triggered by social media. Mr. Kumar's late son Manav suffered immensely from cyberbullying, which acted as a catalyst to take his life. The death of a child is something no parent should ever have to go through. In terms of stress in the psychological sense, it is consistently scored as one of the most, if not the most, difficult things a person would ever have to cope with. It is unimaginable that he lost his only son for one, but at the hands of such nefarious actions carried out through social media makes it even more tragic. It is impossible to relate to what Mr. Kumar, his family, and his community in India are going through, as well as to relate to the losses that many families and communities have had and continue to have. Hence, this book and chapter focus on awareness, information, and solutions.

As such, another motivation for this book is the dire importance of advocating for youth and adolescents who may feel pressured or uncomfortable in the social media space. Being a parent is already the best and most difficult job in the world, so worrying about children's safety in the social media space makes things harder with a digital footprint. Parents, unfortunately, cannot trust that social media platforms will always take the appropriate measures to help overcome social media's dark side. These motivations drive the objectives stated next.

Aim and Objectives of the Chapter and the Corresponding Book

Our aim is broadly to offer suggestions of avenues of future research so that corrective steps are taken to help solve some problems instigated by social media. We hope to bring awareness to the misunderstood impact of social media on human behavior and present it with cases in an empathetic manner. We hope to research concerns that many people know about, but only a few are brave enough to research in a systematic way. More specifically, the objective of this chapter (and the corresponding book) is fourfold:

1) The main objective is to educate and *bring societal awareness* about the darker side of social media for consumers and mental health. In doing so, we acknowledge that a balanced perspective of the pros and cons

of social media is important to examine. Here, we focus mainly on the cons from a darker side lens in order to supplement the literature on the benefits of social media.

2) The second objective is to specify and *illuminate key problems* for consumer well-being and mental health that are intensified by social media presence and usage.
3) The third, and perhaps most important, aim is to *suggest actionable solutions* to the problems stated in each chapter. In doing so, it is our sincere aim to bring comfort to the afflicted. We strive to come from a lens of empathy, compassion, and understanding to social media users who are hurting or suffering.
4) The fourth and final aim is to *provide scholars with future research directions* to expand and extend the research provided in this book. Our intention is to spark interest among scholars on this darker side topic and to provide them with specific research questions to explore in their own thesis, dissertation, journal article, or book.

To be clear, we are not claiming that mental health disorders are caused directly by social media use or presence. Generally speaking, these tend to be individual differences rooted in genetics, life experiences such as trauma, and their living environment. Even without any social media use or presence, many people suffer from these afflictions—especially stress. That said, we believe (based on our own experience as long-term social media users and as academics) that some aspects of social media are toxic for mental health and consumer well-being. In some respects, it is the social media platform itself—its structure, orientation, and algorithms—that is concerning or problematic (Petrescu & Krishen, 2020).

Yet, at the same time, it is other social media users that cause or intensify specific issues. We understand that people may tend to be cruel, mean, heartless, malicious, vindictive, hateful, and hurtful when hiding behind a screen or social media platform. For example, while bullying in face-to-face situations occurs in life, when the bullying is done on a social media page or private message, it may be even more detrimental because there may be a broader audience and a long-term digital footprint. In other words, the cyberbullying evidence may stay on the Internet for years and may haunt the victim forever.

The Duality of Social Media

While this chapter and book largely focus on the cons of social media with respect to mental health, we acknowledge that there are many pros to social media. This duality of social media is complex. In fact, the authors of this chapter are both active social media users across multiple different platforms like millions of others worldwide. We fully acknowledge the benefits and a positive aspect to social media as well—such as bringing old friends together again, finding like-minded online communities, and current information. The term "digital native" refers to someone who has been online and/or on social media since school. Many may remember how social media got started and one of the first social media platforms called MySpace. Everyone who used MySpace got their first friend request from "Tom," who was everyone's first social media friend on that platform. Around the same time, many college students got access to Facebook (now Meta) when one required a college email address to join Facebook. At the start of the rise of social media, it was more positive, intriguing, and novel. It seemed like the best communication tool to entertain, inform, and connect. The social media connections back then (early 2000s) were a sincere and fun way to connect online with past or current classmates. When social media was first gaining acceptance in society, it seemed like a safe space. Early Facebook and MySpace were reminiscent of a high school or college yearbook; the exception was that it was internet-based, interactive, informative, and innovative. Those are clearly pros to social media use. In addition, social media use can be entertaining and a coping mechanism for boredom. Social media can fulfill one's need for cognition. It can fill a void for fulfilling one's curiosity and desire for learning. On a broad scale, social media can strengthen in-person or virtual communities by way of bringing like-minded individuals together. Just as social media brings people together, unfortunately, it can also bring people with different views apart, which is intensified by the divided political spectrum in the United States and across the globe. Now almost 20 years later since social media became popular, we have seriously begun to question the indirect or direct effects of its use.

As seen in Figure 1.1, Americans especially perceive more negative effects of social media and internet use on social well-being (Pew Research, 2023). This research shows a negative impact of social media and the internet index by country. Unsurprisingly, the United States leads this index followed by the Netherlands, Hungary, Belgium, Spain, Canada, and France, each having a negative impact of a social media index of 2.5 or higher.

The dark side of social media is especially salient because many of the social media platforms and internet companies are based in the United States (Meta/Facebook, X/Twitter, Google). Futhermore, there are massive differences in U.S. political ideologies and American's desire to persuade others to hold their political or social views. According to Pew Research (2022a), Americans perceive three things that are distinct from social media and American culture. These three aspects are depicted in Figure 1.2. First, 64% of Americans say that social media has been a bad thing for democracy—far

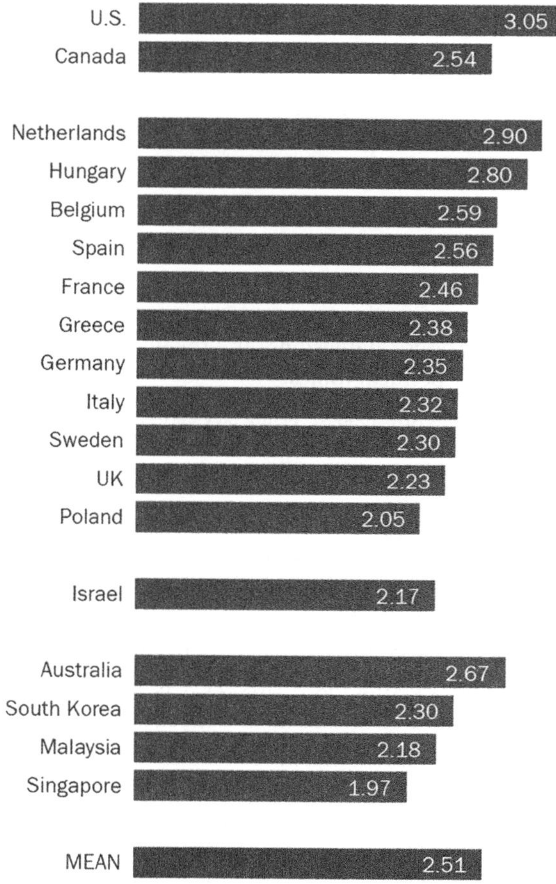

FIGURE 1.1 Americans especially perceive the darker side of social media relative to many other nations.

Credit: Social media seen as mostly good for democracy across many nations, but the United States is a major outlier. Pew Research Center, Washington, D.C. (December 6, 2022)

More Americans see negative political impact of the internet and social media, compared with other countries surveyed

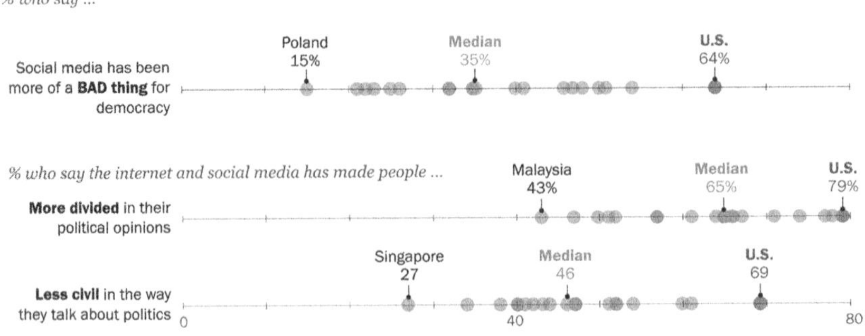

Note: Results for Japan on Q31f are excluded due to a translation error.
Source: Spring 2022 Global Attitudes Survey. Q28. Q31b & Q31f.
"Social Media Seen as Mostly Good for Democracy Across Many Nations, But U.S. is a Major Outlier"
PEW RESEARCH CENTER

FIGURE 1.2 The U.S. is especially prone to having social media impacting our democracy, political divisions, and the way we speak to each other civilly about political topics.

Credit: Social media seen as mostly good for democracy across many nations, but the United States is a major outlier. Pew Research Center, Washington, D.C. (December 6, 2022)

exceeding the thresholds of other countries (the median is only 35%). Second, 79% of consumers say that social media and the Internet have made people more divided in their political opinions, which is statistically well above the overall median of 65%. Third, more Americans say that the way we treat each other on social media is less civilized with respect to how we discuss politics on social media platforms (Pew Research, 2022a).

Many of these effects and unintended consequences are spelled out in the precursor to this book, *The Dark Side of Social Media: A Consumer Psychology Perspective* (Scheinbaum, 2017). That book includes topics such as trolling, digital drama, cyberbullying, eating disorders, addiction, and political unrest. Given the relative youth of social media as an industry, we have little to no precedence of how to understand these issues and solve them in human history. It is thus a paramount time in history, and we are responsible for addressing it. *One Last Jump* is an inspirational, self-help, and motivational book, with applicable lessons to whoever reads it—especially fellow parents in this social media era. Besides parents, youth, investigating agencies, police, and lawmakers will find it useful and worth reflecting upon to help work together and facilitate solutions.

Roadmap of This Chapter and the Book

The organization of this conceptual chapter is as follows. We begin with an overview summary of mental health afflictions and issues intensified by social media. Next, we briefly overview some specific mental health afflictions and issues that we and other scholars believe are *intensified* by social media use, overuse, or presence.

Mental Health Afflictions and Issues Intensified by Social Media

There are negative consequences to consumers and users of social media with respect to mental health (Keles, McCrae, & Grealish, 2020). Specifically, the mental health–related afflictions or issues that most relate to social media use are (a) anxiety, (b) depression, (c) loneliness and isolation, (d) stress, and (e) body image issues/eating disorders (Berryman et al., 2018). Thus, we briefly introduce these potential negative outcomes of too much or toxic social media use.

Anxiety. Defined, "anxiety is an emotion characterized by feelings of tension, worried thoughts, and physical changes like increased blood pressure" (American Psychological Association, 2022a). Social media presence, use, and overuse or addiction can fuel consumers who are prone to be anxious in general to be even more anxious (Keles, McCrae, & Grealish, 2020). Consumers have desires to be self-fulfilled, and in social media spaces, others' display of successes likely spark feelings of anxiousness.

For example, these displayed successes may be in the areas of sharing images or stories of their seemingly perfect personal life. They may also be in the category of showing off wealth, in that social media users may show off their expensive vacations, luxury purchases, or visits to glamorous services or experiences (e.g., spas, sporting events, events with celebrities). These shared "successes" may also be in the work setting. While we most associate sharing professional successes on the social media platform LinkedIn, many people use social media to share their career success (e.g., promotions, publications, graduate school acceptances, and other work-related accolades). Each of these three settings of consumer posts and sharing (personal life, showing off wealth, and professional achievements) can trigger feelings of anxiety, inferiority, and/or inadequacy. While social media use is supposed to bring individuals together and keep people connected, it unfortunately can heighten or elevate anxiety for those who are predisposed. Sadly, anxiety could be related to "Facebook Depression" that is associated with overuse (Berryman et al., 2018).

Depression. Depression is defined as "extreme sadness or despair that lasts more than days. It interferes with the activities of daily life and can cause physical symptoms such as pain, weight loss or gain, sleeping pattern disruptions, or lack of energy" (American Psychological Association, 2022b). Depression is linked with overuse of social media or the wrong type of social media, especially for those who are predisposed to depression or situational depression (Cataldo et al., 2021). Those who are prone to depression or who are already depressed may cling to social media for comfort, togetherness, and community. Yet, as literature suggests, social media use or overuse may intensify the symptoms of depression or be correlated with psychological disorders in young people (Cataldo et al., 2021; Seabrook et al., 2016). Research has shown a relationship between social media use and feeling depressed and isolated in a variety of studies. For example, a comprehensive review paper (Seabrook et al., 2016) found correlations between "negative online interactions" with both depression and anxiety. The links between social media use and depression exist in both young populations (i.e., children, adolescents, and college students) and adult populations. Much of the focus however is on young people (Cataldo et al., 2021).

The literature on depression and social media use has specifically focused on young people, namely children, adolescents, and undergraduate college students. These are important vulnerable populations to study because social media is purportedly intended for adults. Being an adult in the social media era is difficult enough. Now consider the effects and indirect or direct consequences social media brings to youth. This is in part due to children's undeveloped brains, overall lack of life experience, and difficulties in putting small things in perspective. One telling analogy is that social media is like an infinite playground where all the strangers are invited and wearing masks—if they are even real people at all. Youth are indeed a vulnerable population, and their access to (with relative ease) social media is a catalyst for and accelerator of many influences that adolescents have. Although to obtain a social media account, people should be of a certain age (e.g., one must be 13 years old to have an account with Meta), children have the ability to find ways to join social media platforms at young ages and bypass parental consent.

This is problematic, as children's brains are not fully developed, and they do not have the cognitive and or emotional abilities to process the information seen on social media. They also do not yet have the appropriate decision-making capabilities to discern how and what to post, comment on, and reply to. As such, the exposure of certain social media content as well as any backlash from posting or commenting can bring unwanted feelings and depressive symptoms in young children. Scholars have summarized research on how depression is linked with social media use among young individuals (Marino et al., 2018; McCrae et al., 2017). A systematic literature review evaluating the correlation between social media use and children's/adolescent's symptoms of depression shows a significant relationship between social media use among young people and depression (McCrae et al., 2017). For other evidence, a meta-analysis study showed correlations between Facebook (now Meta) use and mental distress in adolescents and young adolescents (Marino et al., 2018). Other meta-analyses have also reported significant correlations among social media use by young individuals and clinical depression (Best et al., 2014).

The literature on social media and depressive symptoms is also prevalent in adult populations who use social media. For instance, greater social media use is greatly associated with higher depressive symptoms (Cunningham et al., 2021). For many, these depressive symptoms include oversleeping, changes in eating habits, loss of interest in activities one generally enjoys, and reduced motivation to engage with others. The research has also focused on older adults (65 years old or older) with respect to social media use and depressive symptoms. More social media use was associated with more symptoms of depression among older people (Cotten et al., 2022). However, not all studies have found significant correlations between social media use frequency and depression or anxiety in older populations. For instance, Hofer and Hargittai (2021) did not find any significant effects in this population. Thus, we are careful again to claim that social media causes depression or specific depressive symptoms. However, based on the growing research that often finds significant relationships between increased social media use and depression in certain populations (young people, adults, and older adults), it is a problem to be concerned about. As depression for many is related to symptoms of wanting to be alone, isolation from activities one generally enjoys, and withdrawal from others in person, we now focus on the aspects of loneliness and social isolation with respect to social media use.

Loneliness and social isolation. Social media use and overuse are also associated with people feeling lonely and socially isolated, despite being "connected" with others online. There is a strong connection between loneliness and social isolation (Berezan et al., 2020). Berezan et al. (2020) relied on self-determination theory to examine Facebook users' hedonic well-being; specifically, they examined social media users with low (vs. high) levels of perceived loneliness. As this study was during the global pandemic, there were external influences that contributed to the many people who were reporting feeling lonely. Using a random sample of Facebook users (n=323) to do fuzzy-set qualitative comparative analyses, they compared the two groups (high vs. low loneliness individuals). For the high loneliness group, they found that interactivity and feelings of belonging are the psychological needs that bring consumers to Facebook (Berezan et al., 2020). At the same time, interactivity and belonging were the rewards for individuals who were in the low loneliness group. Again, this study was in the realm of severe social exclusion.

The social media activity can also trigger the fear of missing out (FOMO) on individuals. This FOMO typically stems from the fear that they are being excluded from experiences gained when they are not on social media. As people's lives and their activities are constantly displayed in their feeds, it is normal for one to experience this FOMO on enjoyment. There were several findings that found direct or indirect positive relationships between FOMO and stress. A decrease in FOMO explains why in some studies where participants were asked to refrain from social media for a few days a reduction in stress was found (Wolfers & Utz, 2022).

Stress. Stress is another factor to consider with respect to mental health, well-being, and social media. Research indicates that stress and social media are correlated in various ways. For instance, scholars have relied on student samples to investigate cycles of toxic social media use and their correlation with satisfaction with life, depression, anxiety, and stress among university students. In their longitudinal study, they found a positive relationship between problematic social media use and insomnia levels and suicide-related outcomes (i.e., thoughts and behavioral attempts up to a year) (Brailovskaia et al., 2021). For the experimental studies, reduction of time spent on social media or quitting social media resulted in an increase in satisfaction with life and reduced symptoms of anxiety and depression (Hunt et al., 2018; Brailovskaia et al., 2021) as well as problematic social media use (Brailovskaia et al., 2021). It has been hypothesized that intense use of social media and problematic social media use can negatively impact one's mental health (Brailovskaia et al., 2021).

Eating disorders and body image issues. Research has also associated social media use with eating disorders: anorexia, bulimia, and orthorexia. These afflictions, which also impact boys and men, are most commonly written on for female populations. One of the major tie-ins to social media is the fitspiration movement, which refers to the use of social media for inspiration to be fit, thin, or have a trim figure (Marks et al., 2020). This is a very popular movement on social media, as "fitspo" has been tagged in over 66 million posts, while "fitspiration" has had almost 18 million posts or tags on Instagram (Marks et al., 2020). Experimental and correlational studies alike show evidence that social media users viewing "fitspiration" content are negatively affected by harmful behaviors related to body image and eating disorders.

Specifically, the association between social media consumers engaging with fitspiration posts on Instagram and body image worries were examined among young adult women from in the United States and Australia (Marks et al., 2020). They found a significant correlation with body image issues and a nonsignificant correlation with overall Instagram use in general (Marks et al., 2020). Other scholars confirm that social media users are fixate and establish excess importance on appearance; in turn, this sparks negative self-appraisals (Tiggemann & Zaccardo, 2015). Undeniably, publicity of fitspiration content impacts people's self-interpretation and as a result can influence eating disorder behaviors (Marks et al., 2020). Rounsefell et al. (2020) conducted a literature review and found a correlation among social media activity, body image, and food decisions by adults in good health.

Similarly, eating disorder risk is higher for adolescents in places where an internalization of idealized body types is present (McCabe & Ricciardelli, 2005). Social media promotes an ideal body type by frequently displaying the images on many social media feeds and there is a positive correlation between exposure to fitness-focused Instagram content and eating disorder risk (Holland & Tiggemann, 2017). This may occur via orthorexia, an obsession with eating "clean" food and in turn, one suffers from anxiety and guilt or shame if they consume unhealthy food (Turner & Lefevre, 2017). Among those with social media accounts, 54% use the accounts to find and exchange food-related experiences, while 42% use social media for guidance on food-related matters (The Hartman Group, 2014). These statistics suggest a potential link between social networking content and susceptibility to eating disorders (Haines & Neumark-Sztainer, 2006). According to a randomized controlled trial, Coates et al. (2019), kids who viewed influencers with unhealthy snacks had a significantly increased caloric intake (448.3 kcals; P =.001) and unhealthy snack intake (388.8 kcals; P =.001) compared to those who saw influencers of nonfood products (357.1 and 292.2 kcals). They also found that children's watching of influencers with healthy snacks did not significantly cause them to eat the snacks (Coates et al. 2019).

While eating disorders can arise when one spends too much time with toxic social media content, social media activity can also increase the likelihood of one experiencing negative body image symptoms. A study of adults examined the relationship between social media activity and body dissatisfaction. After controlling for many factors (i.e., body dissatisfaction, social media use, gender, age, body mass index, ethnicity, relationship status, socioeconomic status), more social media activity predicted more body image dissatisfaction. In turn, more body dissatisfaction predicted higher social media use among men and women (Marques et al., 2022).

These issues might be happening more often than we think where social media is creating detrimental effects on people's lives. Alyssandra, a 15-year-old, accounts for her experiences developing an eating disorder after she found herself addicted to social media. Alyssandra states: "I said I got an eating disorder, and at first when I started the recovery I didn't really think that social media impacted it," Alyssandra says. "And so, I think during the end of eating disorder recovery therapy, I started to realize: social media's the problem. And I'm honestly, like, addicted to social media. Which is not good! Like, every day I find myself on TikTok or Instagram almost every hour during the school day (McCarthy, 2023).

Young teenagers are some of the most vulnerable people to the dark side of social media, especially when the influencers and celebrities they follow constantly photoshop their features in order to look like the "ideal" body type. One of the many examples of this is the case of Livvy Dunne, a popular collegiate gymnast who amassed 4.4 million followers and has been getting backlash for photoshopping her Instagram pictures. With the powerful influence that she has on millions of people, most of whom are college women, critics took to comment on her pictures saying she was creating unrealistic expectations for young girls who are more likely to be influenced by what they see online. Young girls start to idealize these body types when they are scrolling through social media platforms and all they see are influencers photoshopping their bodies, making themselves appear slimmer, and using filters to perfect their skin.

For an extreme case of the social media-based glamourization of eating disorders, a notorious example is that of Eugenia Cooney, a social media influencer. Eugenia is a YouTuber, streamer, and Instagram creator who posts content about various topics such as a gothic lifestyle and cosplay skills. She began livestreaming and then created a YouTube channel dedicated to her gothic style. While her content does not mention or even refer to her dangerously low weight/apparent anorexia, she has received backlash for promoting eating disorders (Herz, 2023). The comments section of her content is full of social media users discussing the shocking thinness and concern about what appears to be a potentially life-threatening disorder. As such, Eugenia is calling for social media users to show concern in a kinder way (Herz, 2023).

Conceptual Framework: The Darker Side of Social Media

In Figure 1.3, we offer a conceptual framework for the darker side of social media. The framework begins by noting key control variables, such as one's preexisting mental health afflictions. Other important controls entail the length of the active time spent in social media sessions as well as a longer-term measure of how many years one has been a dedicated social media consumer. Further, the time of day or night is an important control. Lastly, demographics such as a social media user's age, race, socioeconomic status, and income are important control variables or factors to consider in explaining or predicting negative outcomes relating to or stemming from social media use.

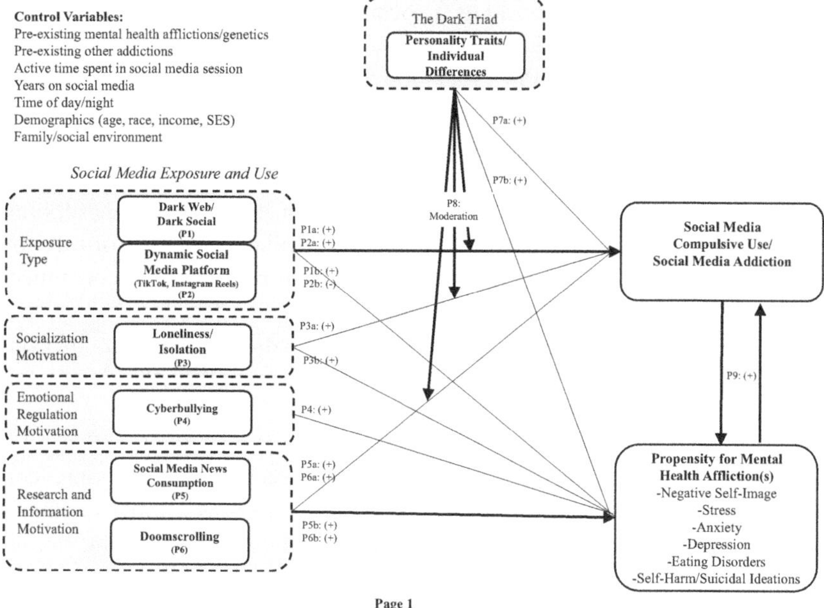

FIGURE 1.3 A conceptal model of Social Media Compulsive Use and Social Media Addiction and Propensity for Social Media-Based Mental Health Afflictions (Close Scheinbaum and Dayan, 2024).

The factors or independent variables of interest are grounded in consumer motivations and consumer psychology—both cognitive and social. For instance, we consider the social media exposure type. Consumers who go on the dark web, especially in dark social media ("Dark Social" as it is referred to in Chapter 4 of this book) may especially be linked to social media overuse, addiction, or various mental health–related afflictions such as negative self-image, anxiety, depression, eating disorders, self-harm, or unfortunately even suicide. This may be intensified when the consumer has dark triad personality traits of Machiavellianism, psychopathy, and/or narcissism.

A second consideration of consumers' social media exposure type entails which social media platform they choose to use and use regularly. Based on secondary research and impending lawsuits against TikTok (such as in Utah), we propose that the algorithms used in TikTok as well as in Instagram/Meta are especially troublesome with respect to social media compulsive use or social media addiction compared to other platforms that are less visual (X/Twitter or LinkedIn, for instance). This may especially be true for those high-in-the-dark triad traits.

Our framework next considers a social media user's socialization motivation. Especially during and soon after a global pandemic, where much of business and society shut down for public health purposes, people are lonelier than ever. Avid or toxic social media use can be a coping mechanism that some lonely people use in order to feel connected, to get some social interactions, and to see or share with others. While this could bring some positive outcomes, such as temporary fulfillment of boredom or fulfilling a fix to "see others," socialization via social media is not a substitute for in-person interactions or relationships. Thus, we propose that consumers who are lonelier (or those who use social media to feel less lonely) are more likely to have some problematic social media compulsions or even addictions—especially if their personality traits lie within the dark triad (Machiavellism, narcissism, psychopathy).

A third broad motivation for social media use entails emotional regulation. Consumers may turn to social media to release anger, hurt, rage, fear, or other negative emotions and even lash out at others as a way to regulate those emotions in an unhealthy way. This is where cyberbullying fits in, because those who use social media to troll, harass, annoy, or hurt others with words may find relief in trolling or cyberbullying as a way to regulate those negative emotions they feel. As such, social media use may become compulsive or addictive, especially if the cyberbully/troll has any of the dark triad personality traits. Again, it is thought that compulsive or addictive use can directly cause or correlate with mental health afflictions (negative self-image, anxiety, depression, eating disorders, and self-harm/suicide).

The final motivation driver of some harmful aspects of social media entails the social media consumers' need or desire for current information or research. Specifically, consumers are now turning to artificial intelligence and similar algorithms used in social media for news or information. Much of this news information is negative—such as topics of political division, wars or foreign conflicts, violence, or worsening economic situations such as inflation. As such, we propose that AI use is associated with, or could even cause rises in, compulsive use of social media, if not addiction to using it. The proposed downstream effects are the mental health afflictions that we have discussed. Again, if a social media user has the dark triad traits, this is especially plausible.

Also, under the motivation of research and information desires, social media users are doomscrolling more than ever. What this means, is that due to the algorithms in social media, when one user clicks on or reads a negative news story (such as about a war), they are more likely to see subsequent content that is related and negative. As an echo chamber of negative or doomsworthy content, social media is a way for consumers to engage in doom scrolling. As such, especially if these people have a preexisting personality trait rooted in Machiavellism, narcissism, or psychopathy, they may be more inclined to engage in compulsive or addictive social media use. As with the other proposed factors, doomscrolling can link to compulsive or addictive social media use with unfortunate downstream consequences on mental health.

Dire Consequences: Cyberbullying, Depression, Negative Self-Esteem, Self-Harm, and Suicide

Cyberbullying is one of the dire consequences that we see of social media use. Almost everyone, at some point in their life, will be exposed to some form of online trolling or bullying behind a screen. In most cases, consumers are exposed to other people (namely celebrities, athletes, politicians, and public figures) getting bullied or trolled online. Yet, in more harmful circumstances, many people are themselves a victim of being mocked online, trolled in a comments section, or made fun of in a social media post. The reason this is more damaging compared to old-school face-to-face bullying is that there is an everlasting digital footprint of cyberbullying for a huge audience to see or read. In many cases, it never goes away and can follow someone their whole life via a simple Google search. As such, cyberbullying is one of the worst manifestations of social media because it can powerfully rob individuals of their human dignity, respect, or even their rights.

Just how prevalent is cyberbullying? It is rampant, and likely underreported, making these figures likely deflated. Over one-third of young individuals self-reported being a direct target or victim of cyberbullying (UNICEF, 2022). This number is on the rise as social media becomes more prolific (Cyberbullying Statistics, 2022). There has been a 70% rise in the quantity of online bullying among teens and children during the pandemic-related lockdown (DigitalTrends.com, 2020). Pew Research has also conducted surveys with respect to cyberbullying's prominence as well as what kinds of things specifically entail cyberbullying these days. Pew Research breaks down the following six distinct behaviors that are considered cyberbullying and then examines relatively how often they occur: physical threats, receiving unsolicited (sexually) explicit content or images, having explicit images of them shared on social media without permission, spreading rumors about them, and name-calling (Pew Research, 2022b). Other cyberbullying or trolling behaviors include when a social media user is frequently being asked about their location, what they are doing, or who they are with; note that this does not include a parent constantly checking in with their child (Pew Research, 2022b).

These behaviors and their relative, self-reported occurrences are shown in Figure 1.4. As can be seen, unfortunately, almost half of teens have experienced one or more of these toxic social media behaviors. The most

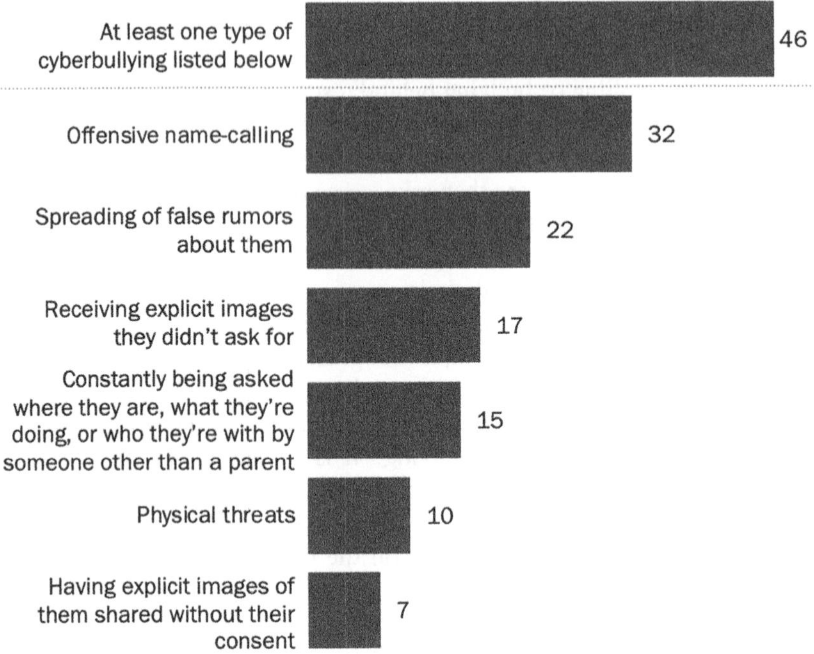

FIGURE 1.4 A darker side of social media is seen in cyberbullying, especially name-calling and spreading false rumors about others.

Credit: Teens and cyberbullying, 2022. Pew Research Center, Washington, D.C. (December 15, 2022)

common type of cyberbullying they have been victim to is offensive name-calling (32% of teens), which is often entangled in hate speech. Another 22% of teens report that there have been fake rumors that have been spread about them on social media (Pew Research, 2022b).

While there is no causal direct evidence that cyberbullying or social media use or addiction definitively causes suicidal ideations or suicide, there have been various unfortunate cases that have associated being cyberbullied via social media with suicide. We note that genetic predisposition to mental health afflictions (anxiety, depression, for example) is an important consideration that we do not take lightly (hence, predisposition of such is a main control variable as proposed in the framework for this chapter). However, there are some associative links between social media and suicide, especially for underdeveloped brains. One such case is about a 15-year-old teenager who committed suicide as a result of being constantly cyberbullied via Snapchat, and as a result, the parents sued the school (Hickey, 2022). Some parents have called for protests to ban social media use by kids who are under the age of 13. As a result, and for a potential solution via regulations, some states in the United States, such as Utah, have legislators suggesting reform or restrictions of TikTok for children.

Cyberbullying relates to those of all ages, genders or gender identities, races, and socioeconomic statuses. Namely, gender and age are associated with teenagers' experiences being cyberbullied; older teenage girls are more likely to be cyberbullied (Pew Research, 2002b). Meanwhile, Black teenagers are almost twice as likely (vs. White or Hispanic teens) to report that they believe their ethnicity or race made them the target of cyberbullying. Similarly, Hispanic or Black teens are more likely (vs. White teens) to report that online abuse is a major problem for teenagers. This breakdown is shown in Figure 1.5.

Proposed solutions to cyberbullying. Many people believe that there are solutions to help curb cyberbullying. Interestingly, teenagers seem to support some reforms or solutions to curb social media use. In fact, almost 75% of teenagers believe that politicians/elected officials and social media companies are not effectively addressing cyberbullying (Pew Research, 2022b). The vast majority of teenagers think that permanent bans from social media apps or websites, along with more or harsher criminal charges can be a solution to divert cyberbullying (Pew Research, 2022b).

One solution, enacted by the state of Texas in the United States is "David's Law" (DavidsLegacy.org, 2023). With David's Law, schools can curb or prevent cyberbullying by empowering school administrators or teachers to look into and address off-campus cyberbullying if it affects the school environment. Specifically, David's Law makes it required for school districts to include cyberbullying in district bullying policies; they must also tell a child's parents or guardians if they are involved in bullying or cyberbullying (regardless of if they are the alleged victim or alleged perpetrator). Importantly, the law also provides for collaboration with law enforcement when very serious (i.e., life-threatening) cyberbullying occurs. For instance, if a student is told to go kill themself via a social media platform, this

Older teen girls more likely than younger girls or boys of any age to have faced false rumor spreading, constant monitoring online, as well as cyberbullying overall

% of U.S. teens who say they have ever experienced__ when online or on their cellphone

	Offensive name-calling	Spreading of false rumors about them	Receiving explicit images they didn't ask for	Constantly being asked where they are, what they're doing, or who they're with by someone other than a parent	Physical threats	Having explicit images of them shared without their consent	Any cyberbullying
U.S. teens	32	22	17	15	10	7	46
Boys	31	16	15	13	10	5	43
Girls	32	29	19	17	10	8	49
White	35	24	16	14	10	6	48
Black	29	17	21	9	11	10	40
Hispanic	29	21	19	21	10	7	47
Ages 13-14	29	20	11	12	10	4	42
15-17	34	24	22	17	10	8	49
Boys 13-14	31	15	11	12	10	3	41
15-17	32	16	18	13	10	7	44
Girls 13-14	25	24	10	12	9	5	41
15-17	36	33	25	20	10	9	54

Note: Teens are those ages 13 to 17. White and Black teens include those who report being only one race and are not Hispanic. Hispanic teens are of any race. Those who did not give an answer are not shown.
Source: Survey conducted April 14-May 4, 2022.
"Teens and Cyberbullying 2022"

PEW RESEARCH CENTER

FIGURE 1.5 Mobile (cell phone based) teen cyberbullying experiences in the U.S. by gender, race, and age.

Credit: Teens and cyberbullying, 2022. Pew Research Center, Washington, D.C. (December 15, 2022)

newer law allows parents and courts legal tools to prosecute horrific cases of cyberbullying or suicide baiting. Last, David's Law supports schools to have educated counselors or rehabilitative services for bullies as well as the victims. This is because they recognize that bullying itself can be or relate to an underlying mental health issue (DavidsLegacy.org, 2023).

Oftentimes, cyberbullying takes advantage of a power imbalance, such as physical, emotional, informational, or other threats to another's mental health or well-being. Examples include students posting information about a classmate living in a homeless shelter, or information their parents are alcoholics. Other examples come in sharing explicit or unflattering photos; especially where one person has a huge social media presence with many followers, one such abusive post could go viral and destroy the victim's reputation. A related solution for cyberbullying is for schools or organizations to maintain an accessible "bullying checklist" to help make sure that incidents of cyberbullying are not dismissed or minimized. This bullying checklist can help assess if and to what extent the incident(s) entailed: (a) physical contact, (b) words-written expression, (c) electronic means, (d) a significant single act that is severe to the victim, and (e) a pattern of acts (DavidsLegacy.org, 2023).

Social Media and Self-Esteem

These solutions are important to address because there are linkages between social media use and self-esteem, especially among youth. Based on a sample from childhood to adolescence (age 10–14 years old), how often they liked or commented on other users' content, termed "other-oriented social media use," predicted reduced self-esteem (Steinsbekk et al., 2021). They also predicted that when young people engage with other people's social media photos or feeds, they would have decreased self-esteem during their transformation from childhood to adolescence (Steinsbekk et al., 2021). This was consistent with their results that showed lower self-esteem when social media is used for other-oriented social media use or for comparing oneself to others (Steinsbekk et al., 2021).

Dark Social: The Dark Web

Besides cyberbullying and the aspects of online abuse, it is worth considering if and how the consumer gets social media information and access. A newer consideration is the dark web, and more specifically dark social media. Research in this book (Chapter 4) shows secondary research that social media users with dark personality traits are more inclined to use dark social media and even conduct fraudulent financial activity via the dark web. The dark web is the platform for the exchange of illegal or unethical information with an anonymous identity.

With the advancement in technology and social media, stock markets worldwide are interconnected. However, the downside is that any mishap in any of the stock exchanges spills over to the other stock exchanges in the world. Market manipulators use the dark web, dark social media, and private communication channels to buy and sell stock tips and price-sensitive information across international markets. Specific details on the dark web and the dark triad personality traits are provided in Chapter 4, along with some high-profile stock market and banking scams that originated from the dark web. There are some very advanced techniques such as deepfakes and voice clones to cheat others in fraudulent ways.

The solutions entail a stronger role of regulators and punishments. The role of regulators becomes vital to safeguard the interest of investors and to make sure that the stock market is a level playing field. The emergence of the dark web and dark social media brings various new challenges for lawmakers to halt social media–based insider trading and scams. As such, there are many risks to consumers who use the dark web, which may entail compulsive use, addiction, and/or eventual mental health symptoms such as anxiety that could stem from the fear of getting caught on the dark web or doing something fraudulent.

Figure 1.6 shows that almost two-thirds of Americans state that they are concerned about a particular social media platform—TikTok.

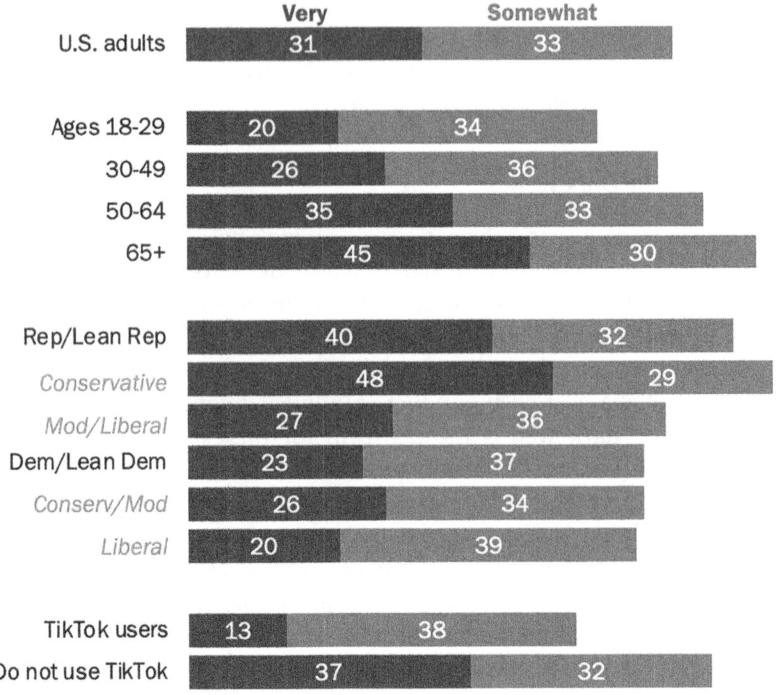

FIGURE 1.6 Despite advertising campaigns highlighting the bright side of TikTok, most American adults clearly agree they are very or somewhat concerned about how TikTok uses data that it collects from its users and/or that it is a clear threat to American security.

Credit: Majority of Americans say TikTok is a threat to national security. Pew Research Center, Washington, D.C. (July 10, 2023)

The concern is how TikTok handles consumer data. Similarly, scholars have warned about data use and privacy concerns from a marketer's lens (Quach et al., 2022). This sentiment is broken down by age, political tendency (ranging from liberal to conservative), and whether they are active users of TikTok. What is notable here is that across these various psychographics and demographics, it is clear that many American adults are very concerned about data use and lack of privacy on the platform (Pew Research, 2023).

The rise in people's use of social media has created a vast amount of data and information available to companies online. This warehouse of easily available information has increased consumer risk of data leaks on the dark web; consumers are vulnerable to cybercrimes namely data theft, privacy, spying, infringement, and theft (Jain et al., 2021). Although some social networking sites like X/Twitter do not enable disclosure of private or financial information, there are experienced hackers who can collect confidential information by going through users' posts and social media shares. With the smallest quantity of personal information posted on social media, one can risk cybercriminals getting their email or passwords (Jain et al., 2021) for the dark web. Creating an account on social networking sites is "free" and something many people do to receive the advantages of social media such as community engagement; however, not all social media content or their application partners are trustworthy, and they can exploit private consumer information by selling them to data brokers without user consent. Hackers can steal confidential information about their targets from social media apps or websites by using various cyberattack techniques (Jain et al., 2021).

The advancement of technology allows people or companies to create artificial intelligence (AI) algorithms or AI-based applications (e.g., deepfakes and generative adversarial networks) that may generate words and images which portray a fake form of reality (Campbell et al., 2022). Deepfakes can look highly believable and real. Deepfakes use AI to imitate the features (e.g., facial features, voice, physical appearance, and/or gender) of the entity that it wants to create (Floridi, 2018; Karnouskos, 2020). For many people, this type of fake content is hard to distinguish from reality, and further advances in technology will, in the future, make it harder to decipher a fake image from a real one (Campbell et al., 2022).

Social Media Self-Comparisons and Self-Discrepancies

Self-comparison appears when individuals give value to their own social or personal worth by comparing themselves to others. Often, social media self-presentation is inauthentic, especially by social media influencers (Audrezet et al., 2020; Swani & Labrecque, 2020; Valsesia & Diehl, 2022). This is oftentimes heightened when people are scrolling through social media, and they start to see individuals posting their lavish lifestyles or bragging about what they have. However, social media self-comparisons can also arise when users come across other users who post seamlessly photoshopped versions of themselves online. With new features being created on social media platforms such as Instagram, Facebook, and TikTok, people now have more options for using filters or effects to blur their blemishes and make their face or body appear smoother or slimmer than it actually is. According to a study done from a sample of children and adolescents, findings suggested that young individuals who often engage in other-oriented social media behavior, liking or commenting on others' posts and pictures, will frequently evaluate other users' ideal versions that they portray online. This can lead them to develop an increase in social comparisons, which ultimately negatively affects self-esteem (Steinsbekk et al., 2021).

Social Media Addiction, Fear, and Anxiety: Social Media News and Doomscrolling

Overuse of social media may bring side effects such as doomscrolling, which is the act of spending an excessive amount of time reading or watching negative content online. When one finds themselves doomscrolling on social media, they can easily become addicted. As a result, one can develop fear and anxiety from the tone of content they consume. A statistically significant relationship was discovered between a more pronounced problematic social media use (PSMU) and lower age, with a higher degree of problematic emotion regulation in all six facets (limited access to emotion regulation strategies, nonacceptance of emotional responses, impulse control difficulties, difficulties engaging in goal-directed behavior, lack of emotional awareness, and lack of emotional clarity). In childhood and adolescence, statistically significant correlations were found between a more pronounced PSMU and lower age, stronger impulsive control difficulties, stronger difficulties engaging in goal-directed behavior, increased procrastination, and higher perceived stress (Wartberg et al., 2021).

According to another study, teenagers who experience social media use (SMU) challenges that resemble addiction are more vulnerable to mental health problems than teenagers who just experience high SMU intensity. It appears that teenage mental health is more negatively impacted by being unable to manage impulses related to SMU, thinking about SMU all the time, feeling upset when SMU is restricted, or placing a high value on SMU than by using social media excessively. In this study, teenagers and adolescents with increased SMU problems reported higher depressive symptoms and lower life satisfaction one year later (Boer et al., 2021).

Discussion and Research Directions on the Darker Side of Social Media for Consumer Well-Being

For future research directions on the darker side of social media for consumer well-being, we offer the framework and propositions for scholars to examine. These propositions can be tested individually or wholly as a predictive model. They could also be tested experimentally, with randomized samples, control groups, and in the design of a randomized controlled trial with more generalizable populations. As one can see from this literature review in this chapter, many of the samples used are convenience samples, or on younger populations. We encourage one or more of these propositions to be studied on a variety of samples, from various countries, and of broader demographics.

Research Propositions for the Dark Side of Social Media and Mental Health

Please refer back to Figure 1.3, which depicts the following propositions as a whole. This is an initial step in research propositions, so scholars are encouraged to adapt these as they see fit or make them easier to measure and empirically test. We also encourage authors to consider the role of causality. Again, as stressed in the forefront of our chapter, we are not implying that all or perhaps any of these predicted relationships are truly causal in nature. More likely, these are associations. Further, we are not clear on the directions of some of these relationships. For instance, while we are thinking about compulsive or even addictive SMU as a dependent variable (or a mediator), it may be considered as an independent variable in related studies. That said, an addictive personality type (or someone who is already clinically addicted to other related things such as television, or video games) may be what drives or helps explain some of the independent variables considered here (such as cyberbullying or doomscrolling). Thus, this framework is not perfect, and there are many modifications to it that could be plausible. Our intention is to spark some more research and scholarly output (theses, dissertations, books, book chapters, journal articles, media articles) that reveal some of the sad truths related to too much or the wrong kind of SMU by the wrong people.

Thus, we offer the following propositions for empirical work on the darker side of social media. Again, scholars are encouraged to modify these as they see fit.

P1a. Consumers who use the dark web are more likely to have compulsive use of social media, and in turn one or more symptoms of a social media–related mental health affliction (negative self-image, anxiety, depression, eating disorders, self-harm, suicidal ideations). OR

P1b. Consumers who use the dark web are more likely to have one or more symptoms of a social media–related mental health affliction (negative self-image, anxiety, depression, eating disorders, self-harm, and suicidal ideations).

P2a. Consumers who use certain social media platforms (TikTok, Instagram) are more likely to have compulsive use of social media, and in turn one or more symptoms of a social media–related mental health affliction (negative self-image, anxiety, depression, eating disorders, self-harm, and suicidal ideations). OR

P2b. Consumers who use certain social media platforms (TikTok, Instagram) are more likely to have one or more symptoms of a social media–related mental health affliction (negative self-image, anxiety, depression, eating disorders, self-harm, and suicidal ideations).

P3a. Consumers who are lonely or who feel isolated are more likely to have compulsive use of social media, and in turn one or more symptoms of a social media–related mental health affliction (negative self-image, anxiety, depression, eating disorders, self-harm, and suicidal ideations). OR

P3b. Consumers who are lonely or who feel isolated are more likely to have one or more symptoms of a social media–related mental health affliction (negative self-image, anxiety, depression, eating disorders, self-harm, and suicidal ideations).

P4a. Consumers who are victims of cyberbullying (or who cyberbully others) are more likely to have compulsive use of social media, and in turn one or more symptoms of a social media–related mental health affliction (negative self-image, anxiety, depression, eating disorders, self-harm, and suicidal ideations). OR

P4b. Consumers who are victims of cyberbullying (or who cyberbully others) are more likely to have one or more symptoms of a social media–related mental health affliction (negative self-image, anxiety, depression, eating disorders, self-harm, and suicidal ideations).

P5a. Consumers who use social media as their primary news source are more likely to have compulsive use of social media, and in turn one or more symptoms of a social media–related mental health affliction (negative self-image, anxiety, depression, eating disorders, self-harm, and suicidal ideations).

P5b. Consumers who use social media as their primary news source often are more likely to have one or more symptoms of a social media–related mental health affliction (negative self-image, anxiety, depression, eating disorders, self-harm, and suicidal ideations).

P6a. Consumers who doomscroll are more likely to have compulsive use of social media, and in turn one or more symptoms of a social media–related mental health affliction (negative self-image, anxiety, depression, eating disorders, self-harm, and suicidal ideations). OR

P6b. Consumers who doomscroll are more likely to have one or more symptoms of a social media–related mental health affliction (negative self-image, anxiety, depression, eating disorders, self-harm, and suicidal ideations).

P7a. Consumers who have a personality trait of Machiavellism, narcissism, or psychopathy are more likely to have compulsive use of social media, and in turn one or more symptoms of a social media–related mental health affliction (negative self-image, anxiety, depression, eating disorders, self-harm, and suicidal ideations). OR

P7b. Consumers who have a personality trait of Machiavellism, narcissism, or psychopathy are more likely to have one or more symptoms of a social media–related mental health affliction (negative self-image, anxiety, depression, eating disorders, self-harm, and suicidal ideations).

P8. A consumer with a personality trait of Machiavellism, narcissism, or psychopathy is especially likely to have social media compulsive or addictive use as a result of (a) exposure type (dark web exposure, TikTok or Instagram platform use), (b) loneliness or feelings of isolation, and (c) doomscrolling.

P9. There is a relationship between social media addiction or compulsive social media use and propensity for mental health affliction(s).

Again, these propositions are a first start, and we sincerely encourage scholars to modify or adapt these ideas of research propositions with empirical research. There may not be causal relationships here, and as such the purported relationships may be associative in nature. Lastly, we encourage more work overall on these topics, and especially more ideas and revisions to the solutions proposed in this chapter as well as in this book.

References

American Psychological Association. (2022a, August). *Anxiety*. https://www.apa.org/topics/anxiety

American Psychological Association. (2022b, August). *Depression*. https://www.apa.org/topics/depression

Appel, G., Grewal, L., Hadi, R., & Stephen, A. T. (2020). The future of social media in marketing. *Journal of the Academy of Marketing Science*, *48*(1), 79–95.

Audrezet, A., De Kerviler, G., & Moulard, J. G. (2020). Authenticity under threat: When social media influencers need to go beyond self-presentation. *Journal of Business Research*, *117*, 557–569.

Berezan, O., Krishen, A. S., Agarwal, S., & Kachroo, P. (2020). Exploring loneliness and social networking: Recipes for hedonic well-being on Facebook. *Journal of Business Research*, *115*, 258–265.

Berryman, C., Ferguson, C. J., & Negy, C. (2018). Social media use and mental health among young adults. *Psychiatric Quarterly*, *89*, 307–314.

Best, P., Manktelow, R., & Taylor, B. (2014). Online communication, social media and adolescent wellbeing: A systematic narrative review. *Children and Youth Services Review*, *41*, 27–36.

Boer, M., Stevens, G. W., Finkenauer, C., de Looze, M. E., & van den Eijnden, R. J. (2021). Social media use intensity, social media use problems, and mental health among adolescents: Investigating directionality and mediating processes. *Computers in Human Behavior*, *116*, 106645.

Brailovskaia, J., Truskauskaite-Kuneviciene, I., Kazlauskas, E., & Margraf, J. (2021). The patterns of problematic social media use (SMU) and their relationship with online flow, life satisfaction, depression, anxiety and stress symptoms in Lithuania and in Germany. *Current Psychology*, 1–12.

Campbell, C., Plangger, K., Sands, S., & Kietzmann, J. (2022). Preparing for an era of deep fakes and AI-generated ads: A framework for understanding responses to manipulated advertising. *Journal of Advertising*, *51*(1), 22–38.

Cataldo, I., Lepri, B., Neoh, M. J. Y., & Esposito, G. (2021). Social media usage and development of psychiatric disorders in childhood and adolescence: A review. *Frontiers in Psychiatry*, *11*, 508595. https://www.frontiersin.org/articles/10.3389/fpsyt.2020.508595

Coates, A. E., Hardman, C. A., Halford, J. C., Christiansen, P., & Boyland, E. J. (2019). Social media influencer marketing and children's food intake: A randomized trial. *Pediatrics*, *143*(4).

Cotten, S. R., Schuster, A. M., & Seifert, A. (2022). Social media use and well-being among older adults. *Current Opinion in Psychology*, *45*(June), in press.

Cunningham, S., Hudson, C. C., & Harkness, K. (2021). Social media and depression symptoms: A meta-analysis. *Research on Child and Adolescent Psychopathology*, *49*, 241–253.

Cyberbullying Statistics. (2022). Retrieved August 13, 2022, from https://enough.org/stats_cyberbullying

David's Legacy. (2023). *Legislation-David's Legacy*. Retrieved October 2023, from https://www.davidslegacy.org/programs/legislation/

DigitalTrends.com. (2020, April 8). Cyberbullying increases amid coronavirus pandemic. Here's what parents can do. *Digitaltrends.com*.

Floridi, Luciano. (2018). "Soft ethics and the governance of the digital." *Philosophy & Technology*, *31*, 1–8.

Haines, Jess, and Dianne Neumark-Sztainer. (2006). "Prevention of obesity and eating disorders: a consideration of shared risk factors." *Health education research*, 21.6, 770–782.

Hartman Group. (2014). *Food & the New Community: How the Internet Changes Food Culture* https://www.hartman-group.com/newsletters/1529252993/food-the-new-community-how-the-internet-changes-food-culture

Herz, J. (2023). Eugenia Cooney's thin figure sparks worry amid eating disorder. *New York Post*. https://nypost.com/2023/08/01/eugenia-cooneys-thin-figure-sparks-worry-amid-eating-disorder/

Hickey, M. (2022). A 15-year-old boy died by suicide after relentless cyberbullying, and his parents say the Latin school could have done more to stop it. *CBS News Chicago*. https://www.cbsnews.com/chicago/news/15-year-old-boy-cyberbullying-suicide-latin-school-chicago-lawsuit/

Hofer, M., & Hargittai, E. (2021). Online social engagement, depression, and anxiety among older adults. *New Media & Society*, *26*(1), 113–130.

Holland, G., & Tiggemann, M. (2017). "Strong beats skinny every time": Disordered eating and compulsive exercise in women who post fitspiration on Instagram. *International Journal of Eating Disorders*, *50*(1), 76–79.

Hunt, M. G., Marx, R., Lipson, C., & Young, J. (2018). No more FOMO: Limiting social media decreases loneliness and depression. *Journal of Social and Clinical Psychology*, *37*(10), 751–768.

Jain, A. K., Sahoo, S. R., & Kaubiyal, J. (2021). Online social networks security and privacy: Comprehensive review and analysis. *Complex & Intelligent Systems*, *7*(5), 2157–2177.

Karnouskos, Stamatis. (2020). "Artificial intelligence in digital media: The era of deepfakes." *IEEE Transactions on Technology and Society*, *1*(3), 138–147.

Keles, B., McCrae, N., & Grealish, A. (2020). A systematic review: The influence of social media on depression, anxiety and psychological distress in adolescents. *International Journal of Adolescence and Youth*, *25*(1), 79–93.

Marino, C., Gini, G., Vieno, A., & Spada, M. M. (2018). The associations between problematic Facebook use, psycho-logical distress and well-being among adolescents and young adults: A systematic review and meta-analysis. *Journal of Affective Disorders*, *226*, 274–281. Elsevier B.V.

Marks, R. J., De Foe, A., & Collett, J. (2020). The pursuit of wellness: Social media, body image and eating disorders. *Children and Youth Services Review*, *119*, 105659.

Marques, M. D., Paxton, S. J., McLean, S. A., Jarman, H. K., & Sibley, C. G. (2022). A prospective examination of relationships between social media use and body dissatisfaction in a representative sample of adults. *Body Image*, *40*, 1–11.

McCabe, M. P., & Ricciardelli, L. A. (2005). A prospective study of pressures from parents, peers, and the media on extreme weight change behaviors among adolescent boys and girls. *Behaviour Research and Therapy*, *43*(5), 653–668.

McCrae, N., Gettings, S., & Purssell, E. (2017). Social media and depressive symptoms in childhood and adolescence: A systematic review. *Adolescent Research Review*, *2*, 315–330.

Mccarthy, Lila. (2023), Feb. 23. Voices of Youth: Battle Creek teen talks with peers about social media's effect on body image, Second Wave Southwest Michigan, https://www.secondwavemedia.com/southwest-michigan/features/Voices-of-Youth-Battle-Creek-teen-explores-social-medias-effect-on-body-image.02223.aspx

Petrescu, M., & Krishen, A. S. (2020). The dilemma of social media algorithms and analytics. *Journal of Marketing Analytics*, *8*, 187–188.

Pew Research. (2022a). https://www.pewresearch.org/global/2022/12/06/social-media-seen-as-mostly-good-for-democracy-across-many-nations-but-u-s-is-a-major-outlier/

Pew Research. (2022b). https://www.pewresearch.org/internet/2022/12/15/teens-and-cyberbullying-2022/

Pew Research. (2023). https://www.pewresearch.org/short-reads/2023/07/10/majority-of-americans-say-tiktok-is-a-threat-to-national-security/

Quach, S., Thaichon, P., Martin, K. D., Weaven, S., & Palmatier, R. W. (2022). Digital technologies: Tensions in privacy and data. *Journal of the Academy of Marketing Science*, *50*(6), 1299–1323.

Rounsefell, K., Gibson, S., McLean, S., Blair, M., Molenaar, A., Brennan, L., & McCaffrey, T. A. (2020). Social media, body image and food choices in healthy young adults: A mixed methods systematic review. *Nutrition & Dietetics*, *77*(1), 19–40.

Scheinbaum, A. C. (2017). *The dark side of social media: A consumer psychology perspective*. Routledge.

Seabrook, E. M., Kern, M. L., & Rickard, N. S. (2016). Social networking sites, depression, and anxiety: A systematic review. *JMIR Mental Health*, *3*(4), 1–18.

Steinsbekk, S., Wichstrøm, L., Stenseng, F., Nesi, J., Hygen, B. W., & Skalická, V. (2021). The impact of social media use on appearance self-esteem from childhood to adolescence–A 3-wave community study. *Computers in Human Behavior*, *114*, 106528.

Swani, K., & Labrecque, L. I. (2020). Like, comment, or share? Self-presentation vs. brand relationships as drivers of social media engagement choices. *Marketing Letters*, *31*(2–3), 279–298.

Tiggemann, M., & Zaccardo, M. (2015). Exercise to be fit, not skinny: The effect of fitspiration imagery on women's body image. *Body Image*, *15*, 61–67.

Turner, P. G., & Lefevre, C. E. (2017). Instagram use is linked to increased symptoms of orthorexia nervosa. *Eating and Weight Disorders-Studies on Anorexia, Bulimia and Obesity*, *22*(2), 277–284.

UNICEF. (2022). *Cyberbullying: What it is and how to stop it*. https://unief.org

Vahratian, A., Blumberg, S. J., Terlizzi, E. P., & Schiller, J. S. (2021). Symptoms of anxiety or depressive disorder and use of mental health care among adults during the COVID-19 Pandemic—United States, August 2020-February 2021. *MMWR Morbidity and Mortality Weekly Report*, *70*(13), 490–494. https://doi.org/10.15585/mmwr.mm7013e2

Valsesia, F., & Diehl, K. (2022). Let me show you what I did versus what I have: Sharing experiential versus material purchases alters authenticity and liking of social media users. *Journal of Consumer Research*, *49*(3), 430–449.

Wartberg, L., Thomasius, R., & Paschke, K. (2021). The relevance of emotion regulation, procrastination, and perceived stress for problematic social media use in a representative sample of children and adolescents. *Computers in Human Behavior*, *121*, 106788.

Wolfers, L. N., & Utz, S. (2022). Social media use, stress, and coping. *Current Opinion in Psychology*, *45*, 101305.

2

COMPULSIVE SOCIAL MEDIA USE AND DISCONNECTION ANXIETY

Predictors and Markers of Compulsive and Addictive Social Media Consumption

Line Lervik-Olsen, Bob M. Fennis, and Tor Wallin Andreassen

Introduction

Social media platforms have revolutionized the way people communicate and interact with each other, making social media use (SMU) an intricate part of consumer social life. In line with Bayer et al. (2020), we define these platforms as "computer-mediated communication channels that allow users to engage in social interaction with broad and narrow audiences in real-time or synchronously" (p. 472). However, the proliferation of SMU—recent estimates have it that around 5 billion consumers worldwide are active social media users (Montag et al., 2023)—has led to the manifestation of certain negative behaviors that are now referred to as the "dark side" of SMU. These behaviors are problematic as they are detrimental to people's well-being (Reinecke et al., 2022). With firms taking on more responsibility through, for example, corporate social responsibility and sustainable consumption and consumers spending more time on social media, the dark sides that are associated with social media demand more attention from academics and leaders. In short, we need to better understand how SMU is associated with individual well-being and digital addiction.

For digital addiction, we align with literature (Kuss & Griffiths, 2017; Maranges et al., 2023; Pellegrino et al., 2022) that conceives of this as disinhibited, partly automatic compulsive and excessive behavior aimed at perpetuating an online presence either active (as in actively posting on social media) and/or passive (frequently checking online content). Thus, the compulsivity of the behavior is a key hallmark of addictive SMU and

DOI: 10.4324/9781003410058-3

therefore will also prominently feature in the research we will discuss in this chapter. Key markers of online compulsivity include excessive use of social media—a high frequency of use, and always being logged in—and a high consumption intensity per online session (see Lervik-Olsen et al., 2023).

Social Media Use, Addiction, and Well-Being

The issue is, and if so, to what extent SMU (and internet use in general) can go "overboard" and may turn into social media addiction is far from new and likely has been around since the advent of the Internet (Katz & Rice, 2002; Lea et al., 1992; McKenna & Bargh, 2000; Li et al., 2015; Lin, Chiang, et al., 2016). Nevertheless, since the proliferation of social media platforms such as Facebook, WhatsApp, Instagram, and TikTok, as well as special-purpose platforms such as LinkedIn and Tinder, the issue has gained momentum and presently features prominently both in scientific (e.g., Valkenburg, 2022; Kuss & Griffiths, 2017; Li et al., 2015; Lin, Chiang, et al., 2016; Pellegrino et al., 2022) and in public debates (e.g., NBC News, 2020).

Because addictive (or compulsive) SMU is intrinsically linked to consumer well-being, addressing this issue essentially requires one to tackle not one but two research questions:

RQ1. What factors, both intrinsic and extrinsic, to the consumer may promote the proliferation of compulsive SMU?
RQ2. Is there a link between features of problematic SMU and consumer well-being (and "ill-being," which is not necessarily its antipode; see Valkenburg, 2022)?

Interestingly, when reviewing the interdisciplinary literature, there seems to be an abundance of studies, reviews, and meta-analyses focused on the second question (e.g., Appel et al., 2020; Meier & Reinecke, 2021; Valkenburg, 2022), but there appears to be a dearth of research on the first question (but see Kuss & Griffiths, 2017; Pellegrino et al., 2022), let alone on research studying the two issues in conjunction.

The research presented in this chapter aims to fill this void. More specifically, across two studies, we aim to explore both intrinsic and extrinsic factors that may contribute to compulsive consumer SMU and its consequence for a specific and proximate type of "ill-being": "disconnection anxiety". For the second study, we take compulsive SMU as our starting point and explore in more detail the types of drivers that may affect the decision to disconnect and its downstream consequences for consumer well-being.

Thus, rather than only zooming in on the problem of consumer compulsivity in this domain, this chapter also aims to shed light on drivers that may offer cues to its solution. As will be discussed in more detail later in the text, the two studies call attention to the roles of *salient motives*—fear of missing out (FOMO) (Study 1) and guilt (Study 2), *external "affordances"* or cues—technological nudges, descriptive social norms (Study 1) and technological disruptions (Study 2), and *previous, established behavioral patterns*—habits (Study 1), compulsive SMU (Study 2) as key antecedents for the formation and perpetuation of problematic SMU (Study 1) and its negative impact on consumer well-being (Study 2).

In the remainder of this introduction, we will discuss the hallmarks of consumer compulsive behavior formation as it applies to SMU, its constituents, antecedent factors, and ensuing consequences for consumer well-being before outlining two causal models that were featured in the two studies reported later in the chapter.

Literature Review

Intrinsic and Extrinsic Drivers of Compulsive Social Media Use

As briefly touched upon earlier in the text, when we speak of SMU addiction, we refer to compulsive, disinhibited social media consumption that is partly automatic and largely unregulated (i.e., more manifest under conditions of low self-control; see Fennis, 2022; Maranges et al., 2023; Reinecke et al., 2022). Indeed, recent research points to the strong association between impaired self-control and what is sometimes euphemistically termed "problematic" or "maladaptive" SMU (Maranges et al., 2023). But how and when does "regular" or "normal' SMU evolve to be "abnormal" and "problematic"? Of note, as alluded to earlier, the impact of SMU on consumer well-being has been the topic of many studies, and by now a substantial number of meta-analyses (see Valkenburg, 2022, for an overview). These studies indicate that SMU does not invariably lead to maladaptive outcomes. Rather, outcomes for well-being can be both positive (i.e., increased social connectivity, improved self-esteem, and greater happiness levels; see, e.g., Yin et al., 2019), and negative (i.e., increased depressive symptoms and anxiety disorders; see, e.g., Cunningham et al., 2021; Yoon et al., 2019). Nevertheless, a closer look at meta-analyses that also include proxies of low well-being shows the highest correlations between such outcomes and problematic, compulsive SMU, rather than either active or passive SMU per se. Thus, these results underscore the relevance and urgency of the topic.

Interestingly, recent research from cognitive neuroscience sheds light on this issue and points to both a behavioral and a motivational path to compulsive behavior (see also Lervik-Olsen et al., 2023). Of note, as a form of compulsive behavior, problematic SMU is not alone, but shares important psychological similarities with other forms of maladaptive, compulsive consumption, such as gambling or substance abuse (see, e.g., Brewer, 2019, for an overview).

Behavioral and Motivational Antecedents of Compulsive Social Media Use

Neuroscience points to the role of *reward-based learning*, known as reinforcement learning or operant conditioning (see Brewer, 2019; Skinner, 1971), as the cornerstone of compulsive social media consumption. To start with, it calls attention to the fact that such consumption is *rewarding*. The ping of the phone, the thumbs up of likes, the retweets of one's messages all send potent reward signals that translate into dopaminergic signals that are received by the brain's ventral and dorsal striatum (cf. Kringelbach, 2005). Indeed, research by Sherman et al. (2018) showed that among adolescent consumers, the ventral striatum became more active after receiving likes compared to dislikes, and given that this region is highly innervated by dopamine, it is plausible that dopamine triggering is the underlying process here, although direct evidence for the role of dopamine release remains scarce (Montag et al., 2023). Nevertheless, this line of work points to the role of external cues that may promise rewards, including proximate cues such as the likes referred to earlier, but also more enabling cues such as the availability of Wi-Fi, push notifications on one's smartphone, and so on. Thus, any model that aims to explain the development of compulsive SMU needs to account for cues that signal reward.

In the research we outline later in the text, we in fact did. That is, in the Lervik-Olsen et al. (2023) study, we gauged the salience of two types of reward cues: technological nudges and consumer engagement cues. Technological nudges included the enabling cues referred to above such as the availability of Wi-Fi, or the possession of a smartwatch and other mobile devices. These types of cues facilitate increased *frequency* of SMU. To gauge cues that may intensify *intensity* of such use we further included cues to consumer engagement (cf. Lindström et al., 2021), for example, engaging in online discussions, leaving comments on company websites, or responding to other consumers' comments.

Interestingly, even singular instances of reward signals can instantiate the psychological state of "desire"—the relatively automatic evaluation of reward-promising stimuli against the background of the consumer's salient needs (e.g., hunger, thirst, sex, or social belonging, Brewer, 2019; Hofmann & Van Dillen, 2012). To the extent that such reward signals fulfill these needs, they turn into wants and desires. Thus, successful reward cues may create a "desire loop" where their presence signals desire, which in turn may increase the salience and motivated attention to such cues. This is the foundation of reward-based learning (Brewer, 2019). That is, each time the consumer encounters a reward cue and experiences a positive affective state, the response to the cue gets reinforced up to the point that the response will be automatic and *habitual* (cf. Lindström et al., 2021). Thus, in terms of the present research, we posited that both types of reward cues may feed into *habitual* social media consumption—repetitive social media consumption that is automatically triggered by encountering any reward-signaling cue (e.g., the ping of one's smartphone). This automatically triggered habitual behavior, in turn, may feed into compulsive SMU (i.e., excessive use and always being logged in) when it becomes unregulated, as when self-control is impaired or the behavior is otherwise disinhibited (see Fennis et al., 2015; Maranges et al., 2023).

The habitual process explained earlier is posited to largely occur outside conscious awareness, but it may be only one of the paths that may ultimately lead to compulsive SMU. Another path that we included in our work is more conscious and motivational in nature and is captured by the *fear of missing out* (FOMO; see Roberts & David, 2020). For this path, the (perpetuation) of compulsive SMU is driven not by *positive* reinforcement (as in the habitual path discussed earlier) but by *negative* reinforcement. More specifically, in our research, we conceive of two normative drivers of this negative reinforcement: descriptive norms and conjunctive norms. Descriptive norms, also known as "social proof" (Anderson & Dunning, 2014; Cialdini & Goldstein, 2004), capture the influence principle of "social proof": the perception of how most similar others choose or behave. The salient perception is that most like-minded other consumers are permanently online, the descriptive norm will reflect this and consequently contribute to a sense that one is missing out on relevant (social) information by not being online.

In addition, an *injunctive* social norm is less concerned with the salient perception of what the perceived majority does, but with what it will approve or disapprove of (cf. Anderson & Dunning, 2014). Thus, an injunctive norm tells one how one *should* behave based on what is important others would approve. We maintain that FOMO is thus increased when there is a salient norm urging that one should (ought to) be online (injunctive norm) as well as a salient perception that most of one's peers are basically always online (social proof).

In sum, in the first study, we describe later, compulsive SMU is conceptualized to be driven by a motivational and a behavioral path, that is, repetitive behavior—habits—on the one hand, and a salient, negatively valanced, motivational driver—FOMO—on the other. Habits, in turn, are posited to be a function of the presence and availability of technological affordances: technological nudges that mainly drive the frequency of SMU, while consumer engagement is posited to drive the intensity of such use (cf. Lindström et al., 2021). The main motivational driver, FOMO is posited to be a function of two types of norms: descriptive norms and injunctive norms that inform the consumer what most other like-minded consumers do and choose (social proof, descriptive norms), and what the normatively "correct" behavior should be regarding SMU (injunctive norms).

This study focuses mainly on explaining the formation and proliferation of problematic SMU, rather than focusing on its downstream consequences for consumer well-being, but still, we included one proxy of potential adverse effects on well-being: anxiety to disconnect.

The formation of the Log Off Movement (https://www.logoffmovement.org/), driven by high school senior Emma Lembke, was a direct response to the negative effect of excessive social media use and the absence of young voices in the discussion on social media advocacy. In line with the concerns raised in the Log Off Movement, for instance, the main objective of the second study we present was to thoroughly investigate the impact of compulsive SMU and other drivers on consumer well-being (see Ronæs & Lervik-Olsen, 2018). In a way, one could argue that the second study starts where the first left off: with compulsive SMU. The main goal of this study was to explore the factors that motivate individuals to disconnect from social media, despite the numerous reasons to be constantly active and the anxiety associated with logging off, as observed in the previous study. By building upon the previous study and conducting a thorough review of existing literature, Ronæs & Lervik-Olsen (2018) identified a series of potential motivators that drive individuals to disconnect from social media. The starting and focal point of this second study, logging off, serves as the main phenomenon to be explored, following the endpoint of the initial study: disconnection anxiety.

Four key motivators emerged as particularly relevant to an individual's decision to disconnect from social media. First, recognizing that their social media use has gone too far and is causing mental distraction, reduced productivity, excessive social media activity, interference with sleep patterns, or otherwise feeling helpless without access to social media could prompt someone to log off. Second, the feeling of guilt associated with being active on social media during family dinners, a child's recital, meetings, or other occasions where they should be present in the moment could drive an individual to log off. Third, when social media use is perceived to interfere with or disrupt social gatherings with friends, relaxation, or work, or when it is deemed inappropriate to use it, a person may be motivated to disconnect.

Finally, perceived stress arising from having too much to do, feeling incapable of managing it all, being off-track, or lacking control can also lead someone to log off from social media.

Consequently, we propose that the decision to log off and the perception of logging off in this study is a function of previous behavior patterns, (compulsive SMU), external cues, or affordances, that is, the extent to which social media devices are perceived to act as disruptors of offline, face-to-face social interactions, and two main, negatively valanced, consumer motivational drivers: the perception of guilt and the experience of stress. In turn, logging off is assumed to have a positive impact on overall consumer well-being in various aspects of life. These positive effects may include better quality of sleep, improved physical and mental health, stronger relationships with others, increased ability to perform daily tasks, greater satisfaction in personal and family life, enhanced enjoyment of life, increased productivity at work, and enriched friendships and relationships, improved sleep quality, and improved concentration.

Our Research

In sum, the two studies reported here delve into the negative consequences of SMU, focusing specifically on two consumer outcomes: digital addiction and individual well-being. Through the two empirical studies, we explore the underlying factors that contribute to compulsive SMU, including indirect antecedents such as habit and FOMO, as well as direct antecedents like excessive use and being always logged in. Additionally, we investigate the impact of logging off on individual well-being, and the factors motivating individuals to log off social media, such as compulsive SMU, guilt, disruptions, and stress.

Study 1

The assumptions from the first study outlined earlier can be summarized as in Figure 2.1. This figure shows the purported antecedents of compulsive social media use (such as excessive use or always being logged in) and in turn disconnection anxiety.

We can observe the depicted routes leading to compulsive SMU and the potential consequence of disconnection anxiety. Disconnection anxiety is considered the ultimate dependent variable in the model. The construct of compulsive SMU, including being always logged in and excessive use, acts as a mediator between habit and FOMO and disconnection anxiety. The formation of habit is influenced by the availability of technology and consumers' engagement with brands in social media. On the other hand,

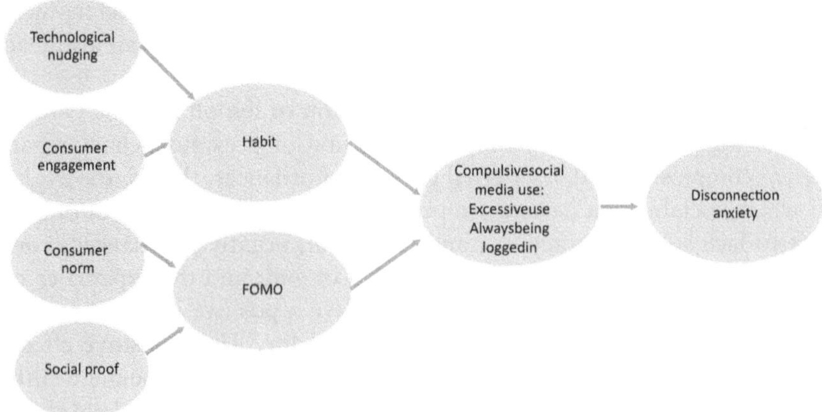

FIGURE 2.1 Conceptual model for study 1.

FOMO stems from an individual's perception of expectations regarding the individual's presence in social media (consumer norms). Additionally, the perception that a majority of one's peers are consistently online (social proof) can contribute to FOMO. The methodological and statistical details are outlined in Lervik-Olsen et al.(2023), and will not be reiterated here, but a summarized overview of the main points will be provided next without going into exhaustive detail.

Method

Study 1 utilized a quantitative research design to test the conceptual model. The researchers developed a questionnaire in line with the classic scale development procedure (Churchill, 1979), in which each variable in the model was operationalized based on validated scales identified through a review of existing literature with minor adjustments made as needed. Some of the scales required adaptation to fit the context, while others were too extensive for the multi-variable model and required a reduction in the number of items. A professional data collection company identified the sample and collected data through computer-aided telephone interviews.

Measures

The questionnaire utilized a Likert-type scale ranging from 1 to 7 to measure each variable in the model. The construct of compulsive SMU was operationalized through two dimensions, that is, being always logged in and excessive SMU. To measure the always logged-in variable, items were selected based on Andreassen et al.'s (2015) work, as well as other sources such as Kolb et al. (2012), referring to the importance and need to be always accessible online, regardless of time and location. Excessive SMU was inspired by Caplan (2005) and measured through items reflecting the urge to be online, difficulty in logging off, and examples of extreme use. The construct of social media habits was operationalized based on Verplanken and Orbell's (2003) work. It involved including questions that addressed automated behavior, difficulties in controlling behavior, and behavior conducted when feeling bored.

To measure FOMO, questions were included about the individual's concern for losing out on relevant information, social activities, and being left out of social networks, aligning with Przybylski et al.'s (2013) operationalization. The scale for measuring technological nudges was operationalized in line with Thaler and Sunstein's (2008) work, reflecting the availability of technology for the purpose of being active in social media. Consumer engagement with brands in social media is in line with Fernandes and Castro's (2020) work and involves incorporating questions about the brand-related activities that individuals engage in in social media.

The measure of social proof aligned with Varian and Shapiro's (1999) and Lin, Zhang, et al.'s (2016) work, resulting in questions about the value of being on social media for the individual and staying in touch with others. Consumer norm was operationalized based on Ajzen and Driver (1992) and in line with Ajzen's (2020) article, resulting in questions about the perceived pressure from family and friends to use and be present in social media. Finally, disconnection anxiety was measured through two items reflecting feelings of uneasiness and disconnection from family and friends when absent from social media, aligning with Spielberger et al.'s (1968/1977) work.

Results and Discussion

The model was tested on data obtained from a representative sample of 600 participants with an average age of 48 years (SD = 16 years). Female participants (n = 316) slightly outnumbered male participants (n = 248). Educational attainment was distributed across three categories—high school, bachelor's degree, and post-graduate degree—with fairly equal representation. The median time spent online per day was 5 hours.

Analytical Procedure

Our conceptual model illustrates the assumed relationships between the antecedents and consequences of compulsive SMU. To be able to test the model properly, we applied the analytical procedure suggested by Anderson and Gerbing (1988). Accordingly, we first tested the measurement model, then the structural model including the assumed relationships between the variables.

Key Findings

Our findings show that all the hypothesized relationships in the model are supported. This confirms that the individual's habit and FOMO both can lead to compulsive SMU. The habit formation is influenced by the availability of technology, but also by consumers' own engagement with brands in social media. FOMO, on the other hand, is affected by the perceived pressure and expectations from family and friends or other close ones and by the social proof of how similar or relevant others choose or behave. The findings further support that compulsive SMU will increase the anxiety of disconnecting from social media. Across all genders, the model was replicated with no significant differences identified, affirming the stability and generalizability of the hypothesized relationships, and underscoring the robustness of the findings in this study.

Compulsive social media consumption can thus lead to reduced well-being for individuals as they might experience a fear of disconnecting professionally and from family and friends if they choose to log off. However, habits formed over time and the FOMO from social activities and networks prevent individuals from logging off. The constant availability and affordability of technology have led to the gradual formation of habits, but it is crucial for marketers to acknowledge their role in shaping unhealthy social media habits through brand engagement. It is equally important to be mindful of how our expectations and fear of missing out can impact others' SMU. In the next section, we will investigate factors that can disconnect the individual from social media.

Study 2

The primary objective of the second study was to examine the factors that motivate individuals to disengage from social media, despite the prevalent incentives to remain consistently connected and spend excessive amounts of time online. The hypothesized relationships tested in Study 2 are outlined in Figure 2.2.

Here, the well-being of individuals is depicted as the dependent variable, indicating that logging off from social media is assumed to positively impact their overall quality of life across various aspects. Logging off serves as a direct antecedent to well-being while concurrently acting as a mediator

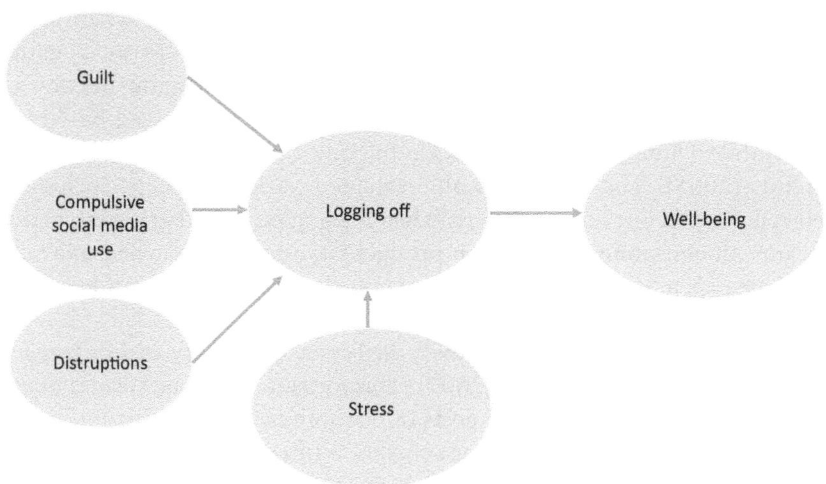

FIGURE 2.2 Conceptual model for study 2.

for mitigating the negative effects of guilt, compulsive SMU, disruptions, and the perception of negative stress on well-being. Individuals who feel guilty about prioritizing social media over being present in social or professional situations are likely to log off, thus improving their life quality. Moreover, individuals who recognize their excessive and unhealthy social media usage as well as those who perceive social media as interfering with and disrupting their social or professional lives are also inclined to log off, thereby positively impacting their well-being.

Method

To achieve the research objectives of their study, Ronæs and Lervik-Olsen (2018) employed a two-stage approach. In the initial stage, they conducted insightful focus group interviews to gain a comprehensive understanding of the context and gather information relevant to identifying pertinent examples and scenarios for the second survey. For a thorough description of the study's methodology and statistical analysis, readers are referred to Ronæs and Lervik-Olsen's (2018) publication.[1] In this summary, the focus will primarily be on highlighting the key findings to prevent repetitive information.

Measures

Guilt was measured using Cohen et al.'s (2011) Guilt and Shame Proneness scale as a foundation. Specific scenarios were created to explore potential instances where individuals might experience guilt when using social media. These scenarios encompassed situations such as social gatherings with friends, attending children's activities, and engaging in conversations with others. Compulsive social media use was assessed based on the Mobile Phone Problem Use scale initially developed by Bianchi and Phillips (2005). The adapted scale evaluated various aspects, including self-reported feelings of uneasiness when logging off, whether social media became all-consuming, impact on productivity, uneasiness when unavailable, time spent on social media, effects on sleep, and feelings of helplessness when not online.

To assess disruptions, we employed the Perceived Quality-of-Life Impact scale developed by Sirgy et al. (2007). This measure involved several questions that examined different aspects of disruptions, such as disruptions in social settings with friends, during relaxation time, at work or school, and at inappropriate times, such as during meetings with colleagues or interactions with students. Perceived stress was operationalized based on the seminal work of Cohen et al. (1983). This led to the inclusion of questions that assessed the frequency of feeling overwhelmed with too much to do, experiencing a sense of incapability in handling tasks, perceiving a lack of control over important aspects of life, and feeling insufficiently up to speed in various domains.

Well-being was assessed using the BBC Well-Being scale developed by Kinderman et al. (2011). This scale encompassed multiple items that measured various domains of life, including sleep quality, physical health, social interactions, ability to perform everyday tasks, personal life, capacity to experience joy in life, self-satisfaction, work functionality, and the quality of friendships and relationships. Finally, logging off was assessed by considering the impact of logging off on social life, availability, the level of uneasiness experienced when logged off, and the feeling of distance from friends while being logged off. These specific items were identified through initial focus group interviews to capture the relevant aspects of logging off from social media.

Results and Discussion

To gather a comprehensive understanding of the subject, two separate focus group interviews were conducted. One group consisted of respondents below 30 years of age, while the other group comprised respondents above 30 years of age. It is noteworthy that gender was equally represented in both interviews.

In the second stage of the study, a survey was administered to a representative sample of 438 participants, of which 246 were female. The survey aimed to capture a diverse range of age groups, although it is important to note that the distribution across age groups was not equal. Specifically, there were 249 respondents between the ages of 18 and 25, 42 respondents between the ages of 36 and 45, and 59 respondents between the ages of 46 and 55.

Interestingly, the analysis revealed variations among these age groups. The youngest age group (18–25 years) demonstrated lower scores in terms of logging off behavior, indicating a higher tendency toward remaining connected to digital devices. Moreover, this same age group showed higher levels of compulsive use. On the other hand, the age group between 46 and 55 years exhibited the least disturbance in terms of their digital device use.

These findings shed light on the differential effects of age on social media behaviors, underscoring the importance of considering age as a significant factor when examining attitudes toward social media usage.

Analytical Procedures

To assess the conceptual model and evaluate the hypothesized relationships between the variables, the researchers utilized the software SmartPLS 3 (Ringle et al., 2015). This software provides advanced statistical analysis tools and allows for a comprehensive examination of the model's structural relationships. By employing SmartPLS 3, the researchers were able to effectively test and validate the proposed framework, ensuring a rigorous analysis of the data. To further investigate potential differences across genders, a multigroup analysis was conducted. This analysis helped determine whether the relationships within the conceptual model differed significantly between different gender groups. This additional analysis added depth to the study's findings and provided valuable insights into potential gender-related differences within the model and served as a comprehensive examination of the data, improving the overall robustness and validity of the study.

Key Findings

First, the study's findings provided support for all the anticipated relationships within the model. Specifically, individuals who acknowledged their compulsive SMU and felt guilt for neglecting other aspects of life showed a perception of disruption in their normal routines and experienced heightened stress levels. These factors, in turn, motivated them to log off from social media platforms. Additionally, the study found that logging off had a positive impact on various aspects of the individual's quality of life.

It is important to highlight that the study's analysis included individuals of all genders, and the results indicated similarities as well as some notable differences among the groups. Specifically, female respondents seem to score higher than male respondents on the degree of experience of guilt, compulsive use, disturbance, and stress. However, the need to log off seems similar. Also, two relationships within the model displayed significant differences in strength between male and female respondents.

It was observed that male participants displayed a stronger tendency to log off due to feelings of guilt compared to female participants. On the other hand, female respondents exhibited a greater inclination to log off when they became aware of their compulsive use, compared to male participants.

These findings highlight the importance of considering gender as a significant factor in understanding individuals' motivations for logging off from social media platforms. The study's ability to identify and examine these gender-related differences provides a more comprehensive understanding of the dynamics at play and enhances the generalizability and applicability of the research findings.

However, it is worth emphasizing that despite the observed differences in specific relationships between gender groups, the overall fit of the model remains strong. This robustness and generalizability of the model signify that the identified relationships and findings are likely applicable to a broader population beyond the specific sample studied. These results enhance the reliability and relevance of the study's findings, further solidifying their validity. It indicates that the proposed framework and its relationships hold value for understanding individuals' motivations to log off from social media and can be regarded as reliable and applicable to diverse populations.

Overall Discussion

SMU has become ubiquitous, but it also has a dark side with consequences for consumer's mental health and well-being. Specifically, anxiety is associated with too much SMU. The negative consequences of SMU can manifest as digital addiction and a decrease in individual well-being. Factors such as habit and FOMO can contribute to compulsive SMU. Recognizing the negative effects of SMU may motivate individuals to log off and boost their well-being. Understanding the negative effects of SMU is crucial for marketers and leaders seeking to promote sustainable consumption, digital well-being as well and quality of life for their customers. We commend the solutions, such as the student-created log-off initiative discussed earlier in this chapter.

We must approach the dark sides of SMU with a balanced perspective, acknowledging both the challenges and the potential strategies to mitigate these negative impacts. This discussion is particularly relevant for leaders, policymakers, and marketers who are in positions to influence societal norms and regulations regarding digital consumption.

One of the primary steps leaders and policymakers can take is to invest in awareness campaigns and educational programs. These should focus on the potential risks associated with excessive SMU, such as digital addiction, mental health issues, and the impact on physical health due to sedentary lifestyles. Education campaigns can also promote digital literacy, helping individuals to critically assess the information they encounter online and understand the importance of maintaining a balanced digital life.

Policies and programs that encourage healthy digital habits can be instrumental. This could include promoting "digital detoxes" and encouraging periods where individuals consciously log off from social media (see Log Off Movement, 2023). Workplaces and educational institutions can play a crucial role by implementing policies that limit unnecessary digital interruptions and respect digital downtime. In some European countries, they are discussing the ban on mobile phones in the classroom. Policymakers should consider the implementation of regulations that require social media platforms to be more transparent about their algorithms and the potentially addictive nature of their features. This could include mandating warnings about excessive use or designing features that actively encourage breaks or limit usage.

Acknowledging the connection between SMU and both physical and mental well-being, it is critical to prioritize the availability of mental health resources. This should encompass the provision of counseling options that target concerns associated with digital use, in addition to a wide range of general mental health support services. Leaders and policymakers should collaborate with technology companies to develop healthier forms of digital interaction. This could involve designing platforms that promote positive social interactions and well-being, rather than algorithms solely focused on maximizing user engagement. Marketers and business leaders can contribute by promoting sustainable consumption patterns. This involves marketing strategies that do not solely rely on constant digital engagement and recognizing the value of products and services that encourage offline interaction and well-being. Continuous research into the effects of SMU is vital. Policymakers and leaders should support studies that explore the long-term impacts of SMU on individual well-being and societal health. This research can inform future policies and interventions.

In conclusion, addressing the dark side of SMU requires a multifaceted approach to solutions that involve education, regulation, support for mental health, collaboration with technology companies, and a commitment to sustainable consumption. Furthermore, marketers can act by considering other forms of marketing communication to supplement their social media marketing. By taking these steps, leaders, marketers, and policymakers can help mitigate the negative consequences of social media use and promote a more balanced and healthier digital environment for individuals.

Note

1 This study is published in Norwegian. The authors can be contacted for explanations in English.

References

Ajzen, I. (2020). The theory of planned behavior: Frequently asked questions. *Human Behavior and Emerging Technologies, 2*(4), 314–324.

Ajzen, I., & Driver, B. L. (1992). Contingent value measurement: On the nature and meaning of willingness to pay. *Journal of Consumer Psychology, 1*(4), 297–316.

Anderson, J. C., & Gerbing, D. W. (1988). Structural equation modeling in practice: A review and recommended two-step approach. *Psychological Bulletin, 103*(3), 411–422.

Anderson, J. E., & Dunning, D. (2014). Behavioral norms: Variants and their identification. *Social and Personality Psychology Compass, 8*(12), 721–738.

Andreassen, T. W., Lervik-Olsen, L., & Calabretta, G. (2015). Trendspotting and service innovation. *Journal of Service Theory and Practice, 25*(1), 10–30.

Appel, M., Marker, C., & Gnambs, T. (2020). Are social media ruining our lives? A review of meta-analytic evidence. *Review of General Psychology, 24*(1), 60–74.

Bayer, J. B., Triệu, P., & Ellison, N. B. (2020). Social media elements, ecologies, and effects. *Annual Review of Psychology, 71*, 471–497.

Bianchi, A., & Phillips, J. G. (2005). Psychological predictors of problem mobile phone use. *Cyberpsychology & Behavior, 8*(1), 39–51.

Brewer, J. (2019). Mindfulness training for addictions: Has neuroscience revealed a brain hack by which awareness subverts the addictive process? *Current Opinion in Psychology, 28*, 198–203.

Caplan, S. (2005). A social skill account of problematic internet use. *Computers in Human Behavior, 26*(5), 1089–1097.

Churchill, G. A., Jr. (1979). A paradigm for developing better measures of marketing constructs. *Journal of Marketing Research, 16*(1), 64–73.

Cialdini, R. B., & Goldstein, N. J. (2004). Social influence: Compliance and conformity. *Annual Review of Psychology, 55*, 591–621.

Cohen, S., Kamarck, T., & Mermelstein, R. (1983). A global measure of perceived stress. *Journal of Health and Social Behaviour, 24*(4), 385–396.

Cohen, T. R., Wolf, S. T., Panter, A. T., & Insko, C. A. (2011). Introducing the GASP scale: A new measure of guilt and shame proneness. *Journal of Personality and Social Psychology, 100*(5), 947–966.

Cunningham, S., Hudson, C. C., & Harkness, K. (2021). Social media and depression symptoms: A meta-analysis. *Research on Child and Adolescent Psychopathology, 49*, 241–253.

Fennis, B. M. (2022). Self-control, self-regulation, and consumer well-being: A life history perspective. *Current Opinion in Psychology*, *46*, 101344.

Fennis, B. M., Andreassen, T. W., & Lervik-Olsen, L. (2015). Behavioral disinhibition can foster intentions to healthy lifestyle change by overcoming commitment to past behavior. *PloS One*, *10*(11), e0142489.

Fernandes, T., & Castro, A. (2020). Understanding drivers and outcomes of lurking vs. posting engagement behaviors in social media-based brand communities. *Journal of Marketing Management, 36*(7–8), 660–681.

Hofmann, W., & Van Dillen, L. (2012). Desire: The new hot spot in self-control research. *Current Directions in Psychological Science*, *21*(5), 317–322.

Katz, J. E., & Rice, R. E. (2002). *Social consequences of Internet use: Access, involvement, and interaction*. MIT press.

Kinderman, P., Schwannauer, M., Pontin, E., & Tai, S. (2011). The development and validation of a general measure of well-being: The BBC well-being scale. *Quality of Life Research*, *20*(7), 1035–1042.

Kolb, D. G., Caza, A., & Collins, P. D. (2012). States of connectivity: New questions and new directions. *Organization Studies, 33*(2), 267–273.

Kringelbach, M. L. (2005). The human orbitofrontal cortex: Linking reward to hedonic experience. *Nature Reviews Neuroscience*, *6*(9), 691–702.

Kuss, D. J., & Griffiths, M. D. (2017). Social networking sites and addiction: Ten lessons learned. *International Journal of Environmental Research and Public Health*, *14*(3).

Lea, M., O'Shea, T., Fung, P., & Spears, R. (1992). 'Flaming' in computer-mediated communication: Observations, explanations, implications. In M. Lea (Ed.), *Contexts of computer-mediated communication* (pp. 89–112). Harvester Wheatsheaf.

Lervik-Olsen, L. L., Andreassen, T. W., & Fennis, B. M. (2023). When enough is enough: Behavioral and motivational paths to compulsive social media consumption. *European Journal of Marketing*. https://doi.org/10.1108/EJM-12-2022-0898.

Li, W., Snyder, S. M., & Howard, M. O. (2015). Characteristics of internet addiction/pathological internet use in U.S. university students: A qualitative-method investigation. *PLoS One*, *10*(2), e0117372.

Lin, X., Zhang, D., & Li, Y. (2016). Delineating the dimensions of social support on social networking sites and their effects: A comparative model. *Computers in Human Behavior, 58,* 421–430.

Lin, Y. H., Chiang, C. L., Lin, P. H., Chang, L. R., Koehler-Waxman, A., & Morahan-Martin, J. M. (2016). Proposed diagnostic criteria for smartphone addiction. *PLoS One, 11*(11), e0163010.

Lindström, B., Bellander, M., Schultner, D. T., Chang, A., Tobler, P. N., & Amodio, D. M. (2021). A computational reward learning account of social media engagement. *Nature Communications*, *12*(1), 1311.

Log Off Movement. (2023). *It's time to log off*. Retrieved November 5, 2023, from https://www.logoffmovement.org.

Maranges, H. M., Haddad, N., Psihogios, S., Timbs, C. L., Gobes, C. M., & Preston, T. J. (2023). Lower self-control is associated with more standard, reputation management, and maladaptive Facebook use. *Journal of Individual Differences, 44*(4), 234–244.

McKenna, K. Y., & Bargh, J. A. (2000). Plan 9 from cyberspace: The implications of the internet for personality and social psychology. *Personality and Social Psychology Review*, *4*, 57–75.

Meier, A., & Reinecke, L. (2021). Computer-mediated communication, social media, and mental health: A conceptual and empirical meta-review. *Communication Research*, *48*(8), 1182–1209.

Montag, C., Marciano, L., Schulz, P. J., & Becker, B. (2023). Unlocking the brain secrets of social media through neuroscience. *Trends in Cognitive Sciences*, *27*(12), 1102–1104.

NBC News. (2020). *A social media addiction is like binge eating. Here's how to find the right diet.* https://www.nbcnews.com/think/opinion/social-media-addiction-binge-eating-here-s-how-find-right-ncna1144586

Pellegrino, A., Stasi, A., & Bhatiasevi, V. (2022). Research trends in social media addiction and problematic social media use: A bibliometric analysis. *Frontiers in Psychiatry*, *13*, 1017506.

Przybylski, A. K., Murayama, K., DeHaan, C. R., & Gladwell, V. (2013). Motivational, emotional, and behavioral correlates of missing out. *Computers in Human Behavior, 29*(4), 1841–1848.

Reinecke, L., Gilbert, A., & Eden, A. (2022). Self-regulation as a key boundary condition in the relationship between SMU and well-being. *Current Opinion in Psychology*, *45*, 101296.

Ringle, C. M., Wende, S., & Becker, J.-M. 2015. *SmartPLS 3*. SmartPLS GmbH. http://www.smartpls.com

Roberts, J. A., & David, M. E. (2020). The social media party: Fear of missing out (FoMO), social media intensity, connection, and well-being. *International Journal of Human–Computer Interaction*, *36*(4), 386–392.

Ronæs, V., & Lervik-Olsen, L. (2018). Logg av mobilen for å logge på livet. *Beta*, *32*(1), 20–40.

Sherman, L. E., Hernandez, L. M., Greenfield, P. M., & Dapretto, M. (2018). What the brain 'Likes': Neural correlates of providing feedback on social media. *Social Cognitive and Affective Neuroscience*, *13*(7), 699–707.

Sirgy, M. J., Lee, D.-J., Kamra, K., & Tidwell, J. (2007). Developing and validating a measure of consumer well-being in relation to cell phone use. *Applied Research in Quality of Life*, *2*(2), 95–124. http://dx.doi.org/10.1007/s11482-007-9033-3

Skinner, B. F. (1971). Operant conditioning. *The Encyclopedia of Education*, *7*, 29–33.

Spielberger, C. D., Gorsuch, R. L., Lushene, R., Vagg, P. R., & Jacobs, G. A. (1977). *State-trait anxiety inventory for adults self-evaluation questionnaire STAI FormY-1 and FormY-2*. Mind Garden. (Original work published 1968)

Thaler, R. H., & Sunstein, C. R. (2008). *Nudge*,. Yale University Press.

Valkenburg, P. M. (2022). Social media use and well-being: What we know and what we need to know. *Current Opinion in Psychology*, *45*, 101294.

Varian, H. R., & Shapiro, C. (1999). *Information rules: A strategic guide to the network economy*. Harvard Business School Press.

Verplanken, B., & Orbell, S. (2003). Reflections on past behaviour: A self-report index of habit strength. *Journal of Applied Social Psychology, 33*(6), 1313–1330.

Yin, X. Q., de Vries, D. A., Gentile, D. A., & Wang, J. L. (2019). Cultural background and measurement of usage moderate the association between social networking sites (SNSs) usage and mental health: A meta-analysis. *Social Science Computer Review*, *37*(5), 631–648.

Yoon, S., Kleinman, M., Mertz, J., & Brannick, M. (2019). Is social network site usage related to depression? A meta-analysis of Facebook–depression relations. *Journal of Affective Disorders*, *248*, 65–72.

PART 2

Social Media–Fueled Fear and Anxiety

Social Media News and the Dark Web

Now that we have addressed some of the broad potential drivers and consequences of SMU that may be associated with mental health concerns for those who are vulnerable to mental health issues or addictions, we move to Part 2. These two chapters entail specific contexts of social media that may bring fear and anxiety or even exposure to fraud and illegal content/behaviors via the dark web, or "Dark Social." In Chapter 3 (Sussman, Looi, Bright, and Wilcox), the authors examine content on X (formerly known as Twitter) as it relates to specific topics during President Donald Trump's transition to the US presidency. As he is a controversial politician, it is a rich context to examine the role of fear in social media news consumption.

Related to fear and anxiety is the dark web. While more is known about the dark web in general, less focus has been on what is called "Dark Social." In Chapter 4, Sadhotra, Patel, and Mishra examine the dark triad (Machiavellianism, narcissism, and psychopathy) as individual differences that relate to specific types of dark web fraud or dark web use in this startling

DOI: 10.4324/9781003410058-4

conceptual chapter that brings awareness to much of the unethical and illegal activity online.

4. The Dark Web: Dark Personality Traits of Machiavellianism, Narcissism, and Psychopathy and Exploiting Stock Markets

   Neha Sadhotra, Samveg Patel, and Prashant Mishra

3

HOW DOES FEAR DRIVE THE NEWS OF THE DAY?

Examining Topic Salience During Trump's Transition of Power

Kristen L. Sussman, Jiemin Looi, Laura F. Bright, and Gary B. Wilcox

Introduction: Fear and Social Media News

X, formerly known as Twitter, has emerged as a highly effective platform for journalists to set the media's agenda (Boynton & Richardson, 2016; Wihbey et al., 2019). Over time, this amalgamation of conversation and content creates a dynamic and hybrid environment of newsmakers and individuals (Pittman & Reich, 2016), which is not only conducive to agenda-setting but also the transfer of emotion (Kramer et al., 2014). In these scenarios, bursts of emotionally charged discourse are met with public attention, thereby subverting the conventional, top-down information flows from the mass media to the public, such that the public is capable of reconfiguring agenda-setting (Walsh, 2021; Boynton & Richardson, 2016). However, the X/Twitter network also comprises vast amounts of information from political elites, news media outlets, journalists, and ordinary users (Boynton & Richardson, 2016) whereas journalists often integrate and engage with non-elite sources in their news production process (Delmastro & Splendore, 2021). Distinguishing between accurate information and misinformation can feel overwhelming (Guo & Vargo, 2020; Jin et al., 2014), making journalists an appealing source for news, as people perceive them to be more trustworthy than corporate news media.

The public's interest in Trump and U.S. politics was reflected in terms of emotionally charged online discourse (Bright et al., 2021). Therefore, to simplify the information-seeking process, individuals may prioritize information on social media based on its *timeliness* (i.e., newest to oldest), their *personal involvement* with issues based on their interest and perceived

DOI: 10.4324/9781003410058-5

relevance, or "*trending*" topics that have garnered regional or global public attention (Kwak et al., 2010). Given the uncertainty exemplified by the series of events occurring under Donald Trump's presidency in the United States and leading up to the 2020 presidential elections, Trump's transition of power in the White House serves as an appropriate and noteworthy research premise to examine the role of online discourse in agenda-setting.

While scholars have extensively replicated the agenda-setting theory to identify its boundary conditions, far fewer studies have analyzed the underlying role of fear as a discrete emotion in the agenda-setting process. Thus, this chapter explores how the discrete emotion of fear and the prominence of topics in the public agenda were exchanged during the time period. Extending traditional agenda-setting research which focuses on prominence and issue salience, media observations were sourced from *Brandwatch*, a social listening tool that connects to social media and their application programming interface (API) to collect all publicly available posts, comments, and online conversations from Brandwatch. The most prominent topic in the discourse was identified before being used as the chapter focus. Time series analysis was then employed to measure the bidirectional relationships between the media and the public agendas, as well as the role of fear in determining those agendas.

Study Context: X (Formerly Known as Twitter)

Apart from helping journalists construct the media agenda, X/Twitter also structures and shapes the public agenda. In particular, users can utilize social tagging (e.g., hashtags and mentions) to enhance the relevance and prominence of specific topics over time (Boynton & Richardson, 2016; Coe & Griffin, 2020; Parmelee, 2014). These affordances increase the visibility of particular issues and attributes, which elevates its status as focusing events (i.e., crises that evoke massive substantial media and public attention; Leiserowitz, 2011) that evoke heightened emotional responses (Weimann & Brosius, 2017). Further, as journalists share news about these focusing events, people also actively contribute to online discourse. User comments regarding the news are especially impactful as their opinions shape how other social media users view the issues and attributes conveyed in the media agenda (Alves et al., 2014). Therefore, X/Twitter is a tool that facilitates the co-creation and dissemination of news between journalists and the general public (Chen et al., 2022; Coe & Griffin, 2020; Kwak et al., 2010).

Agenda-Setting Theory

The agenda-setting theory was introduced in McCombs and Shaw's (1972) seminal Chapel Hill study, which found that patterns in news coverage shape public opinion. Specifically, issues and attributes of objects that were accorded extensive news media coverage were automatically regarded by the public with greater importance (McCombs & Shaw, 1972). Over the decades, agenda-setting effects have been replicated using different research methods (e.g., Boynton & Richardson, 2016; Wanta & Ghanem, 2007). While the agenda-setting theory was originally formulated in the United States, its central tenets are also generalizable to other countries with varied political systems (e.g., authoritarian and partisan governance), media environments with varying press freedom, and cultural values (McCombs & Shaw, 1972).

Levels of Agenda-Setting

The *first level* of agenda-setting focuses on who and what people are thinking about, (McCombs & Shaw, 1972), which is also called the news media's transmission of issue salience to the public (Guo, 2012). The *second level* of agenda-setting examines "how" people think about the issues presented in the news media (Kim et al., 2002; McCombs & Shaw, 1972). Apart from heightening the overall salience of specific societal issues (Weimann & Brosius, 2017), the second level emphasizes specific attributes of a person or object while omitting others (Vu et al., 2019). Like the first level of agenda-setting, the hierarchical order of attributes is compared to determine the transmission of attribute salience (McCombs & Shaw, 1972). Recent research proposes a *third level* of agenda-setting, otherwise called the network agenda-setting model (Guo, 2012; McCombs et al., 2014). While the prior levels of agenda-setting analyzed a unidirectional and primarily linear transmission of issue and attribute salience from the media to the public (or vice versa), the network agenda-setting model explores the bidirectional transmission of media and public agendas (Guo, 2012). The third level of agenda-setting is distinguished by the bidirectional information flows between the media and the public agenda.

Agenda-Setting Effects across News Media Platforms

Overall, the agenda-setting theory is generalizable across varying news media platforms.

However, Chaffee and Metzger (2001) posited that the intensity of agenda-setting effects would differ across media platforms due to differences in formats and technological affordances. Considering these platform-specific differences, recent calls to modernize agenda-setting research have encouraged researchers to assess the unique mechanisms where salience is assigned to specific issues online and in social media. As such, Weimann and Brosius (2017) advocated the need to move beyond issue-only research.

Apart from homophily, Cowart (2020) noted that the effects of repetition are important determinants of conferring issue salience on social media. By approaching the agenda-setting query from the angle of a topic rather than a conventional agenda-setting issue, measurement issues may be mitigated. Tweets comprises keywords, which in turn are amenable to natural language processing techniques that can be useful in determining significant issues (Meraz, 2016). Given Twitter's popularity as a venue for political discussion, topic analysis can then be used as a quantitative methodology for examining topics of political interest in political discussion.

Emotions as Drivers of Agenda-Setting

Further, by using language as data, the words people use in their daily lives reflect who they are and the emotions they feel (Tausczik & Pennebaker, 2010). Emotion scholarship puts focus on the beginning of emotional processing and then examines the effects of behavior (Frijda, 1986). Thus, someone must be exposed to a message before emotionally processing it and altering their behavior (Frijda, 1986). Prior to emotional processing, the message exposure is the original step of the process. Within the emotions literature is a focus on emotional regulation, which is one's ability to influence what emotions they have, when they have the emotions, and how they are experienced and expressed (Gross, 2008). The first part of this emotional regulation process is the cognitive antecedent and the last part pertains to behavioral effects (Frijda, 1986).

Emotion often transfers among people, especially within social media networks. This is apparent by a study entitled the "Experimental Evidence of Massive-Scale Emotional Contagion" (Kramer et al., 2014). This research revealed evidence from a Facebook study showing that emotion can decidedly transfer in a social network among many people. This term is referred to as "emotional contagion" in the psychology literature (Kramer et al., 2014). Their research found that emotions being expressed via a social media feed can influence and transfer to other social media users in their network (Kramer et al., 2014). Coleman and Wu (2010) noted the role of negative emotions in driving the first level (i.e., issue salience) and second level (i.e., attribute salience) of agenda-setting in political issues.

Fear. During the period of Trump's transition of power, fear was likely enhancing the potential agenda-setting effects that were occurring. Fear may serve as an affective attribute in agenda-setting, drawing public attention and instigating online engagement (Coe & Griffin, 2020; Lowry et al., 2003). Coleman and Wu's (2010) study observed a strong correlation between the news media's description of political candidates using emotional-affective attributes and the public's impression of the political candidates. This study also found that negatively valenced emotions (e.g., fear) exerted a greater impact on public perceptions than positively valenced emotions (e.g., joy). Of the discrete negative emotions, fear enhances individuals' perceived relevance and improves recall for news coverage of societal issues, including crime (Lowry et al., 2003) and the September 11 terrorist attacks (Shivananda et al., 1996).

Taken together, the lack of gatekeepers in online discourse and the political turmoil surrounding Trump's presidency would induce fear and heighten individuals' need for orientation (NFO) (Weaver, 1977). Thus, the focus of our chapter and study poses the following:

RQ1: How will the sentiment of online discourse about Trump's transition of power vary across topics?
RQ2: How is issue salience transmitted between media and public agendas in online discourse?
RQ3: To what extent does fear drive agenda-setting in online discourse?

Method

Data Collection

The dataset was sourced using the social media listening platform *Brandwatch*, a software program that collects billions of publicly shared posts, comments, and online conversations from across the internet. *Brandwatch* enables full access to the X/Twitter "firehose" of publicly available data. *Brandwatch* measures "demographics, influential topics and sentiments" and includes text analytics in a user-friendly interface (Batrinca & Treleaven, 2015, p. 109). As a first step in the text analytic process, *Brandwatch* uses Boolean queries to gather unstructured text data based on a specific set of Boolean search criteria. By combining simple terms to form a Boolean expression based on social media mentions and language relating to President Trump, an initial sample of issue topics was sourced. All publicly available social media mentions and language mentioning "Trump" AND "President" were collected to create a sample of observations.

Publicly available online mentions of the keywords occurring between November 1, 2021, and February 7, 2021, were collected at a sample rate of 26% and resulted in an initial sample of 42,352,749 mentions. This time period was selected to capture the full transition of power that occurred between the U.S. presidential election on November 3, 2020, and President Trump's last day in office on January 20, 2021. For the current study, the most prominent topic was studied. In other words, any mention of

"Trump" AND "White House" that occurred on Twitter, Reddit, forums, online news sites, blogs, or Tumblr, were included.

As the biggest source for the data, 79.61% of the conversation volume was sourced from Twitter followed by 15.8% from online news sites, 1.52% from blogs, 1.52% from forums, and about 1% each from Reddit and Tumblr. An online forum is a discussion site where conversations occur in the form of messages and related discussions (i.e., thepoliticsforums.com). Facebook was not included due to API and privacy restrictions of the platform that limits data. For a review of online news sites, the top ten sources are included in the appendix. Globally, approximately 77.03% of the mentions originated in the United States, 4.52% in the United Kingdom, 3.37% in Canada, 1.51% in Australia, 1.42% in India, 1.06% in Nigeria, and less than 1% in all other global locations. Examples of top sources by category can be found in the appendix.

Data Analysis

To examine the salience of topic transfer in relation to the emotion of fear, publicly available data was collected that mentioned Trump. Adhering to agenda-setting studies using computational research methods (e.g., Boynton & Richardson, 2016; Guo & Vargo, 2020; Meraz, 2011; Wanta & Foote, 1994), this study utilizes a series of analytical approaches. First, this study utilizes natural language processing to identify prominent topics that amassed substantial public attention. Then, this study utilized sentiment analysis (refer to Sussman et al., 2023 for a recent example) to focus on tweets with negative emotions. After this, the study conducted regression and time series analysis to determine the developments in media and public agenda. Finally, this study supplemented analyses with Granger causality tests to determine whether the time series for the media agenda was useful in predicting the public agenda.

As a text analytic method, topics are revealed in the language by removing stop words (e.g., a, is, the, etc.) to provide meaningful insight into otherwise unstructured text data. When using text as data, words can provide measures for understanding social behavior, emotion, and attention (Tausczik & Pennebaker, 2010). Given the complexity of the topics, the study selected one focus of "Trump" AND "White House" (e.g., mentions relating to Trump and the White House). This topic was selected based on interest and popularity in the Trump topic mention volume. This approach allows the researcher to take an indirect approach to measuring which topics were most salient about Trump. Trump's tweets have been made public for the purposes of research. However, by identifying topics in the public agenda, the study provides another context for measuring agendas.

After selecting the topic of interest, using a computer-assisted analysis, all online mentions collected were coded before exploring the relationship between online news and affective attribute agenda-setting effects. Predictor variables of fear, impressions, and media agendas were measured for bi-directional, significant relationships. Impressions, which are the total number of potential times a topic was seen by social media users, are provided by X/Twitter's API and used as the outcome measure of attention in the study. Impressions are discussed in our findings as a measure of prominence of agenda-setting in the Trump, White House topic of interest. Impressions have been used for many years in the field of advertising and public relations as an important measure of the success of media in reaching the public. Thus, topic prominence was measured using impressions and is referred to as representing the public agenda throughout the paper. Additional regression, including VAR and time series analysis, was performed using *R* before employing Granger causality tests using the *R* package, "lmtest."

The time series analysis began with a test for unit roots which can indicate an issue of non-stationary data, a potential problem that suggests the possibility of unreliable, spurious results. Issues of non-stationary data can be identified by how the data vary over time by mean, variance, and covariance. To identify and remedy any issue, the Augmented Dickey-Fuller test was applied using the *R* package, "tseries" (Trapletti et al., 2021). Next, the variables that were identified as non-stationary were remedied using a first-differencing technique (Walters, 2018).

For the model, all variables were treated as endogenous because all variables were sourced from one online platform (e.g., Brandwatch). To identify the best lag, the "tsDyn" package in *R* was used (Di Narzo et al., 2022). Then, the best BIC scores identified that the lag of 1 was optimal and selected based on the lowest BIC score of 6641.16. Next, VAR models were run and tested which endogenous variables were the most appropriate in the model before using bi-variate Granger causality tests. Using the "lmtest" package in *R*, the bivariate (two-way) tests were employed (Hothorn et al., 2022). The raw data, including online news stories and fear, as measured in the language, are presented in Figure 3.2. Additional tests are included in the appendix.

Results

RQ1: Topics by Sentiment

The prominent topics identified in this study were selected based on their popularity and were identified within the larger Trump conversation (see Figure 3.1). With interest in the hybrid environment in social media, this study examined the time period and discourse that occurred during President Donald Trump's transition out of the White House (e.g., November 1, 2020, and February 7, 2021). From this dataset, the ten topics that were produced are presented in Table 3.1. Corresponding examples of online mentions and sources are also provided. The study focused on the Trump + White House topic and is discussed in the following section as it relates to the third and fourth research questions of agenda-setting and the attribute of fear.

The online mentions of Trump occurring between November 1, 2021, and February 7, 2021, were collected at a sample rate of 26% and resulted in an initial data set of 42,352,749 mentions. Due to firehose restrictions, datasets this large must be sampled. As the most prominent theme, Donald Trump commanded the two most mentioned topics with 1,600,804 or about 38% of all online mentions in the dataset. Other themes included Washington (9.51% of topics), White House (9.23% of topics), Senate (7.79% of topics), Democrats (7.5% of topics), Capitol (7.17% of topics), President-elect Joe Biden (6.92% of topics) and vice president (6.17% of topics).

TABLE 3.1 Trump Data by Source and Topic

Topic	*Source*	*Description*
President Donald Trump	Twitter	Thank God for President Donald Trump!
White House	Twitter	"Maybe we'll look back from a future world where a woman is in the White House and wonder if experiencing four years on the dark side with Donald got us there a little faster," writes @gailcollins
Democrats	Twitter	I tell you right now I am not budging on what God told me Trump will serve the next four years Those who stole the election will go to prison it will be Democrats and Republicans who will be found out to have had a hand in the evil. Its not over no fat lady singing here!
Capitol	Twitter	"Let's all post photos of the Women's March from 2016 tomorrow. There's no way that Trump supporters are anywhere near organized enough to turn out in the same numbers in cities all across the US, much less the Capitol."

Note: The examples above are intended to illustrate the topics. Online mentions captured by Brandwatch.

A computer-assisted sentiment analysis revealed that data related to the overall sentiment in the online mentions of Trump were overwhelmingly negative with about 91.73% (6,381,398) of online mentions falling into this category. Alternatively, about 8.27% (528,000) of this sample were positive. Negative topics were White House, Trump, U.S., Congress, Senate, Capitol, Republicans, Washington, and Democrats. Interestingly, topics including the White House and Democratic parties (i.e., Republican and Democrat), fell into both negative and positive sentiment, while others were found to be either discretely positive or negative. For instance, Americans, vice president, and President-elect Joe Biden are three topics presented only as positive. On the other hand, Trump appears in both the positive and negative results. Overall, the conversation and media trend negatively. Figure 3.1 shows the Trump data by topic and sentiment.

RQ2 and RQ3: Agenda-setting on X/Twitter

The VAR model results identify four statistically significant Granger-causality relationships in the Trump+White House topic data. The first suggested that the prominence of the topic on Twitter Granger-caused the number of online news stories published on the same topic. The second suggests that fear, as expressed by the public agenda through language on

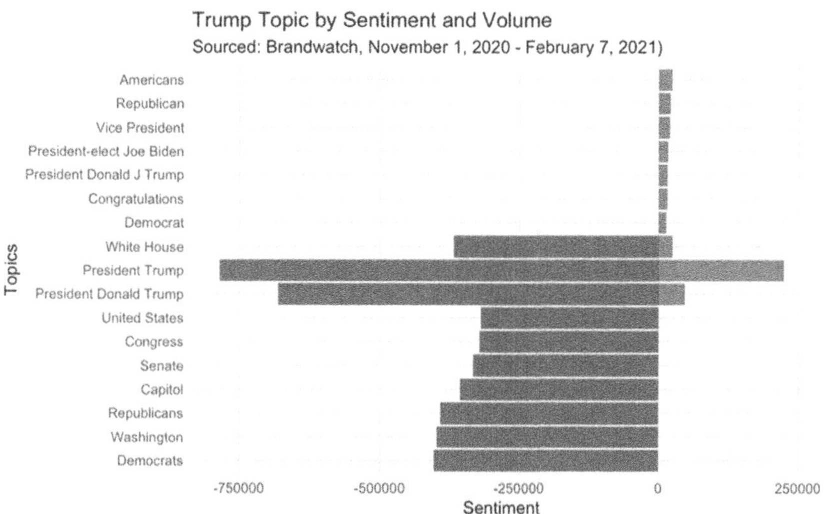

FIGURE 3.1 Trump data by topic and sentiment.

TABLE 3.2 Granger analysis of Trump and White House topics

Bidirectional Tests of Granger Causality	*F*	*p Value*
News Stories to Impressions	0.286	0.594
News Stories to Fear	0.049	0.826
Journalists to Impressions	0.001	0.925
Fear to Impressions	1.011	0.317
Fear to News Stories	0.547	0.461
Impressions to News Stories	3.962	0.049*
Fear to Journalists' Tweets	13.359	<.001***
Impressions to Journalists' Tweets	5.701	0.018*
Impressions to Fear	7.362	0.008**

Note: 1 Impressions are the number of times a message has potentially been seen on Twitter. 2. Emotions were measured using computer-assisted natural language processing based on Ekman and Friesen's six emotions. ***$p < 0.001$, **$p < 0.01$, *$p < 0.05$

Twitter, Granger-caused the number of tweets published by journalists. The third significant relationship suggests that the prominence of the topic also Granger-caused the number of tweets published by journalists on Twitter. The final and fourth significant result found that the prominence of online news stories Granger-caused fear. The Granger-causality results are presented in Table 3.2.

The third research question sought to understand the role of fear in predicting impressions of a particular topic on Twitter, as such time series analysis was used. Impressions, which are the total number of potential times a topic was seen by social media users, were operationalized as a measure of prominence on X/Twitter. The results are presented visually in Figure 3.2.

Discussion

Overall, this study drew upon the societally prominent context of Donald Trump's transition of power to examine the agenda-setting theory's predictive validity regarding online discourse on X/Twitter. Moreover, this study assessed how negative emotions (e.g., fear, NFO) established "pictures in our heads" (Lippmann, 1922), which shaped the construction of the media agenda and its impact on the public agenda. Notably, this study observed that the number of daily online news stories and journalists' tweets determined the salience of specific issues. Additionally, fear played a crucial role in journalists' construction of the media's agenda, which in turn elicited fear among their audiences.

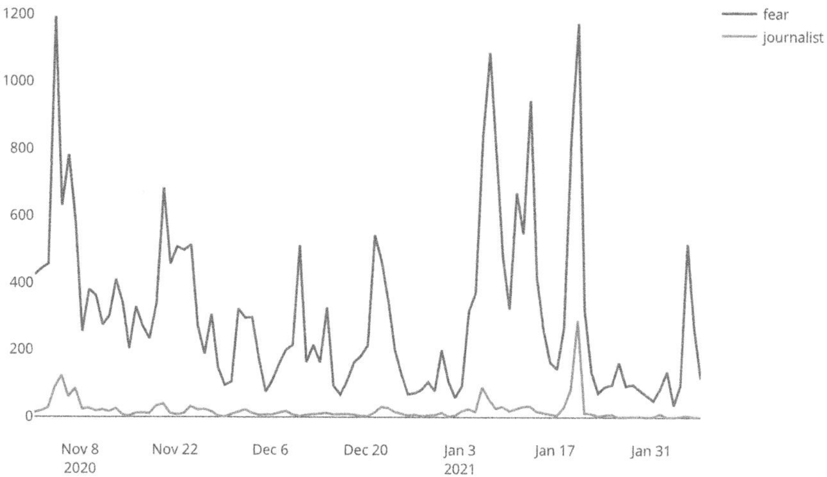

FIGURE 3.2 Time series analysis of impressions (number of times a topic was seen by X users) and fear.

Study Implications

The study's findings present several theoretical and practical implications. First, our findings revealed that the emotion of fear was significant in predicting, and temporally related to the number of tweets (i.e., about the White House and Trump) published by journalists on X/Twitter. This is an important finding considering the influence of journalists on social media. This influence can be measured in terms of the number of connections a journalist has, the number of followers, their measure of centrality, and the prestige of the news publication that employs them (Tauberg, 2022). However, the influence and role that a journalist plays in the social network are unique given the ability to share personal opinions while also holding a distinctive level of trust among their network of followers. Interestingly, fear was not temporally significant in Granger-causing online news stories, which could suggest that journalists are more malleable than traditional news media in their involvement in news distribution. Impressions were significant in Granger-causing fear as expressed by the language in the data. These results engender new questions relating to media effects. Though outside the direct interest of this chapter, these results are interesting and create an opportunity for future research to further explore the effects of polarization in an online media environment.

Second, this chapter has answered calls to expand how modern agenda-setting research examines issues, another aim was to focus on topics instead of traditional issues. To do this, online media mentioning "Trump" AND "White House" provided the first object, or topic, of research interest.

After identifying the topic of focus, the study analyzed the relationships between the emotion of fear and the prominence of the topic in both the public and news media agendas. Unique to this study, impressions were identified to Granger-cause the number of online news stories published on the topic, the number of tweets from journalists (on the topic), and the amount of fear in the public's agenda. Fear, on the other hand, was found to Granger-cause only journalists' tweets. Again, this supports the previous finding that their voices hold a special position in the network.

Perhaps most interesting was the lack of support for traditional agenda-setting occurring in the online environment. There was no positive relationship found between online news stories and the prominence of the White House topic in Trump discourse. Because the study examined online-only media on X/Twitter, online news sites were operationalized as traditional media. However, when measuring the relationship between the prominence of the topic and the number of news stories published about the topic, there was evidence of Granger causality. A positive relationship was found in both the measure of impressions to the number of journalists' tweets and the number of impressions to online news stories published. This suggests that both journalists' and news media's agendas are set by the prominence of a topic on X/Twitter.

Coleman et al. (2009) describe agenda-setting as "the process of the mass media presenting certain issues frequently and prominently with the result that large segments of the public come to perceive those issues as more important than others" (p. 147). X/Twitter considers impressions as a representation of the number of times a message was potentially seen on their platform. Therefore, the measure of prominence of a topic was operationalized using impressions. As impressions increase and reach more people, the result is an increase in the frequency that the message is seen. Impressions, or the prominence of the topic, were found to Granger-cause news stories, journalists' tweets, and fear. This suggests evidence in support of previous literature which has shown that more coverage of an issue relates to how important people find the issue (Mustapha, 2012; Coleman et al., 2009).

For political campaign managers, impressions play an important role in messaging and relate to driving awareness and strategic goals of persuasion. On social media, platforms like Facebook, X/Twitter, and LinkedIn, now make measures of reach, impressions, and frequency readily available. In news media, agenda-setting effects can be limited by the slower, less frequent publishing schedule found in television, print, or even online news sites (Boynton & Richardson, 2016; Guo & Vargo, 2020; Harder et al., 2017). Thus, research suggests that both speed and immediacy are key influencing factors to set the agenda (Conway et al., 2015). Common to social media marketing as well as personal use of social media, speed and agility can result in increased reach and engagement among communities (Conway et al., 2015). Agenda-setting literature has also suggested more focus on networks (e.g., Guo, 2012; Meraz, 2011), in an effort to better understand intermedia effects. The results also support research that has shown X/Twitter as a platform dominated by news media and the need to measure "who follows whom" in relation to intermedia effects between journalists (Conway et al., 2015; Guo & Vargo, 2016).

Limitations and Future Research

Despite the research contributions, the findings should be interpreted with the following caveats. First, this study relies heavily on computational data that has been analyzed using a "black box" analysis. Therefore, the research and outcomes contain some sampling errors that are not generalizable across the population and should be further analyzed using hand-labeled training data from human coders. Naturally, the goal of social science is to recognize patterns in human behavior and consequently, these findings should continue to be rigorously tested across methods and groups. Second, the measures used in the study are extracted from natural language and therefore the data itself was not created for scientific inquiry. Thus, some control is lost in the study creating its own set of limitations (Wu & Taneja, 2021). Further, X/Twitter itself can have sampling errors when used generally in social media research and has been shown to only represent a small minority of people. One in five X/Twitter users are representative of the broader population and are younger and likely to identify as a democrat (Wojcik & Hughes, 2019).

Notably, with the emergence of terms like angry populism and Trump's resulting U.S. headlines, the former president's use of media at times could be interpreted as satirical. After the Capitol Riots, social media organizations made a broad move to permanently ban Trump from use of their platforms, with many accusing that his misuse had contributed to inciting violence at the Capitol on January 6, 2021; recent studies, though, have suggested that hate groups have become more difficult to track as they move online (Southern Poverty Law Center, 2021). While advocates of Trump may recognize his ability to mobilize groups of people, it is also plausible that these far-right acts of violence have ultimately engaged an entirely new audience outside of the traditionally politically involved citizen.

Conclusion

This study aimed to better understand how "pictures in our heads" (Lippmann, 1922) are both experienced and transferred in an online media environment. The focal predictors of interest included the news agenda, measured by the number of daily online news stories published and the number of daily tweets from journalists on X/Twitter, as well as the public agenda. To measure the public agenda and to extend agenda-setting research beyond the first level in a meaningful manner, the secondary focus was on the emotion of fear and was examined in relation to the news and public agendas. Time series analysis and Granger causality tests were employed to test temporal relationships between the news media and public agendas.

Relatively few studies ground their agenda-setting effects in an online media context alone. Recognizing the need for more focus in this area, this study uses six sources of publicly available online data to provide a sample of online discourse. Contemporary agenda-setting research has traditionally relied on "two countervailing trends" including those that explicate key theoretical concepts and those that expand into new domains (McCombs & Valenzuela, 2020, p. 157). Some issues of the traditional theoretical application of agenda-setting have been called to light and seek an expansion of the definition of news sources, differentiation of agendas, and segmentation of issues (Weimann & Brosius, 2017). In recognition of these issues, the current study expands agenda-setting research beyond its traditional measure of issue salience and focuses on a subtopic of interest—online media coverage regarding Trump's transition of power in the White House.

References

Alves, F., Caeiro, S., Azeiteiro, U. M., De Kraker, J., Kuijs, S., Cörvers, R., & Offermans, A. (2014). Internet public opinion on climate change: A world views analysis of online reader comments. *International Journal of Climate Change Strategies and Management*, 6(1), 19–33.

Batrinca, B., & Treleaven, P. C. (2015). Social media analytics: A survey of techniques, tools and platforms. *Ai & Society*, *30*, 89–116.

Boynton, G. R., & Richardson, G. W., Jr. (2016). Agenda-setting in the twenty-first century. *New Media & Society*, *18*(9), 1916–1934. https://doi.org/10.1177%2F1461444815616226

Bright, L. F., Sussman, K. L., & Wilcox, G. B. (2021). Facebook, trust and privacy in an election year: Balancing politics and advertising. *Journal of Digital & Social Media Marketing*, *8*(4), 332–346.

Chaffee, S. H., & Metzger, M. J. (2001). The end of mass communication? *Mass Communication & Society*, *4*(4), 365–379.

Chen, E., Deb, A., & Ferrara, E. (2022). #Election2020: The first public Twitter dataset on the 2020 US Presidential election. *Journal of Computational Social Science*, *5*(1), 1–18. https://doi.org/10.1007/s42001-021-00117-9

Coe, K., & Griffin, R. A. (2020). Marginalized identity invocation online: The case of President Donald Trump on Twitter. *Social Media+Society*, *6*(1), 2056305120913979. https://doi.org/10.1177/2056305120913979

Coleman, R., McCombs, M., Shaw, D., & Weaver, D. (2009). Agenda-setting. In *The handbook of journalism studies* (pp. 167–180). Routledge.

Coleman, R., & Wu, H. D. (2010). Proposing emotion as a dimension of affective agenda setting: Separating affect into two components and comparing their second-level effects. *Journalism & Mass Communication Quarterly*, *87*(2), 315–327.

Conway, B. A., Kenski, K., & Wang, D. (2015). The rise of Twitter in the political campaign: Searching for intermedia agenda-setting effects in the presidential primary. *Journal of Computer-Mediated Communication, 20*(4), 363–380. https://doi.org/10.1111/jcc4.12124

Cowart, H. (2020). What to think about: The applicability of agenda-settings in a social media context. *The Agenda-Setting Journal*, *4*(2), 195–218.

Delmastro, M., & Splendore, S. (2021). Google, Facebook and what else? Measuring the hybridity of Italian journalists by their use of sources. *European Journal of Communication*, *36*(1), 4–20.

Di Narzo, A., Aznarte, J., & Stigler, M. (2022). tsDyn: Nonlinear time series models with regime switching. *R package version 11.0.2*.

Frijda, N. H. (1986). *The emotions*. Cambridge University Press.

Gross, J. J. (2008). Emotion regulation. *Handbook of Emotions*, *3*(3), 497–513.

Guo, L. (2012). The application of social network analysis in agenda-setting research: A methodological exploration. *Journal of Broadcasting & Electronic Media, 56*(4), 616–631. https://doi.org/10.1080/08838151.2012.732148

Guo, L., & Vargo, C. (2020). "Fake news" and emerging online media ecosystem: An integrated intermedia agenda-setting analysis of the 2016 US presidential election. *Communication Research,* *47*(2), 178–200. https://doi.org/10.1177/0093650218777177

Harder, R. A., Sevenans, J., & Van Aelst, P. (2017). Intermedia agenda-setting in the social media age: How traditional players dominate the news agenda in election times. *The International Journal of Press/Politics*, *22*, 275–293.

Hothorn, T., Zeileis, A., Farebrother, R., Cummins, C., Millo, G., Mitchell, D., & Zeileis, A. (2022). Lmtest: Testing linear regression models. *R package version 0.9-40*.

Jin, F., Wang, W., Zhao, L., Dougherty, E., Cao, Y., Lu, C. T., & Ramakrishnan, N. (2014). Misinformation propagation in the age of twitter. *Computer*, *47*(12), 90–94.

Kim, S. H., Scheufele, D. A., & Shanahan, J. (2002). Think about it this way: Attribute agenda-setting function of the press and the public's evaluation of a local issue. *Journalism & Mass Communication Quarterly, 79*(1), 7–25. https://doi.org/10.1177%2F107769900207900102

Kramer, A. D., Guillory, J. E., & Hancock, J. T. (2014). Experimental evidence of massive-scale emotional contagion through social networks. *Proceedings of the National Academy of Sciences*, *111*(24), 8788–8790.

Kwak, H., Lee, C., Park, H., & Moon, S. (2010, April). What is Twitter, a social network or a news media? In *Proceedings of the 19th international conference on world wide web* (pp. 591–600).

Leiserowitz, A. (2011). Editorial, environment: Science and policy for sustainable development. *53*(6), 2–15. https://doi.org/10.1080/00139157.2011.623033

Lippmann, W. (1922). *The world outside and the pictures in our heads*. MacMillan Co.

Lowry, D. T., Nio, T. C. J., & Leitner, D. W. (2003). Setting the public fear agenda: A longitudinal analysis of network TV crime reporting, public perceptions of crime, and FBI crime statistics. *Journal of Communication*, *53*(1), 61–73.

McCombs, M., & Valenzuela, S. (2020). *Setting the agenda: Mass media and public opinion*. John Wiley & Sons.

McCombs, M. E. & Shaw, D. L. (1972). The agenda-setting function of mass media. *The Public Opinion Quarterly*, *36*(2), 176–187.

McCombs, M. E., Shaw, D. L., & Weaver, D. H. (2014). New directions in agenda-setting theory and research. *Mass Communication and Society*, *17*(6), 781–802. https://doi.org/10.1080/15205436.2014.964871

Meraz, S. (2011). Using time series analysis to measure intermedia agenda-setting influence in traditional media and political blog networks. *Journalism & Mass Communication Quarterly*, *88*(1), 176–194.

Meraz, S. (2016). An expanded perspective on network agenda-setting between traditional media and Twitter political discussion groups in 'everyday political talk.' *The Power of Information Networks*, 66–87.

Mustapha, L. K. (2012). Agenda-setting theory: A reflective and visionary analysis. *Critique and Application of Communication Theory*, 85–108.

Parmelee, J. H. (2014). The agenda-building function of political tweets. *New Media & Society, 16*(3), 434–450. https://doi.org/10.1177%2F1461444813487955

Pittman, M., & Reich, B. (2016). Social media and loneliness: Why an Instagram picture may be worth more than a thousand Twitter words. *Computers in Human Behavior, 62*, 155–167. https://doi.org/10.1016/j.chb.2016.03.084

Shivananda, S., Lennard-Jones, J., Logan, R., Fear, N., Price, A., Carpenter, L., & Van Blankenstein, M. (1996). Incidence of inflammatory bowel disease across Europe: Is there a difference between north and south? Results of the European Collaborative Study on Inflammatory Bowel Disease (EC-IBD). *Gut*, *39*(5), 690–697.

Southern Poverty Law Center. (2021). *The year in hate and extremism 2020: Hate groups became more difficult to track*. https://www.splcenter.org/news/2021/02/01/year-hate-and-extremism-2020-hate-groups-became-more-difficult-track-amid-covid-and#.YJv1HoztFKQ.twitter

Sussman, K. L., Bouchacourt, L., Bright, L. F., Wilcox, G. B., Mackert, M., Norwood, A. S., & Allport Altillo, B. S. (2023). COVID-19 topics and emotional frames in vaccine hesitation: A social media text and sentiment analysis. *Digital Health*, *9*. https://doi.org/10.1177/20552076231158308.

Tauberg, M. (2022, May 4). The most influential journalists on Twitter. *Medium*. Retrieved March 4, 2023, from https://medium.com/the-shadow/the-most-influential-journalists-on-twitter-f04e14435db7

Tausczik, Y. R., & Pennebaker, J. W. (2010). The psychological meaning of words: LIWC and computerized text analysis methods. *Journal of Language and Social Psychology*, *29*(1), 24–54.

Trapletti, A., Hornik, K., & LeBaron, B. (2021). Tseries: Time series analysis and computational finance. *R package version 0.10-49*.

Vu, H. T., Jiang, L., Chacón, L. M. C., Riedl, M. J., Tran, D. V., & Bobkowski, P. S. (2019). What influences media effects on public perception? A cross-national study of comparative agenda-setting. *International Communication Gazette*, *81*(6–8), 580–601. https://uk.sagepub.com/en-gb/journals-permissions

Walsh, J. P. (2021). Digital nativism: Twitter, migration discourse and the 2019 election. *New Media & Society*, 14614448211032980. https://doi.org/10.1177%2F14614448211032980

Walters, T. (2018, January 30). Time series analysis in R part 2: Time series transformations | DataScience+. *Datascience+*. Retrieved March 23, 2022, from https://datascienceplus.com/time-series-analysis-in-r-part-2-time-series-transformations/

Wanta, W., & Foote, J. (1994). The president-news media relationship: A time series analysis of agenda-setting. *Journal of Broadcasting & Electronic Media*, *38*(4), 437–448.

Wanta, W., & Ghanem, S. (2007). Effects of Agenda-setting. In R. W. Preiss, B. M. Gayle, N. Burrell, M. Allen, & J. Bryant (Eds.), *Mass media effects research: Advances through meta-analysis* (pp. 37–51). Lawrence Erlbaum Associates Publishers.

Weaver, D. H. (1977). Political issues and voter need for orientation. In D. l. Shaw & M. E. McCombs (Eds.), *The emergence of American political issues* (pp. 107–119). St. Paul: West.

Weimann, G., & Brosius, H. B. (2017). Redirecting the agenda. *The Agenda-Setting Journal*, *1*(1), 67–102.

Wihbey, J., Joseph, K., & Lazer, D. (2019). The social silos of journalism? Twitter, news media and partisan segregation. *New Media & Society*, *21*(4), 815–835. https://doi.org/10.1177%2F1461444818807133

Wojcik, S., & Hughes, A. (2019). Sizing up Twitter users. *PEW Research Center*, *24*, 1–23.

Wu, A. X., & Taneja, H. (2021). Platform enclosure of human behavior and its measurement: Using behavioral trace data against platform episteme. *New Media & Society*, *23*(9), 2650–2667.

APPENDIX

1. Top ten sources by online media source category

Top Sources by Category			
Bogs	*Forums*	*News Sites*	*Twitter*
thegateway pundit.com	democraticunder ground.com	yahoo.com	cnnbrk
oann.com	thepoliticsforums.com	msn.com	CNN
rawstory.com	justplainpolitics.com	pressfrom.info	nytimes
wordpress.com	debatepolitics.com	headtopics.com	BBCWorld
google.com	thegatewaypundit.com	dailymail.co.uk	Reuters
thehill.com	advfn.com	thehill.com	FoxNews
townhall.com	dcurbanmom.com	foxnews.com	JoeBiden
nationalfile.com	xnxx.com	politicalwire.com	WSJ
populist.press	bodybuilding.com	washingtonpost.com	TIME
weebly.com	delphiforums.com	democraticunder ground.com	washingtonpost

2. The Boolean query code for Trump data that was used to source social media discourse relating to him is included here: "Trump" AND "President"

3. Tests of ACF and PACF

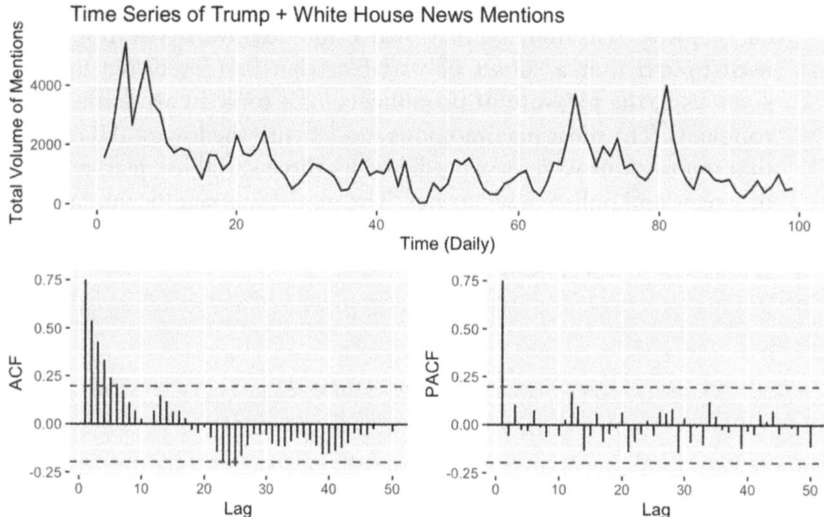

FIGURE 3.3 Tests of ACF and PACF: Total Volume of X Mentions and a Time Series Analysis of Trump and White House News Mentions.

4. Decomposed Time Series of News Stories on Trump, White House

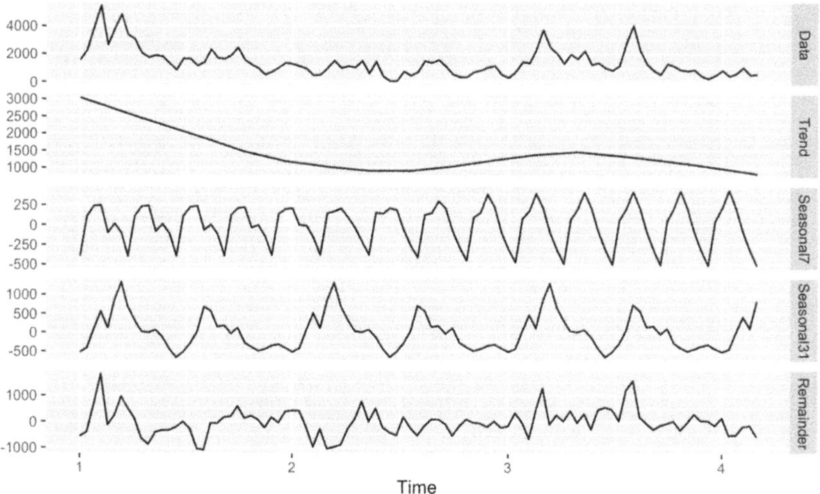

FIGURE 3.4 Data, Trends, and Seasonal Views (Decomposed Time Series) of News Stories on Trump and the White House.

5. Multiple linear regression

Using stepwise selection, both forward and backward selection were used to arrive at a subset of variables that best predicted impressions (e.g., the measure of prominence of a topic in an online environment). The most parsimonious model with the lowest AIC found that impressions were best predicted by three variables: fear, number of tweets and online news stories. The model was significant, and the three variables predicted about 81.65% of the variance in the model [$F(3, 95) = 140.9$, $p < .001$, $R^2 = 0.817$].

4

THE DARK WEB

Dark Personality Traits of Machiavellianism, Narcissism, and Psychopathy and Exploiting Stock Markets

Neha Sadhotra, Samveg Patel, and Prashant Mishra

Introduction to the Dark Web and Dark Social Media

The Internet and social media have collectively transformed the world by connecting people and providing numerous amounts of information at consumers' fingertips. Yet, a problem remains, in that beyond the familiar surface web lies the "dark web," a platform that is largely hidden and less traceable. It is especially correlated with those with personality types and disorders relating to psychopathy, narcissism, and manipulation. As the word "dark" suggests something that cannot be seen, dark web is a hidden part of the Internet that is only accessible using special software. The dark web represents a small fraction of the Internet that is intentionally hidden and inaccessible through conventional search engines. Web browsers do not index the contents of the dark web, the dark web allows the users and website operators to maintain their identity anonymously without sharing their location information. The exact year of the emergence of the dark web is unknown, but it began in the early twenty-first century. In 2012 Alexis C. Madrigal, an editor at *The Atlantic*, coined the term "dark social" in an article titled "Dark Social: We Have the Whole History of the Web Wrong." He used the term to describe the sharing of online content through private channels that are not traceable by analytics tools. The goal of this conceptual chapter is to provide a broad overview of the dark web, social media, and the linkages between dark personality traits and usage of the dark web to exploit the stock market returns.

The dark web is an overlay network that uses non-standard internet protocol but requires software like the Onion Router, known as TOR. TOR

DOI: 10.4324/9781003410058-6

anonymizes users by encrypting and routing their internet traffic through a network of volunteer-operated servers. This routing obscures the source and destination of online activities, offering a higher level of privacy and anonymity versus the surface web. Dark social media refers to social media content that does not have digital referral information about the source. People use dark social media for privacy, anonymity, censorship avoidance, or illegal activities.

There are social media platforms on the dark web, with all the functions similar to a regular social media platform where users can create their own profile page, have friends and followers, write posts, create blogs, and discussion forums. The profiles on dark social media are unidentifiable. Dark social media uses private communication channels for exchange of information. When the user uses dark social media through the specialized browser, it sends the information through multiple nodes all across private networks before reaching a particular site and hence the location and IP address of the user cannot be traced. The content shared on regular social media platforms like Meta (Facebook) and X (Twitter) is visible to anyone in the form of posts and interactions, whereas dark social media platforms prioritize privacy and anonymity.

However, the term "dark" in dark social media does not always refer to anything malicious or illegal. Instead, it signifies the lack of visibility and traceability of the origin of the information source. The usage of dark social media platforms is a topic of interest to marketers to understand how content is being shared and consumed online about their products and services. As the link shared on dark social media platforms masks the referral point identity and shows as the direct link, it is difficult for marketers to understand the impact of specific campaigns.

Dark social media platforms and the dark web have gained more attention in recent times with the evolution of online communication and the growing importance of privacy in the digital age. Dark social media platforms play a significant role in the spread of information and content, and they have garnered concern due to their association with illicit activities. Although there are people advocating the use of the dark web and dark social media platforms for some good reasons like whistleblowing, the right of speech to express one's opinion and free journalism in some of the countries with tight censorship and lesser freedom, the emergence of dark social media platforms has given rise to larger threats. Dark social media platforms are full of advertisements for illegal products and services. The purpose of regular social media platforms is to socialize, share personal experiences and moments of life, build networks and connections with like-minded people, and communicate from an identified source. Whereas the prime purpose of dark social media platforms is to have anonymous communication.

The dark web's anonymity feature can be empowering and problematic. On the one hand, they offer an avenue for individuals to exercise their right to free speech, bypass censorship, and protect their online activities from surveillance. Journalists, activists, and dissidents in repressive regimes can use the dark web to communicate and disseminate information safely. On the other hand, the same features also enable cybercriminals, terrorists, and other malicious actors to operate with reduced risk of identification or apprehension. The dark web is primarily used for ransomware, political discussion, terrorism, cryptocurrency services, fraud-related activities, to name a few. It is often associated with illegal activities, such as drug trafficking, weapons sales, hacking services, and various forms of cybercrime. The dark web is a haven for criminal activities.

However, it is again important to note that not everything on the dark web is illegal, and there are legitimate uses for anonymous browsing and communication. The dark web provides anonymity to its users, which can attract individuals engaged in illicit activities or those who have concerns about privacy and security. It is crucial to understand that accessing and engaging in illegal activities on the dark web is against the law in many jurisdictions. Engaging with the dark web without proper knowledge and precautions can expose individuals to significant risks, including cyberattacks, scams, and legal consequences. The risk of using dark social media is that if the user's computer is not properly protected, information stored on the user's computer can be stolen. One of the most well-known aspects of the dark web is its hidden marketplaces. These marketplaces enable the trade of illegal goods and restricted services, including drugs, firearms, stolen data, counterfeit currencies, and hacking tools. Commercial websites on the dark web use cryptocurrency like bitcoin as the payment method, further contributing to the anonymity of buyers and sellers.

Dark social media platforms create a new set of challenges for regulators, as it is difficult to track the origin and spread of content shared on these platforms. The content on dark social media appears as direct traffic in website analytics, making it difficult to find the exact digital referral point. The dark web continues to intrigue and challenge our understanding of the Internet's capabilities. It represents a complex ecosystem with both legal and illegal dimensions. While it facilitates privacy and provides opportunities for individuals in oppressive environments, it also harbors illicit activities that pose risks to individuals, businesses, and societies at large. Effectively addressing the challenges posed by the dark web requires a comprehensive approach that balances privacy, security, and legal considerations. By fostering collaboration, technological advancements, and awareness, we can strive to navigate the hidden dimensions of the Internet responsibly and ensure a safer digital landscape for all.

Literature Review: Personality

Personality, the essence that shapes our thoughts, emotions, and behavior, is a multifaceted construct that has intrigued psychologists and philosophers for centuries. The study of personality delves into understanding the unique and enduring patterns of traits, characteristics, and behaviors that distinguish individuals from one another. This section aims to explore the intricacies of personality, unraveling its origins, dimensions, and the various theories and perspectives that have shaped our understanding of personality.

Personality

Personality is a complex and multifaceted topic that has been studied in various fields, including psychology, genetics, and neuroscience. The development of personality involves a combination of genetic, biological, environmental, and social factors. From a genetic standpoint, certain personality traits are believed to have a hereditary basis, meaning they can be influenced by an individual's genetic makeup. Twin and family studies have provided evidence for the heritability of certain personality traits, suggesting that genetics play a role in shaping personality. Biologically, personality is also influenced by brain structure and functioning. Different brain regions and neurotransmitters are associated with specific personality traits. For example, the prefrontal cortex is involved in decision-making and impulse control, which are relevant to traits like conscientiousness and self-control. Environmental factors, such as parenting styles, cultural influences, and life experiences, also contribute to the development of personality. Childhood experiences, in particular, can have a significant impact on personality formation. Environmental factors interact with genetic predispositions, shaping and influencing the expression of personality traits. Social factors, including socialization, peer relationships, and cultural norms, further contribute to the development of personality. In today's world, we have more friends and followers on social media platforms than real-life friends. We learn and adopt behaviors, attitudes, and values through their interactions on social media platforms. Personality is a complex interplay of these various factors, and there is ongoing debate and research about what personality types turn to social media or the dark web specifically.

Dimensions of Personality

Multiple theories and models have attempted to describe the dimensions of personality. One widely recognized framework is the Five-Factor Model

(FFM), also known as the Big Five, which proposes five broad dimensions of personality:

1. **Openness to experience:** This dimension reflects a person's level of openness, curiosity, and receptiveness to new ideas, experiences, and emotions. Individuals high in openness tend to be imaginative, creative, and open-minded, while those low in openness may be more conventional and prefer routine. These five dimensions of personality provide a framework for describing and understanding individual differences in personality traits.
2. **Conscientiousness:** Conscientiousness refers to the extent to which a person is organized, responsible, disciplined, and goal-oriented. Those high in conscientiousness are typically diligent, reliable, and self-disciplined, while individuals low in conscientiousness may be more spontaneous and less focused on long-term goals.
3. **Extraversion:** Extraversion measures the level of social engagement, assertiveness, and positive energy in individuals. Extraverts are outgoing, energetic, and tend to seek social interaction, while introverts are more reserved and prefer solitary activities or smaller social gatherings.
4. **Agreeableness:** This dimension relates to a person's tendency to be cooperative, compassionate, and considerate toward others. Individuals high in agreeableness are generally empathetic, trusting, and value harmony, while those low in agreeableness may be more skeptical, competitive, or assertive in nature.
5. **Neuroticism (i.e., emotional stability):** Neuroticism represents the extent to which an individual experiences negative emotions, such as anxiety, moodiness, and vulnerability to stress. People high in neuroticism may be more prone to worry and emotional instability, while those low in neuroticism tend to be more emotionally resilient and stable.

Another dimension of personality, popularly known as the psychodynamic perspective of personality, emphasizes the influence of unconscious processes and childhood experiences on shaping an individual's personality. It originated from the work of Freud, who proposed a complex theoretical framework to explain human behavior and personality development. The key concepts in the psychodynamic perspective include the following:

- **Unconscious mind:** According to Freud, the unconscious mind contains thoughts, memories, desires, and impulses that are outside of conscious awareness but still influence behavior. These unconscious processes are believed to shape personality and can manifest through dreams, slips of the tongue, and other forms of symbolic expression.

- **Id (instinct), ego (reality), and superego (morality):** Freud proposed a structural model of the mind consisting of three components. The id operates on the pleasure principle and represents basic, instinctual drives and desires. The ego operates on the reality principle and seeks to balance the demands of the id and the constraints of the external world. The superego represents internalized societal rules, moral values, and conscience.
- **Defense mechanisms:** Defense mechanisms are unconscious psychological strategies that individuals employ to cope with anxiety and protect themselves from distressing thoughts or emotions. Examples of defense mechanisms include repression (blocking out painful memories), projection (attributing one's undesirable thoughts or feelings to others), and denial (refusing to acknowledge reality).
- **Psychosexual stages of development:** Freud proposed a series of psychosexual stages that individuals progress through during childhood, each associated with a different erogenous zone and developmental task. These stages include the oral, anal, phallic, latent, and genital stages. Unresolved conflicts or fixations at any stage can lead to personality traits or issues later in life.
- **Early childhood experiences:** The psychodynamic perspective emphasizes the significance of early childhood experiences, particularly the parent–child relationship and the resolution of conflicts during the psychosexual stages. Freud believed that unresolved conflicts and experiences during this period could have a lasting impact on personality development.

The psychodynamic perspective has evolved and been modified by subsequent theorists, such as Carl Jung, Alfred Adler, and Erik Erikson. While some aspects of Freud's theories have been subject to criticism and empirical challenges, the psychodynamic perspective continues to contribute to our understanding of personality and psychological processes.

Exploring Dark Personality Traits

Personality, though a complex and multi-dimensional construct, is a captive field of study that offers insights into the core of human behavior and individual differences. Understanding personality is crucial for personal growth, effective interpersonal relationships, and even therapeutic interventions. Some people have personality quirks that might make interacting with them challenging. Even if they may be erratic, haughty, or overbearing, with careful management one can enhance their talents, counteract the problematic aspects of their behavior, and reestablish team unity. However, there are some other traits and behaviors, known as "dark personality traits," which are characterized by socially aversive behaviors and motivations. Dark personality traits refer to a collection of interrelated traits that exhibit negative and socially undesirable qualities. These traits share common features such as manipulation, callousness, and self-centeredness, although each trait presents its unique manifestations.

Paulhus and Williams (2002) introduced the term the "Dark Triad" to describe three dark personality traits that are associated with problematic behaviors but also can vary within nonclinical populations. These three traits are Machiavellianism, narcissism, and psychopathy. Later, Chabrol et al. (2009) found that sadistic traits were predictive of delinquent behavior even after accounting for the Dark Triad traits. Consequently, they proposed the inclusion of sadism, forming the "Dark Tetrad." The concept of the Dark Triad (or Tetrad) has provided a useful framework for studying dysfunctional personality traits that can lead to interpersonal harm, even in individuals without a clinical disorder. However, this framework may be overly restrictive, potentially causing researchers to overlook other dark personality traits that can be maladaptive and harmful to relationships.

Dark Triad and Social Media

Out of the socially undesirable personality types mentioned in Kowalski (2001), three have received significant empirical focus: Machiavellianism, narcissism, and psychopathy. Because people with such personalities may exhibit difficulties in being sociable in real life, they may be more inclined to communicate via social media or even private channels. The Dark Triad is shown in Figure 4.1.

Machiavellianism. Machiavellianism refers to a manipulative and cunning personality, originating from Niccolò Machiavelli, an Italian political philosopher who wrote the book *The Prince* in 1513. The book was perceived as endorsing the shady practices of diplomacy's guile and deceit. In his book, Machiavelli discussed the nature of power, politics, and leadership, often advocating for the use of ruthless tactics to maintain and expand one's authority. People with high levels of Machiavellianism are typically skilled in manipulating others to further their own agendas. They tend to be strategic, calculating, and willing to use deceit and manipulation to achieve their goals. Duplicity, manipulation, self-interest, and a lack of both feeling and morality are characteristics of Machiavellianism, referring to a manipulative and strategic approach to social interactions.

Narcissism. Narcissus was a Greek hunter who died after falling in love with his own image in water; he is said to have inspired what we call narcissism. The characteristics of narcissists are self-centered, brash, haughty,

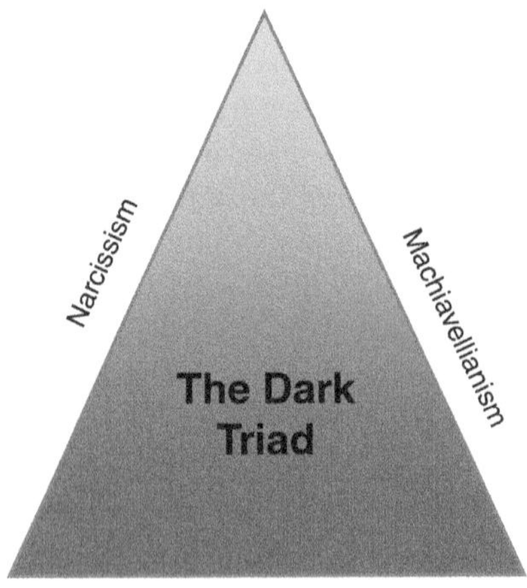

FIGURE 4.1 The Dark Triad: narcissism, Machiavellianism, and psychopathy.

lacking in empathy, greedy, and overly sensitive to criticism. Narcissism is characterized by grand self-importance, constant need for admiration or affirmation, and a lack of empathy. Individuals with narcissistic traits exhibit grandiosity, arrogance, and an intense need for recognition. They are often attention-seeking and may turn to social media posting and commenting for constant attention. They often prioritize their own needs and goals over the well-being of others, leading to interpersonal difficulties and shallow relationships.

Psychopathy. Characteristics of psychopathy include antisocial behavior, manipulation, and irritability. They also include a lack of empathy and regret after doing something cruel or calculating. It is crucial to understand that there is a difference between having psychopathic features and actually being a psychopath. An actual psychopath is frequently associated with committing or planning a violent crime. Psychopathy involves a lack of remorse, shallow emotions, and a propensity for impulsive and antisocial behavior. Psychopathic individuals display a disregard for societal norms, manipulative tendencies, and a reduced capacity for empathy toward others. They often exhibit superficial charm, deceitfulness, and a predisposition toward aggression or criminal behavior. It may not always be easy to spot a psychopath, especially on social media—where they often lurk and use charm to display a superficial representation that is in no way authentic.

Despite their varied origins, the personalities that make up the "Dark Triad" share common characteristics. All exhibit varying degrees of socially malevolent traits, such as self-promotion, emotional detachment, deceitfulness, and aggressiveness. The connections among these traits have been recognized in the literature (Heilbrun et al., 1998). The development of measures for all three constructs has enabled empirical studies within non-clinical populations. As a result, there is empirical evidence demonstrating the overlap between (a) Machiavellianism and psychopathy (McHoskey et al., 1998), (b) narcissism and psychopathy (Gustafson & Ritzer, 1995), and (c) Machiavellianism and narcissism (McHoskey, 1995). These associations suggest the possibility that in non-clinical samples, the constructs of the Dark Triad may be equivalent.

Moreover, some studies propose the inclusion of a fourth dimension, known as sadism, to complement the Dark Triad (van Geel et al., 2017; Buckels et al., 2013). Sadism fulfills the requirements of "callousness or impaired empathy" while additionally introducing a distinctive aspect not encompassed by the Dark Triad traits, namely, an inherent enjoyment derived from causing harm to others (Paulhus et al., 2020).

Assessment of Dark Personality Traits

Defining a novel personality construct is a distinct endeavor from effectively assessing it. Addressing this challenge, a group of psychologists, led by Delroy Paulhus from the University of British Columbia in Canada, devised a comprehensive 28-item questionnaire to gauge the individual traits of narcissism, Machiavellianism, psychopathy, and sadism. Below are the statements they formulated for assessment purposes. Respondents are required to rate their agreement or disagreement on a 5-point scale, ranging from strongly disagree to strongly agree. The measures of dark personality traits (Paulhus et al.) are in Table 4.1.

Despite consisting of 28 items, the researchers discovered that this scale demonstrated consistent accuracy in predicting individuals' authentic values pertaining to the four specific personality dimensions under investigation. Jones and Paulhus (2014) introduced the Short Dark Triad (SD3), a more abbreviated measure for assessing dark personality traits. Dark personality traits, including narcissism, psychopathy, and Machiavellianism, are associated with negative interpersonal behaviors. Again, these people may turn to social media to hurt others with words (cyberbullying), to say mean things on others' social media profiles, and to show off their material possessions or their seemingly exceptional qualities.

Over the past decade, the Dark Triad has garnered significant attention in personality psychology due to its association with various negative outcomes and behaviors. Furnham et al. (2013) have done an in-depth

TABLE 4.1 Measures of Dark Personality Traits (Paulhus et al.)

Machiavellianism Measures

1. *It is not wise to let people know your secrets.*
2. *Whatever it takes, you must get the important people on your side.*
3. *Avoid direct conflict with others because they may be useful in the future.*
4. *Keep a low profile if you want to get your way.*
5. *Manipulating the situation takes planning.*
6. *Flattery is a good way to get people on your side.*
7. *I love it when a tricky plan succeeds.*

Narcissism Measures

1. *People see me as a natural leader.*
2. *I have a unique talent for persuading people.*
3. *Group activities tend to be dull without me.*
4. *I know that I am special because people keep telling me so.*
5. *I have some exceptional qualities.*
6. *I'm likely to become a future star in some area.*
7. *I like to show off every now and then.*

Psychopathy Measures

1. *People often say I'm out of control.*
2. *I tend to fight against authorities and their rules.*
3. *I've been in more fights than most people of my age and gender.*
4. *I tend to dive in, then ask questions later.*
5. *I have been in trouble with the law.*
6. *I sometimes get into dangerous situations.*
7. *People who mess with me always regret it.*

Sadism Measures

1. *Watching a fistfight excites me.*
2. *I really enjoy violent films and video games.*
3. *It is funny when idiots fall flat on their faces.*
4. *I enjoy watching violent sports.*
5. *Some people deserve to suffer.*
6. *Just for kicks, I have said mean things on social media.*
7. *I know how to hurt someone with words alone.*

analysis of the Dark Triad and explored the relationships between the Dark Triad traits and various outcomes across different domains. Their study highlights that individuals high in the Dark Triad traits are more likely to engage in delinquent behaviors, aggressive acts, and unethical practices. Additionally, they tend to exhibit lower levels of job performance, relationship satisfaction, and overall well-being. Factors such as a lack of empathy, manipulative tactics, self-enhancement strategies, and an inclination toward short-term gains at the expense of others contribute to the detrimental effects of the Dark Triad.

Moreover, Rogoza et al. (2022) explore the integration of dark personality traits into existing models of personality. The study provides an overview of dark personality traits, including the widely recognized traits of Machiavellianism, narcissism, psychopathy, and sadism. These traits are typically associated with a lack of empathy, manipulative tendencies, and a propensity for exploiting others. The authors emphasize the importance of studying dark traits within a comprehensive framework of personality, as opposed to treating them as separate constructs.

To facilitate the integration of dark traits into broader models of personality, we consider two models of personality structure. One, the FFM, includes dimensions of extraversion, agreeableness, conscientiousness, neuroticism, and openness to experience; it has been widely used in personality research. The authors propose that incorporating dark traits as additional dimensions within the FFM or as facets within existing dimensions could enhance its explanatory power.

Next is the HEXACO model by Ashton and Lee, which stands for honesty, emotionality, extraversion, agreeableness, conscientiousness, and openness to experience. It expands upon the FFM by including a sixth dimension of honesty-humility, provides a potential framework for incorporating dark traits. The authors suggest that dark traits can be conceptualized as maladaptive manifestations of specific HEXACO dimensions, such as low honesty-humility or low agreeableness. The paper also explores the measurement of dark personality traits, highlighting the challenges associated with self-report measures due to social desirability biases and the inherent difficulty of capturing subtle manifestations of dark traits. The authors discuss alternative measurement approaches, including informant reports, behavioral observations, and projective techniques, that may provide more accurate assessments of dark personality traits. Finally, the paper emphasizes the importance of studying dark personality traits in relation to their functional implications, such as their influence on interpersonal relationships, organizational behavior, and mental health outcomes.

By incorporating dark traits into broader models of personality, researchers can gain a more comprehensive understanding of their underlying mechanisms and develop effective interventions for mitigating their negative consequences. By integrating these traits into comprehensive frameworks, researchers can advance our understanding of their nature, measurement, and functional implications, ultimately contributing to the development of strategies for managing and mitigating the negative effects of dark personality traits.

Dark Personality Traits and Risk-Taking Behavior

A person with dark personality traits is more likely to demonstrate highly risk-taking behaviors. There is a strong correlation between the Dark Triad traits and the propensity to take financial risks, attitudes toward risky driving, health-risk behaviors like substance use and unsafe sex, problematic media use, and other abnormal behaviors like aggression, bullying and cyberbullying, and crime. Different perspectives on how Machiavellianism, psychopathy, and narcissism affect dangerous behavior have come to light. Both psychopathy and narcissism are highly detrimental factors when it comes to engaging in risky activities. However, there are some distinctions between them in terms of their risk patterns. Moreover, psychopathy is the most socially undesirable trait, showing a stronger association with behavioral dysregulation and proactive aggression compared to the other two factors. On the other hand, narcissism is closely linked to ego threat and reactive aggression.

In contrast, the relationship between Machiavellianism and risk-taking activities has yielded mixed findings. While some studies indicate that Machiavellianism is strongly associated with specific risky behaviors, such as aggression, others have not found significant connections. Nonetheless, Furnham et al. (2013) suggest that the relationships between dark traits and risky behaviors may vary depending on the specific type of risky behavior being examined. In a person-centric approach, it is important to acknowledge that not only the relationships but also the composite levels of scores on each of these factors may differ depending on the particular type of risky behavior under investigation.

The majority of studies have focused on examining a single type of risky behavior or have compared the dark traits to other personality traits, such as impulsivity or sensation seeking, in order to shed light on their relationship with risky behaviors. To gain a better understanding of individual differences concerning the dark triad and the implications for risk behavior, it is crucial to design and conduct studies that encompass different types of risky behavior.

The literature analyzing the relationship between professional risk managers' dark triad personality traits and their selective hedging activities (risk-taking behavior) suggests that persons with dark personality traits are more likely to engage in selective hedging than those without. This effect is pronounced for older, male, and less-experienced risk managers (Pelster et al., 2023). The dark personality traits are associated with increased sensation-seeking and risky behaviors (Crysel et al., 2013).

Managers with pronounced dark personality traits are more likely to indulge in risky derivative strategies. Involvement in a derivative market provides the narcissistic manager with a convenient stage for bold and decisive action that generates a continuous supply of attention (Bajo et al., 2022). Identifying the dark triad traits helps to predict individuals' propensity to take financial, investment, and gambling risks (Sekścińska &

Rudzinska-Wojciechowska, 2020), to predict employee behaviors in the workplace (Neo et al., 2018), to predict a series of undesirable firm's outcomes, such as extreme and fluctuating organizational performance (Chatterjee & Hambrick, 2007) or reduced investment performance (ten Brinke et al., 2018).

Implications of Dark Personality Traits for Society

Dark personality traits have far-reaching implications for individuals and society. At the individual level, these traits can hinder personal relationships, impede personal growth, and lead to a lack of emotional fulfillment. Dark personalities are often associated with problems in the workplace, such as poor teamwork, manipulation of colleagues, and unethical behavior. Moreover, dark personality traits can have severe consequences for society. Individuals with these traits may engage in criminal activities, manipulation of others for personal gain, or abuse positions of power. Their actions can undermine trust, destabilize social structures, and create toxic environments that perpetuate harm.

Dark personality traits represent a distinct and concerning aspect of human behavior. By exploring the nuances and manifestations of narcissism, psychopathy, and Machiavellianism, one can gain valuable insights into the detrimental impact these traits can have on individuals and society. Recognizing and addressing dark personality traits is essential for fostering healthier relationships, nurturing empathetic communities, and creating a more harmonious and compassionate world.

As technology advances, online platforms have become prevalent and offer new avenues for individuals to engage in harmful behaviors. Understanding the link between dark personality traits and online antisocial behaviors is crucial for addressing the negative impact of such behaviors in virtual communities. Dark personality traits can manifest in online interactions, leading to harmful behaviors such as cyberbullying, trolling, harassment, and online deception. There are multiple studies investigating the relationship between dark personality traits and antisocial online behaviors. Moor and Anderson (2019) reveal consistent positive associations between dark personality traits and various forms of online aggression, harassment, and manipulative behaviors. Individuals high in dark traits are more likely to engage in cyberbullying, spreading hate speech, identity theft, online stalking, and engaging in deceptive practices. It also reveals the underlying mechanisms that contribute to the link between dark personality traits and antisocial online behaviors. The study highlights factors such as a lack of empathy, reduced self-regulation, thrill-seeking tendencies, anonymity, and the absence of immediate consequences in online environments.

These factors create an environment conducive to the expression of dark traits and facilitate engagement in harmful online behaviors. The research also considers the role of gender and age in the relationship between dark personality traits and online antisocial behaviors. It suggests that males tend to exhibit higher levels of dark traits and engage in more overt forms of online aggression, while females may display more covert forms such as relational aggression or spreading rumors. There is a consistent association between dark personality traits and various forms of antisocial behavior in online environments.

There is a need for a deeper understanding of the developmental pathways and etiology of the Dark Triad traits. Additionally, the examination of potential protective factors, interventions, and strategies for managing individuals high in the Dark Triad is really important. Understanding the Dark Triad traits and their implications can contribute to a better understanding of individuals' behavior and inform interventions aimed at mitigating the negative consequences associated with these traits.

Jonason and Zeigler-Hill (2018) have investigated the underlying social motives associated with dark personality traits. Their work uncovers the fundamental motivations that drive individuals with dark personality traits to engage in socially harmful actions. The three fundamental motives that are common among individuals with dark personality traits are power, status, and control. Power refers to the desire to dominate and exert influence over others. Individuals with dark traits often seek positions of authority and use their power to manipulate and exploit others for personal gain. Status reflects the need for social recognition, admiration, and superiority. Those with dark personality traits are driven by a constant desire to be admired, respected, and feared by others. They engage in behaviors aimed at elevating their social standing and maintaining a sense of superiority.

Control represents the urge to manipulate and control the environment and people around them. Individuals with dark traits strive to exert control over others' thoughts, emotions, and actions. They employ various tactics, such as deception and coercion, to maintain dominance and manipulate social situations to their advantage. These social motives are distinct from the motives exhibited by individuals without dark personality traits. Individuals with dark traits often engage in complex and strategic behaviors that align with multiple motives simultaneously. Understanding the fundamental social motives associated with dark personality traits has important implications for predicting and managing negative social behaviors. By recognizing the underlying motivations, practitioners can develop targeted interventions to mitigate the harmful effects of dark personality traits in various settings, such as workplaces, relationships, and social interactions.

Managing Dark Traits

Managing dark personality traits requires a multi-faceted approach, and how they use social media is important to consider. Awareness and understanding of these traits are crucial for identifying and mitigating their negative impact via social media. Psychological assessments, counseling, and therapy can help individuals with dark personality traits develop healthier coping mechanisms, improve emotional regulation, and foster empathy and prosocial behaviors. In the realm of society, education and awareness campaigns can promote an understanding of dark personality traits and their consequences. Effective measures to prevent and address the harm caused by these traits include robust legal frameworks, ethical guidelines in professional settings, and the cultivation of empathy and emotional intelligence at both individual and societal levels. While sometimes these people should not be so active on social media, it is unfortunately difficult to manage, and these people may be inherently drawn to social media for an audience.

Dark Personality Traits and Stock Market Efficiency

Just as those with dark personality traits may be drawn to social media for an audience, they may also be inclined to indulge in risky activities. The investment in stock market is by very nature a risky investment asset class. Individuals with higher scores on dark personality traits are ready to exploit others for their personal gains and stock market investment is one such place where it is always a zero-sum game. For someone to make a profit, the other person has to lose the money. Investors with dark personality traits are greedy to get higher returns and have higher motivation to get involved in stock market manipulation. Before making an investment, investors generally analyze all relevant and publicly available information about the company. Much of this information is on social media as well, with specific audiences that post and share tips and tricks about the stock market.

The theory in financial economics known as the Efficient Market Hypothesis (EMH) was proposed by Eugene Fama in 1970. The EMH suggests that stock markets are efficient in processing all publicly available information. It proposes that the stock price incorporates all publicly available information and reflects the fair value of the company's stock. According to EMH, it is not possible for investors to consistently outperform the market by exploiting the mispriced investment opportunity. The stock market rapidly and accurately incorporates the newly released information. This means it is extremely difficult, if not impossible, to consistently beat the market and generate abnormal returns by timing the markets. Hence, for someone to make extraordinary returns in the stock market, needs to have privy information about the listed companies. Specifically, investors with dark personality traits are likely to look after such information to become wealthy in a short span of time. It is very unlikely to get such price-sensitive information on publicly available websites. Hence, the preferred marketplace for such illegal information sharing is dark social media platforms.

The EMH classifies the market efficiency in three categories as follows:

- **Weak form of efficiency:** It suggests that current price reflects historical price and volume information about companies' stock and they cannot be used to generate excess returns.
- **Semi-strong form of efficiency:** In addition to historical price and volume information, all publicly available information is incorporated into the current stock price. Hence, investors look for private and confidential information about the companies, if not from public sources then definitely from dark social media platforms, to be ahead of others in getting information, analyzing that information, and exploiting the investment opportunity before everyone else comes to know about that price sensitive piece of information.
- **Strong form of efficiency:** It suggests that all public and private information is incorporated into the current stock price. If the market is a strong form of efficiency, it is an indication of insider trading activity in the stock market.

The literature on EMH is controversial. Some researchers support the original proposition of Fama (1970) and believe that the stock market follows a random walk and hence it is not possible to find the difference between fair value and price or predict the trends via technical analysis. On the other hand, many studies find the market anomaly and support that investors can generate excess returns than the average market returns. Even successful investors like Warren Buffet are examples of stock prices deviating from their fair value. Most of the financial intermediaries use financial models to identify the undervalued stocks.

However, critics of the EMH argue that markets are not perfectly efficient due to factors such as behavioral biases, market frictions, and information asymmetry, which can create opportunities for skilled investors to outperform the market. It is important to note that while the EMH provides a useful framework for understanding market efficiency, it remains a topic of ongoing debate among economists, academics, and practitioners in the field of finance.

The assumption of traditional finance models is that investors are rational. It is being challenged by behavioral finance literature, suggesting that investors are not rational and they do have emotions and biases. Human beings by very nature are greedy and desire to get higher returns than average market returns by exploiting market anomalies or looking for critical information about the companies to make the better-informed decision to maximize the wealth. In this process of finding critical price-sensitive information at times, investors cross ethical boundaries and seek private confidential information. Investors with dark personalities are more prone to use the dark web and dark social media platforms to search for insider information to be ahead of others to earn excess returns.

Dark Personality Traits and Stock Market Scams

Most of the stock market scams across the world are examples of extreme greediness to become a billionaire by manipulating stock prices, deceiving investors, launching fraudulent schemes, or siphoning off funds from the market. The personality types exhibited by most of the persons involved in these scams are very similar to the dark personality traits. Some of the biggest scams in India are as follows. Here are examples of high-profile cases in both India and the United States that involve individuals with dark personality traits. Each has been implicated in financial fraud and many of these cases relate to social media as a way to recruit, communicate with, or deceive others. Table 4.2 contains some notable scams, their approximate dates, and a description of the scam or fraud.

On a frequent basis, many receive spam emails, personal messages, and public posts on social media platforms, and SMS on mobile phones. Some of the common themes in this communication are claiming to provide a multi-bagger stock investment opportunity, informing that you won the lottery, someone wanting to transfer funds from abroad to your country, business investment opportunity, asking to share bank account details, sending links to click to avails exclusive offers and discount and many more. If all these activities are carried out publicly on regular websites and social media platforms, despite having surveillance of regulators, just think of what can happen on the dark web and dark social media platforms, which are completely anonymous and private. Fraudsters use dark social media platforms to launch Ponzi schemes, it is a form of financial fraud that lures investors' hard-earned money.

Insider Information in Investment Management

As per the Securities and Exchange Board of India (SEBI), the regulatory body for the securities and commodity market in India, all price-sensitive financial information should be disseminated only through stock exchanges

TABLE 4.2 Notable Financial Scams and Descriptions

Scam Name (Date)	*Description*
The Harshad Mehta scam of 1992	A broker used fake bank receipts to borrow money from banks and inflate the prices of stocks, leading to a stock market crash and investors losing up to 4000 crore.
The Ketan Parekh scam of 2001	A broker engaged in circular trading using funds from banks and other institutions to manipulate the prices of a few stocks, causing a market crash and a loss of ₹40,000 crore.
The Satyam scam of 2009	The Satyam scam of 2009, where the chairman of Satyam Computer Services Ltd. faked the company's accounts and revenues to inflate the share price and siphon off funds, causing a loss of ₹14,000 crore and eroding investor confidence in the financial markets.
The Bernie Madoff Ponzi scam of 2009	Bernie Madoff was an American financier and former chairman of the NASDAQ stock exchange. Madoff orchestrated one of the largest Ponzi schemes in history, defrauding investors out of billions of dollars. He exhibited traits of psychopathy and Machiavellianism, manipulating investors and showing a lack of remorse for his actions. Madoff was convicted in 2009 and sentenced to 150 years in prison.
The Elizabeth Holmes/ Theranos scam of 2022	Elizabeth Holmes was the founder and former CEO of Theranos, a healthcare technology company. Holmes claimed that her company's technology could perform a wide range of medical tests using a small amount of blood, but the claims were later exposed as fraudulent. She exhibited traits of narcissism, using her charisma and persuasive skills to deceive investors and the public. Holmes was charged with multiple counts of fraud. She was convicted by a jury in San Jose, California, and began her 11-year prison sentence in 2023.
The Allen Stanford/ Stanford Financial Ponzi scam of 2012	Allen Stanford was an American financier and former chairman of Stanford Financial Group. Stanford orchestrated a massive Ponzi scheme through his bank, defrauding investors of billions of dollars. He displayed traits of narcissism and manipulation, using his social status and connections to deceive investors. Stanford was convicted in 2012 and sentenced to 110 years in prison.
The Jordan Belfort/Wolf of Wall Street Scam of 1999	Jordan Belfort, also known as the "Wolf of Wall Street," was a former stockbroker and founder of Stratton Oakmont brokerage firm. Belfort engaged in securities fraud and money laundering, defrauding investors through pump-and-dump schemes. He exhibited traits of narcissism and psychopathy, displaying a reckless and self-centered lifestyle. Belfort served 22 months of prison time as part of an agreement to give testimony against many partners in the fraud.

to make it accessible to the general public at the same point in time. It is illegal for an investor to trade based on private and insider information. Market manipulators use dark social media platforms and private chat groups like WhatsApp and Telegram to share stock tips to buy and sell stocks and unpublished price-sensitive information about companies. It gives an unfair advantage to investors who use this information to trade before it becomes publicly available, potentially violating the rule of front running and insider trading. It is illegal to share and receive confidential information and trade based on this type of insider information.

Given the kind of vigilance activity run by the stock market regulators, it is not easy for someone to share and receive confidential information about companies. Hence, the preferred marketplace for the exchange of private confidential price-sensitive information is dark social media platforms, which do not have any digital referral information about the source. As it is difficult for regulators to trace the identity of the person engaged in such illegal activity on dark social media platforms, fraudsters get the free hand to market confidential information about publicly listed companies. Even the payment for such type of illegal activity mostly happens through cryptocurrency like bitcoin, which increases the difficulty of regulators to trace the identity.

People with dark personality traits are more likely to use private channels on dark social media websites to share insider information and other price-sensitive information about the company, which may lead to market manipulation. It is illegal to share insider information with others if one has access to it, and the person who possesses the insider information is not allowed to trade based on that information to take the undue advantage of having prior information about the company. Hackers use remote access to the servers to access confidential information. They launch malware to access the company's confidential information. Software vendors usually patch malware, and IT teams often fail to deploy patches that make company information vulnerable.

Stock tips on dark social media are not reliable and may be illegal. Some of the sources like insider trading forums on dark social media are selling stock tips by falsely claiming that they have access to material non-public information about listed companies. Some other dark social media platforms serve as a marketplace of stolen financial information about individual persons such as bank account details, credit card information, or identity documents that can be used for fraud and money laundering activities. Some dark social media platforms also sell malware that can be used to infect systems and servers of companies or access the private and confidential information stored in companies' networks.

Most of the financial transactions on dark social media platforms accept cryptocurrency as a tender to buy and sell illegal goods and services. Many countries do not recognize cryptocurrency as a legal tender for payment. Use of dark social media platforms makes the user vulnerable to the risk of theft of their cryptocurrency. Cryptocurrency provides anonymity, privacy, and security for dark web users and vendors. However, cryptocurrency can also be volatile, risky, and subject to hacking or theft. Some sources on dark social media promote their own trading platform for trading cryptocurrencies and other digital assets. They claim to have faster, more secure, and anonymous transactions for users. However, these platforms can also be highly unreliable, scams, or illegal. Insider trading on the dark web violates securities laws and regulations that aim to protect investors and ensure fair and efficient markets. Insider trading can also harm the reputation and performance of the companies involved, as well as the trust and confidence of the public. Insider trading can result in large fines, prison time, and embarrassment for the perpetrators.

Fraudulent Investment Schemes on Dark Social Media

According to a report from Kaspersky, a cybersecurity firm, India is among the top five countries in the Asia Pacific region based on the usage of dark social media to share price-sensitive information. Stock market fraud is a crime to misrepresent information to investors and misguide the decision-making process. Scammers commit financial frauds on dark social media platforms like offering fake investment plans and stock investment advice. Some examples of stock market fraud are listed in Table 4.3.

These activities can result in severe legal consequences for both the buyers and sellers of such services. Users should stay away from such fake investment offers and fraud plans on dark social media platforms. If someone encounters suspicious activity or fraud, one should report it to regulators anonymously for investigation. Scammers sell stock market tips and investment advice to their followers on dark social media platforms, but this can be risky and unreliable. There are many cases of market manipulations using dark social media platforms to spread false and misleading information about listed companies.

Stock market regulators regularly try to create investor awareness about such misleading schemes and increase financial literacy among investors. Most of them clearly say to read the offer documents carefully and do your own research using all publicly available information before investing in the stock market. The credibility of the source of information is vital for successful stock market investing. In the case of dark social media platforms, where the source is non-identifiable, the accuracy and correctness of

TABLE 4.3 Stock Market Fraud Types and Explanations

Stock Market Fraud	*Explanation*
Pump-and-dump schemes	Fraudsters use dark social media or other platforms to spread false or misleading information about a stock to create a dummy demand, inflate its price, and then sell their own shares at a high price.
Insider trading	Fraudsters use confidential, non-public information about a company or its securities to trade for their own benefit or stock tips others who trade on that information.
High-yield investment fraud	Fraudsters offer investments with high returns and low risks, but the investments are either nonexistent or worthless.
Ponzi schemes	Fraudsters use money from new investors to pay returns to earlier investors, creating an illusion of profitability and legitimacy.
Theft of personal financial information	Criminals steal users' personal financial information and use it to illegally withdraw money from the user's account or transfer the money from the user's account to their own account. At times, fraudsters also sell the stolen financial details on dark social media platforms.
Investment fraud	Scammers mislead users by selling lucrative investment opportunities as multi-bagger investment plans that can make users wealthy in a short span of time. Most of them are fake promises and hidden facts about investments.
Money laundering	Money launderers use platforms on the dark web to sell or transfer items purchased with laundered funds. They also use services like crypto mixing or stolen crypto wallets to hide the source and destination of their illicit money.

information are doubtful. One must not use dark social media platforms to seek price-sensitive information otherwise; one is vulnerable to financial scams such as those listed in Table 4.3.

Impact of the Dark Web on the Surveillance Role of Regulator

Regulators across the world try to maintain the stock market as a level playing field for every investor. They keep a close monitoring system to ensure transparency in the stock market. With the emergence of private communication channels where the messages are encrypted and dark social media platforms allowing users to exchange insider information without revealing the original identity, the role of regulators become quite challenging. Regulators use undercover agents to catch manipulators who misuse dark social media platforms to share insider information.

In one such incident, the Federal Bureau of Investigation (FBI) in 2021 caught a Greek citizen who was selling insider information about companies listed on the NYSE and NASDAQ stock exchanges, on the dark social media website called AlphaBay Market. The person was selling insider information about companies using various subscription plans like daily, weekly, and monthly. He was accepting payment in bitcoins. He was claiming himself as an office clerk working in a trading branch at a hedge fund firm. The FBI used the undercover agents to communicate with the person involved in this illegal activity. The FBI found that the person had access to confidential quarterly earnings reports and information about upcoming mergers and acquisitions. The undercover agent had a voice chat with the person and he made an actual payment using bitcoin to get the clue to trace the real identity of the person. While tracing the account used to receive the bitcoin payments and the account opening information like photo and passport used as identity proof documents, the FBI caught a Greek citizen named Apostolos Trovias. He has been extradited to the United States to face trial for getting involved in security fraud and money laundering.

Another such example is James Roland Jones, who used the moniker "Millionaire Mike" and pleaded guilty to insider trading. He was buying information from the dark web with the goal of profiting from illegal tips about the listed companies in the United States. From 2016 to 2017, he used to illegally purchase names, dates of birth, and Social Security numbers to open a fraudulent brokerage account. Through those accounts, Jones traded on tips, one of which was provided to him by an undercover FBI agent. Jones is based in Redondo Beach, California. In a parallel civil case, the U.S. Securities and Exchange Commission (SEC) accused Jones of selling fake tips about companies, with the regulator saying it was its first-ever enforcement action tied to securities law violations on the dark web. Several people paid Jones about $27,000 combined in Bitcoin transactions, ultimately trading on his fake tips. This case shows that the SEC can and will pursue securities law violators wherever they operate, even on the dark web," David L. Peavler, director of the SEC, said in a statement.

Another example is from the Indian market, where SEBI, caught a gang of operators who were using private communication channels like Telegram and other dark social media platforms with more than five million subscribers to spread false or misleading information about listed companies in India. This gang of operators bought large stakes in a few stocks and then used dark social media platforms to create a misleading demand and inflate the stock price to an unsustainable level. Then, they sold their stocks and booked abnormal profit. SEBI raided their premises and seized evidence of the scam.

To prevent such scams, regulators promote a whistleblower framework and encourage people to anonymously report the illegal sharing of confidential information on private chat groups so that they can inquire about it and penalize the wrongdoers. The two leading stock exchanges of India, Bombay Stock Exchange (BSE) and the National Stock Exchange (NSE), have set up a system for anyone to tip off through a toll-free phone number, email, or report directly on their websites. Once the tip-off is received, the stock exchanges analyze the trade history for possible manipulation and if suspected, they refer the matter to SEBI, which is the regulatory body of the Indian stock market. Regulators have also increased the vigilance on social media platforms and if need be they ask telecom companies to share call data to probe the suspects further. Regulators also use social media analytics and artificial intelligence (AI) to track various dark social media websites. Alerts generated by these tools are closely monitored and passed onto surveillance teams for further inquiry.

As per the SEBI law, only registered investment advisors (RIAs) can provide investment advice to investors. Regulators closely monitor the dark social media platforms and they have taken action against many persons and entities who are providing investment tips without proper registration as investment advisors. Regulators are taking action against scammers who are selling stock tips on dark social media. One should be mindful and avoid such risky and unethical practices. Stock market regulators with the help of the telecom regulator body try to curb the fraudulent bulk SMS from non-registered firms to entrap the investor with false and misleading promises of financial gains. Stock market regulators warn investors to be vigilant of misleading schemes and not to rely on stock tips from unverified online sources. Regulators run various investor awareness campaigns to protect the interests of the investors. However, regulators have yet to put a law banning the use of dark social media platforms for illegal financial activities.

Earning returns in the stock market is not an exception to it. One should only use trusted data sources to collect the relevant information to analyze the stock of the company and perform sufficient due diligence before making an investment. The dark social media platforms as a source of information are certainly unreliable sources. Hence, one must refrain from using dark social media to seek stock tips or investment advice. Investors should also know their risk appetite to select what types of investment products are suitable based on their risk appetite.

Dark Social Media Platforms and Banking Frauds

The use of dark social media platforms not only leads to stock market scams but may also cause banking fraud. Banking fraud can be classified into the following different categories based on their modus operandi:

- **Phishing:** Fraudsters create a fake website that looks like a legitimate one, such as a bank's website, and trick customers into entering their security credentials, which are then used to access their accounts. Fraudsters use the dark social media platforms to share the links of fake websites. The use of dark social media protects fraudsters from being caught because it is difficult to find their identity in the absence of a digital reference point.
- **Vishing:** Fraudsters call or approach customers over the phone or dark social media platforms pretending to be bankers, officials, or agents and persuade them to share confidential information such as passwords, OTPs, PINs, and CVVs by citing an urgency or an offer.
- **Frauds using online sales platforms:** Fraudsters pose as buyers on online sales platforms and instead of "paying the seller," they use the UPI app's "request money" option and ask the seller to authorize the request by entering the UPI PIN. Money is transferred to the fraudster's account when the seller enters the PIN.
- **Frauds due to the use of unknown/unverified web links:** Fraudsters circulate certain app links that appear similar to the existing apps of authorized entities and ask customers to download them. These apps may contain malware or spyware that can steal customer data or access their accounts.

To prevent banking fraud, customers should be vigilant and aware of the common types of fraud and their signs. They should also follow some basic safety tips such as:

- Do not share your security credentials with anyone or disclose them over the phone, email, or social media platforms.
- Do not click on unknown or suspicious links or download unverified apps.
- Do not authorize any UPI request money transactions unless you are expecting them.
- Check your bank statements and transaction alerts regularly and report any discrepancies immediately.
- Use strong passwords and change them periodically.
- Use secure internet connections and devices for online banking.
- Do not use dark social media platforms that may steal confidential information like passwords stored on your devices.

Innovative Scam Techniques

With the growth in digital ecosystems, online fraud cases are rising exponentially. Fraudsters use innovative techniques to con victims to fulfill their criminal agenda like using private communication channels and dark social media platforms. Scammers keep adopting innovative ways to steal money from victims. Hackers use chatbots to generate spear-phishing emails, fake websites, fake posts, fake profiles, and fake consumer reviews, or to help create malware, ransomware, and prompt injection attacks on dark social media platforms.

Nowadays, fraudsters are using deepfakes and voice clones to facilitate imposter scams, extortion, and financial fraud. Hackers send the voice clone as an audio message over dark social media threatening a victim creating a misleading emergency about a loved one in the family and asking for money or confidential information. A voice clone is a synthesized voice of a person created using AI technology. AI voice cloning is becoming better, cheaper, and more accessible in recent times with the boom in generative AI. Microsoft introduced Vall-E, a generative AI-based voice simulator that can replicate someone's voice and create responses with the user's unique voice tone if it has a three-second or more audio sample. Scammers are leveraging this type of tool to dupe users. Some of us regularly share our voice in the form of content in short videos or even voice notes on social media platforms. Scammers use this technology to scrape voice data, get it to AI algorithms, and generate cloned voices as a way to conduct scams and extort money. AI voice-cloning technology plays with people's emotional connection and a sense of urgency, to increase the likelihood of us falling for the scam. Generative AI is helping create sophisticated social engineering attacks.

Federal Trade Commission warned consumers that bad actors are using the technology to supercharge "family-emergency schemes," scams that fake an emergency to fool a concerned loved one into forking over cash or private information.

Conclusion and Solutions for Consumers

There are solutions. For voice-based scams, families can have a code word to make sure that a scammer is not using a loved one's voice to extort money or information. Dark social media platforms can have many suspicious and unsafe web links and attachments, so another solution is to be hypervigilant as to what to click on- even if it looks normal. If users click on those links or download attachments, they may expose the users to malicious websites. Thus, a solution is to have more information and education as to how to notice and handle such malice on social media or the dark web. Dark social media platforms are full of hackers and scammers who can easily perform their illegal and unethical activities without sharing their identities. At the same time, regulators and law enforcement agencies use undercover agents to monitor, exploit, and arrest such fraudsters.

Another solution is to be aware of the risks before considering using dark social. Usage of dark social media can expose users to the following risks:

- **Psychological risk:** Dark social media can cause depression, anxiety, jealousy, loneliness, and other negative emotions. It exposes the users to disturbing, violent, or illegal content that can traumatize the users.
- **Security and privacy risk:** Dark social media can expose users to malware, phishing attacks, and threats of personal and confidential information or data breaches.
- **Performance and productivity risk:** Dark social media can lead to addiction, wastage of time, distraction, and procrastination, which can affect users' performance and productivity. Engaging in illegal activities on dark social media can result in legal consequences and reputational damage for users.

Hence, users should refrain from using dark web and dark social media platforms and take sufficient measures to protect themselves from fraudsters.

For specific solutions, here are some suggestions to keep oneself safe from the risks of dark social media platforms:

1. The first and easiest solution ***is not to use dark social media and dark web if possible***. However, if a user plans to access dark social media for some positive intent, they should take care of the following points.
2. If need be, users should access dark social media platforms through safe web browsers and tools. ***Beware of clicking on malicious or fake links***.
3. ***Use a virtual private network (VPN)***, it adds an extra layer of security and privacy. It hides your IP address, location, and identity so it is difficult for someone to spy on you or track your online activities.
4. ***Use robust antivirus protection***; it can protect your system from threats such as malware and viruses.
5. ***Do not disclose your identity and other personal information on dark social media*** platforms. Users should never share their name, address, mobile number, bank account details, or credit card details.
6. ***Do not use the same username and password across different websites*** on the regular web and dark social media platforms.

7. ***Beware of financial and phishing scams.*** Users should not get trapped by offers and requests that involve money, cryptocurrency, and other financial transactions on dark social media platforms. Most of them may try to trick you by stealing financial information or money from your account.
8. ***Do not engage in activities where others are doing illegal things on dark social.*** Users should avoid accessing any content that is unethical, immoral, and illegal on dark social media platforms. These activities are not only harmful and dangerous, but they may attract legal punishments from law enforcement agencies.

References

Bajo, E., Jankensgård, H., & Marinelli, N. (2022). Me, myself and I: CEO narcissism and selective hedging. *European Financial Management*, *28*(3), 809–833.

Buckels, E. E., Jones, D. N., & Paulhus, D. L. (2013). Behavioral confirmation of everyday sadism. *Psychological Science*, *24*(11), 2201–2209.

Chabrol, H., Van Leeuwen, N., Rodgers, R., & Séjourné, N. (2009). Contributions of psychopathic, narcissistic, Machiavellian, and sadistic personality traits to juvenile delinquency. *Personality and Individual Differences*, *47*(7), 734–739.

Chatterjee, A., & Hambrick, D. C. (2007). It's all about me: Narcissistic chief executive officers and their effects on company strategy and performance. *Administrative Science Quarterly*, *52*, 351–386.

Crysel, L. C., Crosier, B. S., & Webster, G. D. (2013). The dark triad and risk behavior. *Personality and Individual Differences*, *54*(1), 35–40.

Fama, E. F. (1970). Efficient capital markets: A review of theory and empirical work. *Journal of Finance*, *25*(2), 383–417.

Furnham, A., Richards, S. C., & Paulhus, D. L. (2013). The dark triad of personality: A 10-year review. *Social and Personality Psychology Compass*, *7*(3), 199–216.

Gustafson, S. B., & Ritzer, D. R. (1995). The dark side of normal: A psychopathy-linked pattern called aberrant self-promotion. *European Journal of Personality*, *9*(3), 147–183.

Heilbrun, K., Hart, S. D., Hare, R. D., Gustafson, D., Nunez, C., & White, A. J. (1998). Inpatient and post discharge aggression in mentally disordered offenders: The role of psychopathy. *Journal of Interpersonal Violence*, *13*(4), 514–527.

Jonason, P. K., & Zeigler-Hill, V. (2018). The fundamental social motives that characterize dark personality traits. *Personality and Individual Differences*, *132*, 98–107.

Jones, D. N., & Paulhus, D. L. (2014). Introducing the short dark triad (SD3) a brief measure of dark personality traits. *Assessment*, *21*(1), 28–41.

Kowalski, R. M. (2001). *Behaving badly: Aversive behaviors in interpersonal relationships*. American Psychological Association.

McHoskey, J. (1995). Narcissism and Machiavellianism. *Psychological Reports*, *77*(3), 755–759.

McHoskey, J. W., Worzel, W., & Szyarto, C. (1998). Machiavellianism and psychopathy. *Journal of Personality and Social Psychology*, *74*(1), 192.

Moor, L., & Anderson, J. R. (2019). A systematic literature review of the relationship between dark personality traits and antisocial online behaviours. *Personality and Individual Differences, 144*, 40–55.

Neo, B., Sellbom, M., Smith, S. F., & Lilienfeld, S. O. (2018). Of boldness and badness: Insights into workplace Malfeasance from a triarchic psychopathy model perspective. *Journal of Business Ethics, 149*, 187–205.

Paulhus, D. L., Buckels, E. E., Trapnell, P. D., & Jones, D. N. (2020). Screening for dark personalities. *European Journal of Psychological Assessment*, *37*(3), 208–222.

Paulhus, D. L., & Williams, K. M. (2002). The dark triad of personality: Narcissism, Machiavellianism, and psychopathy. *Journal of Research in Personality*, *36*(6), 556–563.

Pelster, M., Hofmann, A., Klocke, N., & Warkulat, S. (2023). Dark triad personality traits and selective hedging. *Journal of Business Ethics*, 1–26.

Rogoza, R., Kowalski, C. M., Saklofske, D. H., & Schermer, J. A. (2022). Systematizing dark personality traits within broader models of personality. *Personality and Individual Differences*, *186*, 111343.

Sekścińska, K., & Rudzinska-Wojciechowska, J. (2020). Individual differences in dark triad Traits and risky financial choices. *Personality and Individual Differences, 152*, 109598.

ten Brinke, L., Kish, A., & Keltner, D. (2018). Hedge fund managers with psychopathic tendencies make for worse investors. *Personality and Social Psychology Bulletin*, *44*, 214–223.

van Geel, M., Goemans, A., Toprak, F., & Vedder, P. (2017). Which personality traits are related to traditional bullying and cyberbullying? A study with the Big Five, dark triad and sadism. *Personality And Individual Differences*, *106*, 231–235.

PART 3

Social Media Self-Discrepancies and Unhealthy Self-Comparisons

While the previous part focused on fear, anxiety, and the dark web, we now shift to Section 3, which entails the psychology of when we compare ourselves to others on social media and the mental health outcomes or associations. In Chapter 5, Mukherjee and Roy illuminate three aspects of the conceptual chapter—the social media exposures, the effects of social media use from a mental health or consumer well-being lens, and the proposed solutions.

5. In the Mirror, Darkly: Negative Effects of Social Media on Self-Discrepancy and Consumer Well-Being

   Ashesh Mukherjee and Arani Roy

One such interesting context that relates to unhealthy self-thoughts or self-comparisons is with food and by association body image, weight, and body perceptions. In Chapter 6, Peter, Mendini, Krishen, and Zeng examine social media content and food-related photos and postings on Instagram. They explore popular hashtags, such as #foodporn, and empirically analyze them with respect to consumer well-being or mental health. They show the duality of food-related posting, as there are some positive aspects. The darker side though relates to self-esteem and body issues and eating disorders to maintain what the authors find as unhealthy "Thinspiration."

6. The Dark Side of Instagram of Food: The Duality of Food-Related Social Media Posting

   Paula C. Peter, Monica Mendini, Anjala Krishen, and Qin Zeng

DOI: 10.4324/9781003410058-7

5

IN THE MIRROR, DARKLY

Negative Effects of Social Media on Self-Discrepancy and Consumer Well-Being

Ashesh Mukherjee and Arani Roy

"For now we see in a mirror, darkly": 1 Corinthians 13–12

Social media is omnipresent in our daily lives. Around 5 billion people around the world use social media, spending an average of two to three hours each day on platforms such as Facebook, Instagram, TikTok, Snapchat, Twitter, YouTube, LinkedIn, and WhatsApp (Statista, 2023). Social media has improved our lives in many ways, with people of all ages using social media to interact, date, share, learn, and stay in touch. But alongside its benefits, concern has been rising that social media has a dark side that harms consumers, brands, and social cohesion. This chapter draws on research in marketing, consumer behavior, and psychology to shine a light on this less-visible underbelly of social media. The central thesis of this chapter is that social media is a dark mirror in which consumers look at themselves and see different types of self-discrepancies such as lack of resources, lack of control, lack of intelligence, and lack of power. These self-discrepancies, in turn, have negative effects on consumers such as increased stress, anxiety, depression, envy, materialism, stereotyping, low self-esteem, low self-control, and maladaptive consumption. Fortunately, these negative effects are not inevitable; the chapter offers several suggestions for sidestepping the pitfalls and thereby reaping the full benefits of social media.

The rest of this chapter is organized as follows. First, we set the stage by tracing the evolution of social media from its early days to its multifaceted role in life today. Second, we introduce self-discrepancy as a central

DOI: 10.4324/9781003410058-8

psychological construct that is key to understanding the effect of social media on consumers. Third, we discuss research showing that the use of social media increases different types of self-discrepancies which, in turn, have negative effects on consumer well-being. Finally, we outline actions that can be taken by consumers and social media platforms to combat the negative effects of social media on consumer well-being.

Evolution of Social Media

Social media has evolved over the years. It is no longer simply a way to connect with others but has also become a means to share opinions, gather information, and interact with firms. This evolution is reflected in the greater diversity of social media platforms in the marketplace today. While the original platform of Facebook remains popular, others offering functions other than just social connections have emerged over time. For example, Instagram and Pinterest offer social connections through the sharing of audiovisual rather than verbal content. TikTok and YouTube Shorts offer curated short videos made by content creators from around the world. Patreon and OnlyFans allow people to support their favorite artists online. People can interact directly with social media influencers such as sports stars, musicians, reality television personalities, and movie stars. Brands have also leveraged this channel to interact with consumers and understand consumer sentiment about their offerings in real time. Consumers, in turn, feel empowered as they can tag the social media handle of a brand while posting their queries and complaints.

In parallel with new usage situations, the frequency of use of social media has exploded in recent years driven by factors such as lower cost of internet access, greater utility from use, greater ease of use, increased entertainment value, and increased use of social media during the COVID-19 pandemic to counter isolation. For example, Instagram has gone from 2 billion to 3.5 billion users in the last three years and a single social media post by Dwayne Johnson or Cristiano Ronaldo can reach more than 300 million people (Data.ai insights). Social media has worldwide reach because of low international barriers to entry for digital platforms and reduced internet access costs around the world.

It needs to be acknowledged that social media serves many good purposes. The United Nations refugee organization has used its Facebook page to communicate with refugees about shelter and asylum. People used #covidhelp and #covidresources hashtags on Twitter during the pandemic to ask for oxygen and COVID treatment. Many people get their news primarily from Twitter and Facebook and thereby stay updated on the go about current events. People use LinkedIn to find jobs and stay informed about the latest advances in their professional fields. People can quickly find information on social media about the work culture of a prospective employer or the quality of an educational institute one intends to join. Consumers who are dissatisfied with a firm's products or services can now easily contact the firm through social media to seek redress or publicize the lack of response from the firm. At the same time, there is a darker side of social media reported in the media such as wasting time, trolling, cyberbullying, and spreading fake rumors. This chapter sheds new light on the darker side of social media by focusing on the psychological construct of self-discrepancy. Specifically, we describe research showing that social media increases different types of self-discrepancies which, in turn, leads to negative effects on consumer well-being.

Self-Discrepancy

Self-discrepancy is defined as the incongruity between how one currently perceives oneself and how one desires to view oneself (Mandel et al., 2017). In other words, self-discrepancy is the gap between one's current and ideal selves. For example, there could be a gap between an individual's current level of income and her ideal level of income. Another example would be a perceived gap in the level of control one currently has over daily decisions and the level of control one desires to have. Similarly, the gap between one's current level of power in the workplace and the ideal level of power wished for is another example of self-discrepancy. As illustrated by these examples, self-discrepancy can arise in different domains such as resources, control, power, intelligence, social belongingness, and physical attractiveness.

Past research has shown that self-discrepancy can influence a range of consumption behaviors. For example, it has been shown that individuals experiencing isolation or lack of social belongingness tend to make riskier financial decisions (Duclos et al., 2013a). Other research has shown that self-discrepancy in the domain of intelligence can influence product choice (Gao et al., 2009; Kim & Rucker, 2012). Similarly, self-discrepancy in other domains has been shown to lead to consumption behaviors that help address the discrepancy in question (Stone et al., 1997). For example, it has been shown that self-discrepancy in the form of physical appearance influences appearance-boosting consumption (Park & Maner, 2009). Self-discrepancy in the form of resource scarcity increases the consumption of scarce products (Sharma & Alter, 2012). Self-discrepancy in the form of masculinity increases preference for masculine products (Willer et al., 2013). Self-discrepancy in the form of lack of power increases the choice of status products (Rucker & Galinsky, 2008) and self-discrepancy in the form of control increases the choice of utilitarian over hedonic products (Chen et al., 2017a, 2017b).

Social Media, Self-Discrepancy, and Consumer Well-Being

This chapter argues that the use of social media can increase self-discrepancy and consequently reduce consumer well-being. Notably, self-discrepancy due to social media use can take different forms such as resource scarcity, loss of power, insecurity about physical appearance, lack of intelligence, feelings of loneliness, and loss of control. For example, when a person sees a Facebook post of a friend's new luxury car purchase, they might think about not having enough money. Similarly, when a person sees a family member's LinkedIn post about a recent job promotion, they might think of not having enough power. Social media posts highlighting new degrees and certifications obtained by peer group members could lead to inferences about one's lack of intelligence. Artfully edited pictures posted on Instagram can make people question their own physical attractiveness. In general, social media provides people with new frames of reference that represent an ideal life—an ideal place to live, an ideal amount of money to have, or an ideal level of power to exercise over others. Furthermore, these ideal states are omnipresent on people's phones that accompany them throughout the day. These ideal states are also disseminated worldwide through the Internet across socio-economic classes and national boundaries. As a result, people frequently observe self-discrepancies on social media between their actual states and the large number of ideal states visible online. In the following sections, we discuss eight types of self-discrepancies that are increased by social media namely resource scarcity, perceived control, power, physical appearance, social belongingness, gender identity, mortality salience, and perceived intelligence. We then describe the negative effects of these self-discrepancies on consumer well-being as well as ways to mitigate these negative effects.

Self-Discrepancy: Resource Scarcity

Resource scarcity has been defined as a discrepancy between one's current level of resources and a higher, more desirable reference point (Cannon et al., 2019). In other words, resource scarcity is the feeling of not having enough. Research shows that individuals often experience resource scarcity in their daily lives which, in turn, affects outcomes in both personal and consumption contexts (Blocker et al., 2023; Cannon et al., 2019; Mehta & Zhu, 2016; Roux et al., 2015). For example, individuals might feel resource scarcity toward the end of the month when their bank balance is running low. People might feel resource-scarce following large purchases such as buying a car or paying for a hotel reservation. Reading about recessions or job losses in the media can trigger feelings of not having enough. Notably, resource scarcity is not limited to lack of money—lack of time, digital resources, food, or water are all forms of resource scarcity. For example, people could feel resource scarcity in terms of time when they feel they do not have enough time to complete required tasks or catch an upcoming flight.

Browsing social media can lead to feelings of resource scarcity. For example, feelings of resource scarcity in terms of money can be highlighted by exposure to social media posts about others' consumption such as images of new cars or houses, travel videos, or descriptions of stay in luxury resorts. Others posting their opinions about an upcoming recession or deficits in national budgets can trigger thoughts of not having enough savings. Others posting about their financial success may lead to feelings of not having enough money. Social media users often come across posts where their peers' current standard of living appears to be resource abundant. For example, Instagram posts about hosting a birthday party at an expensive resort may lead to others thinking about their own relatively inadequate level of resources for such celebrations. Social media posts by celebrities feature lifestyles that are more desirable than audiences' current lifestyle thus triggering a sense of not having enough. Seeing their peers living in resource-rich environments, traveling, or getting promoted acts as reminders of a gap between the individual's current resource level and a higher, more desirable resource level. Repeated exposure to these gaps on social media is likely to result in an increased perception of resource scarcity over time.

Resource scarcity has been shown to have a range of negative effects in both personal and consumption contexts. In personal contexts, feelings of resource scarcity bring harsher moral judgments (Pitesa & Thau, 2014) and heightened arousal (Zhu & Ratner, 2015). These consequences highlight the detrimental effects of resource scarcity on consumer welfare in personal contexts. In consumption contexts, feelings of resource scarcity have been shown to reduce purchase-related word of mouth (Paley et al., 2019), increase preference for high-status products (Kamakura & Du, 2012), and increase favorability toward range marketing offers (Fan et al., 2019).

For example, participants in the Fan et al. (2019) study who were in the resource scarcity condition read an article claiming that five natural resources (e.g., water, oil, natural gas) would soon run out. In contrast, participants in the control condition read an article describing the visual capacities of monkeys. After reading and summarizing articles, participants were given the option of doing a bonus task for an additional financial reward. The financial reward was framed as either a point offer where each participant would get a $.20 payment or a range offer where each participant would get an amount between $.10 and $.30 depending on the number of participants in the bonus task. A chi-square test showed that when the range offer was presented, more participants in the resource scarcity condition (98.1%) chose to participate in the bonus task compared to control participants (76.9%). In contrast, there was no difference in the participation rate for the bonus task between the resource scarcity (89.1%) and control condition (85.0%) when the point offer was presented.

Notably, these findings indicate that resource scarcity could lead to suboptimal financial choices by consumers. For example, range offers often lead to lower discounts compared to point offers and individuals experiencing monetary scarcity could therefore end up paying a higher price to purchase products. Further, resource scarcity has been shown to induce unpleasant effects (Sharma & Alter, 2012), and decrease life satisfaction. These negative emotional consequences of resource scarcity are also likely to reduce consumer well-being. Notably, these negative effects are likely to be more pronounced on social media platforms that emphasize visual content such as Instagram or Pinterest. Similarly, negative effects are likely to be stronger on social media platforms that frequently update their content such as Twitter or LinkedIn.

Self-Discrepancy: Perceived Control

People often experience a lack of control when they feel they can't affect the outcomes of a task they are engaged in. For example, when an individual misses a meeting due to bad traffic or postpones travel due to bad weather, she might feel that she doesn't have enough control over life. Although environmental factors are often the reason for people to feel a lack of control, interpersonal factors can also reduce one's perceived level of control. For example, people in organizations experience a lack of control when they cannot complete a project due to organizational reasons. Students might experience a lack of control when they see examination questions from topic areas that have not been covered in class.

The use of social media can lead to feelings of low control. Sports fans reading news on Twitter about their favorite sports team selling an important player could trigger feelings of low control. Testimonials from employees on LinkedIn about getting fired from companies can trigger thoughts of not having enough control over outcomes in life. Reading about how peers have been able to achieve their financial goals, dream jobs, or perfect houses can make social media users reappraise their control over outcomes in life. Social media posts about the future of employment and the economy can make people feel they are not in control of their lives. Reading about wars or natural disasters can make people feel that their locus of control is largely external rather than internal. In general, social media posts often highlight how others are in control of their lives in contrast to a lack of control in one's own personal environment.

Lower perceived control has been shown to influence outcomes in both personal and consumption contexts (Friesen et al., 2014; Mandel et al., 2017; Whitson & Galinsky, 2008). Researchers have shown that perceived control is important for subjective well-being (Whitson & Galinsky, 2008), with high control leading to positive emotions and mental health (Kay et al., 2010; Landau et al., 2015) and low control leading to negative emotions and anxiety (Kay et al., 2010; Tangney et al., 2018; Whalen, 1998). As far as personal behavior is concerned, loss of control has been shown to increase belief in conspiracy theories (Whitson & Galinsky, 2008) and horoscope predictions (Wang et al., 2012). These findings suggest that low control encourages suboptimal judgment and decision-making in terms of superstitious and irrational thinking. As far as consumption is concerned, loss of control has been found to increase preference for high-effort products (Cutright & Samper, 2014), utilitarian products (Chen et al., 2017a), and brand leaders (Beck et al., 2020). Since people have an innate desire to be in control, loss of control motivates people to engage in compensatory behavior to reestablish control (Landau et al., 2015). There are three major ways in which people seek to restore lost control, namely reducing perceptions of randomness (Cutright, 2012; Landau et al., 2015), bolstering personal agency (Chen et al., 2017b; Cutright & Samper, 2014), and affiliating with an external high-control entity (Beck et al., 2020; Kay et al., 2010). For example, the study reported by Beck et al. (2020) manipulated perceived control with a writing task. Participants in the low control condition were asked to write about an incident in life where they had low control while participants in the high control condition wrote about an incident where they had high control. Participants were then asked to choose a gift certificate worth $25 for either a brand leader (i.e., McDonald's) or a brand non-leader (i.e., Wendy's). Results revealed that more participants in the low control condition (50%) compared to the low control condition (33%) chose the brand leader. These consumption choices driven by loss of control can be suboptimal when the brand leader does not have the highest quality or the best price in the marketplace. Similar to other forms of self-discrepancy, loss of control has negative emotional consequences in terms of lower mood and life satisfaction, which implies a reduction in consumer well-being.

Self-Discrepancy: Power

Power has been defined as asymmetric control over valued resources in social relations (Keltner et al., 2003). People with lower power in social relationships are generally dependent on those possessing high power for making important decisions in daily life. In an organizational context, employees can feel powerless when they are dependent on others for work-related decisions. In a family context, people could experience a lack of power when they feel that their life choices are circumscribed by those who are older than them. Research has shown that incidental stimuli in the environment can also affect an individual's perceived level of power. For example, reading words such as "comply," "obey," and "submit" can lead to thoughts of not having enough power (Smith & Trope, 2006). From a physical perspective, sitting positions have been shown to affect feelings of power (Carney et al., 2015). From a broader social perspective, social class is an antecedent of power with higher social class generally associated with greater power (Yu & Blader, 2020; Anderson et al., 2012).

Social media use can lead to feelings of low power. People often see social media posts on LinkedIn about their friends and peers acquiring power by getting promotions or winning leadership awards. These posts can lead to discrepancies between the level of power one currently possesses and the level of power one would ideally like to possess. Seeing others' Instagram accounts increase their follower counts can lead to feelings of low power when one's own follower count is stagnant. When individuals see peers wearing luxury clothes and dining at expensive restaurants; they may mentally associate their peers with a certain social class. This can lead to thoughts of disparity between one's own social class and others' social class, leading to self-discrepancy in power. Perceived lack of power can arise from exposure to Twitter posts. For example, Twitter posts about people getting fired or being forced to act against one's wishes can lead to feelings of powerlessness. This is illustrated by a video in India that went viral on Facebook, Twitter, and LinkedIn in June 2023. This video shows a senior employee of one of India's largest financial entities misusing his power by using abusive language towards fellow employees. This incident led to extensive online discussion about the powerlessness of junior employees in corporate settings in India.

Research shows many detrimental effects of lack of power. Lack of power drives people to buy expensive products that signal status (Rucker et al., 2012) as well as larger-size items (Rucker & Galinsky, 2008). Lack of power has been shown to reduce one's confidence (Briñol et al., 2007), increase anxiety (Kim et al., 2020), and increase complaining tendencies (Popelnukha et al., 2021). In one study, Kim et al., 2020 manipulated the level of power through a recall task. In the low power condition, participants were asked to recall an incident where someone else had power over them while participants in the high control condition were asked to think of an incident where they had more power over others. Participants in low-power conditions showed higher levels of anxiety than participants in high-power conditions. Like other forms of self-discrepancy, loss of power has also been associated with reduced subjective well-being (Yu & Blader, 2020). Notably, these negative effects of social media use on perceived power and subsequent judgment and decision-making are subject to a vicious cycle of reinforcement. As people see social media posts that reduce their perceived power, they are likely to compensate by posting their own success stories. These posts, in turn, will magnify a selection bias online whereby only positive posts of success proliferate on social media over time. Perceived lack of power due to social media use might be higher at certain points in time. For example, people looking for jobs might browse platforms such as LinkedIn more often and thereby experience greater self-discrepancy in the domain of power.

Self-Discrepancy: Physical Appearance

As noted earlier, self-discrepancy can arise in different domains such as physical appearance, gender identity, affiliation, or intelligence. Of these, physical appearance is particularly important since appearance is visual in nature and can be assessed quickly in daily life with minimal cognitive effort. Since individuals are said to be cognitive misers (Simon, 1986; Corcoran & Mussweiler, 2010), information related to physical appearance is likely to be easily processed and hence have a significant effect on judgments and decisions. The importance of physical appearance has also been reinforced in the process of evolution. Research in evolutionary psychology suggests that humans are hardwired by natural selection to automatically infer the value of potential mates by external signs of health and symmetry that, in turn, become culturally encoded into standards of attractiveness (Crawford & Krebs, 2013).

If evolution and biology have made us vigilant about appearance, social media has made it easier than ever before to compare our appearance with others. Many social media platforms such as Facebook, Instagram, Snapchat, TikTok, and YouTube are largely visual in nature and put the visual appearance of others front and center for users. Contrast this with the relatively fewer people we had daily visual contact with before the advent of social media. When we are regularly exposed to others' appearance on social media, these act as reference points for self-discrepancy by allowing easy comparison with our own appearance. An important aspect of social media is that it encourages upward, rather than downward social comparisons. Upward social comparisons are comparisons where others are seen to be better than us which, in the domain of attractiveness is when others are seen to be more attractive than us. Try this the next time you are on Facebook or Instagram: look at the pictures or videos posted and see if you can spot anyone looking less than good. People spend hours curating their personal pictures and videos before posting them on social media using filters and video editing tools earlier available only to professional film editors. Furthermore, the prospect of posting one's pictures and videos online motivates people to invest in clothes, makeup, and even plastic surgery to have that Instagram-ready face and body. This is a fundamental expression of human nature since self-enhancement—the drive to look good in the eyes of others—is one of the strongest human motives (Kwang & Swann, 2010). Consistent with this idea, it has been shown that people tend to share self-enhancing facts with friends and family whereas they share their mistakes and losses only with close relatives and friends (Zheng et al., 2020).

What might be the effect of continuous exposure to attractive people on social media from a young age? A likely outcome is that social media users will compare their imperfect selves with the idealized images they see online and experience self-discrepancy in the domain of physical attractiveness. Research shows that such self-discrepancy can have negative effects both in the short and long term. In the short term, self-discrepancies can produce negative emotions such as anxiety, dissatisfaction, disappointment, or dejection (Packard & Wooten, 2013). Similarly, Heine et al. (2006) have shown that experiencing self-discrepancies has a psychological cost in terms of distress and negative arousal. We examined this issue in a research study where half the participants were asked to log into their personal Facebook account and browse at their own pace for twenty minutes while the other half were asked to browse CNN for twenty minutes (Mukherjee, 2018). Participants then completed a questionnaire measuring different emotions such as pride, anger, joy, and envy. We wanted to find out which emotions were most strongly associated with browsing social media, compared to other types of websites. We found that, of all the emotions we measured, it was envy that was most strongly associated with social media browsing. This finding is consistent with other research showing that envy is the emotion most strongly associated with upward social comparisons (Mussweiler et al., 2004).

In the longer term, self-discrepancy in physical appearance has been shown to reduce self-esteem especially when appearance is an important basis of self-esteem (Braun & Wicklund, 1989; Richins, 1991; Valkenburg et al., 2021). Lack of self-esteem, in turn, can motivate compensatory behavior both directly in the domain of physical attractiveness as well as indirectly in other domains of daily life. When individuals seek direct resolution of self-discrepancy, they might purchase products and services that address the source of self-discrepancy (Heine et al., 2006; Tesser & Cornell, 1991). For example, it has been shown that consumers experiencing self-discrepancies in weight or appearance show increased interest in joining a gym or undertaking plastic surgery (Schouten, 1991). Notably, of these two options, it is no secret which one is easier to pursue or more likely to provide immediate benefits in terms of improved appearance. Extensive research on goal pursuit shows that self-control is a fragile thing and weight gain is a wicked problem that is extremely difficult to address with diets and gyms (Walls, 2018). This leaves plastic surgery, pharmaceutical products, makeup, clothes, and camera filters as surer paths to reducing self-discrepancies in physical appearance. These have significant costs for individuals, not just in money but also in terms of health risks and psychological fragility that comes from a superficial appearance-based foundation for self-esteem. Cosmetic procedures are also subject to the consistency principle which states that taking one small step towards a goal makes it much easier to take the next steps towards the same goal (Cialdini et al., 1995). This is why plastic surgery is a seductive siren call; do it once and you may find yourself going back for more and more.

Research has demonstrated other negative effects of appearance self-discrepancy on people's shopping behavior. It has been shown that individuals cope with self-discrepancy by behaving in ways that shorten the gap between ideal and actual in a symbolic manner (Rucker et al., 2012). For example, Gollwitzer et al. (1982) reported that MBA students who did not have objective indicators of success were more likely to show symbolic indicators of success (e.g., branded clothing or jewlrey). Similarly, individuals facing self-discrepancy in physical appearance may end up spending more money on high-priced brands such as Abercrombie & Fitch or Victoria's Secret that are often represented by attractive models in the media.

Since compensatory behavior following self-discrepancy can be fluid in the sense of being exercised in different domains, it is possible that the appearance of self-discrepancy can lead to a habit of "shopping therapy" and overspending with its negative implications in terms of increased consumer debt. This would be consistent with research showing that escapism is a common response to self-discrepancy. For example, it has been shown that people increase their consumption of food and drink when they perceive that they are below societal standards (Heatherton & Baumeister, 1991). Given the unhealthy ingredients in mass-marketed food and drink, increased consumption of food and drink is likely to lead to weight gain, medical problems, and a vicious cycle of negative self-discrepancy in physical appearance.

A more unusual response to self-discrepancy in physical appearance might be dissociation, disengagement, or rejection of societal standards of attractiveness, and escape into alternative subcultures that promise liberation from conventional social standards (Steele et al., 2002). Since niche subcultures are easy to find on social media, this would complete the circle of social media prompting self-discrepancy as well as providing a community that addresses the self-discrepancy regardless of whether it is a right community from a long-term point of view.

Finally, contextual factors can magnify the effects of social media on appearance self-discrepancy and their downstream negative consequences. For example, it has been shown that the personality trait of perfectionism is increasing among individuals due to greater parental helicoptering during childhood, competition in the education system, and uncertainly in the labor market (Curran & Hill, 2019; Fioravanti et al., 2022). Since perfectionist individuals have chronically high ideal states, they should be vulnerable to the negative effects of social media outlined earlier. Other research has shown that individualist cultures are more concerned about gaining self-esteem than collectivist cultures (Heine et al., 2006; Morrison & Johnson, 2011). As self-esteem can be based in part on physical appearance, this suggests that people in individualist cultures should be more vulnerable to the negative aspects of social media outlined earlier.

Self-Discrepancy: Social Belongingness

The use of social media can increase self-discrepancy in social belongingness which, in turn, can have negative effects on people. There are at least three paths through which social media can influence one's sense of social belongingness, that is, one's social connection to other people in the real world. First, the widespread adoption of smartphones and tablets together with the lower cost of mobile Internet has reduced intra-family interaction and distanced family members from one another. In an earlier era, families would often have dinner or watch television together which gave ample opportunity for talking to each other. In contrast, everyone in the family now has their own device in hand with a world of entertainment and social media curated to maximize online engagement. Similarly, if you look around any coffee shop, you will find atomized individuals each with a screen and earphones insulating them from others.

Second, the strength of connection we have with others on social media can be on a continuum from weak ties to strong ties (Valenzuela et al., 2018). As the number of people, we are connected to on social media increases, average tie strength is likely to decrease given the difficulty of maintaining close relationships with a larger number of people. We may have a lot of friends on Facebook or followers on Instagram but are likely to know only a few of them well. Third, research has shown that people are more often "lurkers" than "posters" on social media, that is, people mostly observe others' behavior passively online rather than actively participate in online conversations (Schlosser, 2005). Passive presence is likely to further reduce the likelihood of forming strong connections with people in person.

People have an innate need to both establish and maintain social relationships with others (Baumeister & Leary, 1995), and hence social media use can hurt people by increasing self-discrepancy in social belongingness. In a study published in *American Psychologist*, researchers from Carnegie Mellon University examined the amount of time people spent interacting with other family members before and after the installation of a computer with internet access (Kraut et al., 1998). During the two-year longitudinal study, family interaction declined dramatically, and this drop was directly proportional to the increase in internet use. Ironically, many participants justified their increased time online by saying they needed to "stay in touch" with more distant friends and relatives, while they increasingly ignored those they were living with. This may be one of the contributors to an epidemic of loneliness and depression that seems to be spreading in tandem with internet use in general and social media use in particular (Pittman & Reich, 2016).

Research has shown that self-discrepancy in social belongingness, that is, experiencing of social exclusion, leads to feelings of social pain including nervousness and discontentment in general (Mead et al., 2011) as well as neural activity perceived as physical pain (Eisenberger et al., 2003). In fact, Randles et al. (2013) have argued that both social and physical pain are in the same dorsal anterior cingulate cortex of the human brain. Self-discrepancy in social belongingness has also been shown to influence consumption behavior. One stream of research has found that people who feel excluded from social groups are more likely to purchase products that signal status or in-group membership (Dommer & Swaminathan, 2013; Duclos et al., 2013b). Since status-signaling products are usually more expensive, this is likely to increase financial pressure and debt load on individuals over time. Another stream of research has shown that experiencing social exclusion increases purchases of nostalgic products since this reinforces their sense of connection with significant others in the past (Loveland et al., 2010). Notably, other research has shown that reminders of compensatory consumption following self-discrepancy can lead to increased rumination about self-discrepancy (Lisjak et al., 2015). Thus, it is possible that surrounding oneself with nostalgic products to counter feelings of social exclusion can backfire by making one's current social isolation more salient.

Social exclusion can be understood not just as a personal disengagement from one's desired social groups but also as the exclusion of one's in-groups from the larger fabric of society. Charles et al. (2009) found that lower income and racial groups spent a larger fraction of their money on conspicuous consumption to presumably counteract the perception of being low status. This can create a negative spiral of the most disadvantaged groups wasting their financial resources on short-term wasteful purchases rather than long-term beneficial investments to improve their lives. Research has also shed light on when the negative effects of self-discrepancy on social belongingness are most likely to manifest themselves. For example, it has been shown that positive mood acts as a resource that allows individuals to process negative information in depth and thereby make judgments and decisions based on more complete information (Raghunathan & Trope, 2002). If so, then a positive mood could help people cope with self-discrepancy in the form of social exclusion, and thereby make better decisions about ways to increase their social connections.

Finally, self-construal could determine the extent to which social exclusion has negative effects on judgments and decisions and control (Jia & Wyer, 2022). Self-construal refers to how individuals view themselves in relation to others, with individuals having a primarily independent or interdependent self-construal (Rose Markus & Kitayama, 1991; Spassova & Lee, 2013). Individuals with an independent self-construal put a high value on self-reliance and autonomy, while individuals with an interdependent self-construal value relationships with other people. Based on these definitions, the negative effects of social exclusion are more likely to emerge for those with an interdependent self-construal than those with an independent self-construal.

Self-Discrepancy: Gender Identity

Social media use can increase self-discrepancy in gender identity which, in turn, can have negative effects on individuals. Gender identity, sometimes referred to as an individual's psychological—as opposed to biological—sex, has been defined as the fundamental, existential sense of one's maleness or femaleness (Spence, 1984). To the extent that gender is culturally derived, gender identity should be ground in cultural understandings of masculine or feminine behaviors (Firat, 1991). There are at least three ways in which social media use can influence one's gender identity, especially at a young age when personal identities are being formed. First, anonymity on social media offers a safe space for discussing issues related to gender identity with others, thereby crystallizing thoughts about this topic over time. Second, seeing examples of others "coming out" with a new gender identity can provide social validation and social proof for one's own course of action in the future. Third, many people get their news from social media. Since issues related to gender identity have become more prominent in the news cycle, they are likely to be at the top of news feeds. Fourth, we can be whoever we want to be on social media, with an assumed name and avatar that is very different from what we are in the real world. As such, social media use makes it easy for us to try out and practice alternative gender identities before transitioning into the real world.

Self-discrepancy in gender identity can have negative effects on both immediate measures of psychological well-being as well as longer-term behaviors. In the short term, research indicates that self-discrepancy in gender identity leads to higher psychological pressure as well as internalization of problems (Yunger et al., 2004). In the longer term, research has investigated the effects of self-discrepancy in gender identity on consumption behaviors. White and Argo showed that when women faced a self-discrepancy in gender identity, those who scored low on collective self-esteem were more likely to choose a gender-neutral magazine over a feminine, identity-confirming magazine (White & Argo, 2009). In other words, people experiencing gender self-discrepancy cope by avoiding products or services related to self-discrepancy and going to products completely unrelated to self-discrepancy. Similarly, Lisjak et al. (2015) showed that self-discrepancy favored cross-domain choices, that is, choices in product categories not related to self-discrepancy. These findings are important by showing that self-discrepancy in gender identity can blind people to potentially useful products and services only because they are reminders of a painful psychological state. Other research has shown that when individuals experience identity-based self-discrepancy, they are more likely to forget ads related to the domain of self-discrepancy (Dalton & Huang, 2014). Such motivated forgetting of information can be harmful by making it more difficult for individuals to gather relevant information that is likely to benefit them in the long run. It is apparent that some men are more feminine than masculine, while some women are more masculine than feminine; social media has played an important role in this transition by increasing the salience of self-discrepancy in gender identity and thereby influencing consumption behavior and well-being.

Self-Discrepancy: Mortality Salience

The use of social media can increase self-discrepancy in mortality salience which, in turn, can have negative effects on people. Mortality salience is defined as the extent to which the idea of death is salient in people's minds (Greenberg et al., 1986). Fear of death is inherent to the human condition and rooted in human nature. Reminders of mortality are all around us in this age of terrorism, pandemics, and global warming. These reminders of mortality are magnified by social media since the algorithms underlying social media platforms highlight danger and threats to increase users' engagement and thereby maximize profits.

Research has shown that increased mortality salience has negative effects on affective responses as well as judgment and decision-making. In terms of affect, Lambert et al. (2014) reported four studies showing that mortality salience manipulations—compared to control—increased negative affect, especially with respect to fear and terror-related sentiments. Mortality salience can also influence consumption behavior. For example, in the aftermath of the terrorist attacks on the U.S. (September 11, 2001), many Americans' engaged in excessive consumption; this overconsumption was seen in more buying of luxury products (White & Leung, 2002), bargain shopping, stockpiling, and overconsuming sugar (Hubler, 2001) to cope with the mortality that comes for us all. Mandel and Smeesters (2008) conducted a series of experiments that showed that research participants who were reminded of their impending mortality were more likely to purchase and eat food compared to participants in the control condition, with this effect being stronger for low self-esteem compared to high self-esteem participants. Similarly, Ferraro et al. (2005) showed that individuals exposed to a mortality salience prime were more likely to eat chocolate cake rather than fruit cake especially when they were low on body self-esteem. Given the increase in obesity rates around the world, these findings suggest that mortality made salient by social media use can create a cycle of unhealthy eating and consequent psychological as well as physiological problems. Other research has found that consumers exposed to death-related information show increased interest in luxury compared to non-luxury brands (Mandel & Heine, 1999) and spend more on hedonic items such as clothing and entertainment (Kasser & Sheldon, 2000). These findings suggest that mortality made salient by social media can further entrench materialism as a cultural value and increase pressure to spend beyond one's means.

Self-Discrepancy: Perceived Intelligence

People sometimes feel they lack the required degree of intelligence to succeed in life. As such, perceived intelligence is another domain where people can feel self-discrepancy. Notably, using social media can exacerbate feelings of being unintelligent. While browsing social media platforms, we often come across posts about others' academic success which increases the salience of what we have not been able to achieve in our academic endeavors. Career success stories posted by others highlight how others have been intelligent enough to achieve greater success than themselves. As more and more people post about their accomplishments, social media could indicate a higher level of intelligence for others than for us.

Research has explored the effects of low perceived intelligence on subsequent judgment and behavior. For example, when people feel they are not intelligent enough they are more likely to buy a fountain pen than a candy bar (Gao et al., 2009). Scoring poorly on an exam has been shown to induce feelings of low perceived intelligence (Mandel et al., 2017) which in turn leads to higher music consumption (Kim & Rucker, 2012). Mandel et al. (2017) showed that a lack of perceived intelligence can lead individuals to highlight their degrees or diplomas in a salient manner using conspicuous frames. These research results show how a perceived lack of intelligence can lead to suboptimal behaviors such as distracting or distancing oneself from the domain of intelligence.

Solutions for Combating the Dark Side of Social Media

Figure 5.1 depicts an overview of self-discrepancy with respect to social media exposure to consumers, its effects on individuals (such as their mental health and well-being), and proposed solutions. Next, we outline these solutions with respect to actions by individuals as well as companies.

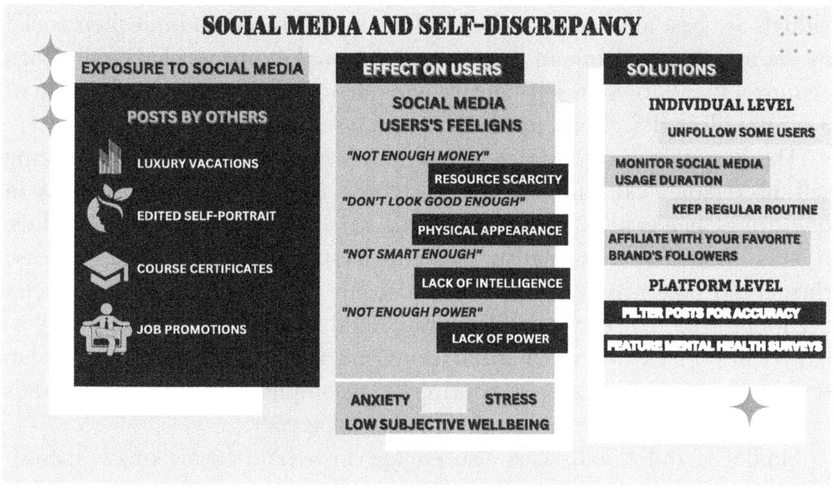

FIGURE 5.1 Social media increases different types of self-discrepancies which, in turn, leads to negative effects on consumer well-being.

We have seen in this chapter that social media use can magnify different types of self-discrepancies such as resource scarcity, loss of control, powerlessness, lack of intelligence, increased mortality salience, reduced physical attractiveness, gender identity-related discrepancies, and lack of social belongingness. These self-discrepancies can then reduce consumer well-being in many ways. However, the good news is that individuals and social media platforms can take actionable steps to combat this dark side of social media as described in the following sections.

Solutions—Actions by Individuals

Individuals can take several steps to mitigate negative discrepancies arising from browsing others' posts on social media. First, individuals could aim to reduce the number of hours they spend on social media platforms and thereby minimize exposure to others' posts on these platforms. Research indicates that monitoring one's behavior can increase self-control (Heatherton & Baumeister, 1991) and hence counting the hours one is spending on social media platforms can help reduce social media use. Technology can create a record of one's exposure to social media platforms. For example, smartphone apps allow users to keep track of time spent browsing different platforms and set an upper limit on the amount of time one can spend on a given platform. Such apps can be used by individuals to limit their social media use and hence reduce their exposure to posts by others that increases self-discrepancy. Notably, research on precommitment indicates that individuals are best advised to make binding commitments to limit their social media use ahead of time in their "cold" rational moments. This will guard against a breakdown in self-control when temptation strikes in the form of TikTok videos, Facebook updates, or Instagram stories.

The literature on self-discrepancy shows that individuals experiencing self-discrepancy can take a range of actions to restore the discrepancy in question (Chen et al., 2017a; Han et al., 2015; Mandel et al., 2017). Thus, if individuals are aware that social media use can increase self-discrepancy, they could take prophylactic steps to ensure that these self-discrepancies are minimized. For example, if an individual thinks that they are likely to experience a lack of control after seeing social media posts, they can plan to complete a short exercise routine or accomplish small personal goals every day to maintain their sense of personal agency.

Similarly, individuals can also engage in several forms of compensatory behavior on social media platforms. Posting something online that the individual has expertise in could be a way to signal self-efficacy and intelligence to oneself as well as others. Association with powerful entities has been shown to provide a vicarious sense of power, agency, belonging, and control (Beck et al., 2020). Thus, in the context of social media, a self-discrepant individual could repost something posted by a big brand or a celebrity to bask in reflected glory. For example, associating with an international soccer club's Twitter account by retweeting their posts or engaging in conversations with other fans based on something they posted could provide a sense of agency and belonging. Literature also suggests that loss of control and feelings of uncertainty can be mitigated through seeking structure (Cutright, 2012). This sense of structure could come from having a routine for the day which would compensate for loss of control induced by social media exposure. Beyond these compensatory actions, individuals could deliberately dissociate from the source of self-discrepancy. For example, unfollowing others whose posts are creating self-discrepancy is a simple way to dissociate from the source of discrepancy. These dissociative actions can also be taken at the platform level, by going on short weekend breaks without any electronic devices or signing up for longer meditation retreats designed to reconnect participants with human rather than digital interaction.

Solutions—Actions by Social Media Platforms

Social media platforms can take several steps to ensure that users have positive rather than negative experiences, and thereby gain customer gratitude and long-term loyalty. Many self-discrepancies are caused by the positive self-presentation motivation of other social media users as expressed through their posts. For example, individuals can be tempted to post their own academic or career success stories on social media platforms to appear successful to others. These success stories could induce feelings of lack of intelligence or powerlessness among other social media users, and repeated exposure to such posts is likely to magnify the gap between other's high states and one's own comparatively lower states in different domains of life. As an aside, these success stories may or may not even be real. For example, social media influencers often buy fake followers or arrange for paid photoshoots in private jets to artificially boost their perceived wealth.

First, social media platforms could start by ensuring that people post real stories and share accurate personal information online. This can be done using human fact-checkers as well as artificial intelligence tools to detect fake information in posts. Further, social media platforms could require users to give more detailed information about their academic and career achievements which can help readers distinguish between fake and authentic claims. As discussed earlier, browsing social media can have negative consequences for emotional well-being and mental health. Therefore, social media platforms could administer surveys to monitor the mental well-being of their users. The results of these surveys could then be made public along with contact information for mental health support. Social media platforms could restrict certain types of advertising that have especially deleterious effects on self-discrepancy and well-being. For example, research shows that a lack of social belongingness leads to higher financial risk-taking (Duclos et al., 2013a, 2013b) and mortality salience leads to food overconsumption (Mandel & Smeesters, 2008). Thus, advertising for lottery tickets or high-calorie food could be restricted on social media to mitigate their especially negative effects on consumer welfare in this context.

Resource scarcity has been shown to increase competitive behavior (Roux et al., 2015) and lack of power has been shown to increase stereotyping (Rucker & Galinsky, 2008). These outcomes are synonymous with increased hate and bullying in the context of social media. As such, social media platforms should take more proactive steps to control hateful behavior when self-discrepancies are strongest in user's minds. Research shows that humor is an effective antidote for the negative effects of fear appeals in advertising. Specifically, humor reduces arousal induced by fear advertising and thereby increases the likelihood of desirable actions such as using sunscreen lotion and reducing smoking (Mukherjee & Dubé, 2012; Alden et al., 2000). Thus, users of social media might benefit by watching humorous content online while browsing social media to counteract the negative consequences of high-discrepancy material. More fundamentally, social media users should educate themselves about the psychological pitfalls of interacting with others online. To be forewarned is to be forearmed—thus understanding the psychological dangers of social media is the first step toward lessening bias in one's judgments and decisions (Srivastava & Raghubir, 2002).

This chapter mainly focused on the negative effects of self-discrepancies on consumer well-being. We would like to end on a positive note by highlighting some positive implications of self-discrepancies both for profit and for not-for-profit firms. For example, resource scarcity has been shown to increase charitable donations (Roux et al., 2015) as well as local consumption (Roy & Mukherjee, 2023). Therefore, social media platforms should feature advertisements for charities and local sellers to capture these beneficial effects of self-discrepancy. Loss of control has been shown to increase the preference for utilitarian products (Chen et al., 2017a) and high-effort products (Cutright & Samper, 2014). Therefore, firms offering such products should advertise on social media since people experiencing loss of control on social media are more likely to positively evaluate advertisements for these types of products.

References

Alden, D. L., Mukherjee, A., & Hoyer, W. D. (2000). The effects of incongruity, surprise, and positive moderators on perceived humor in television advertising. *Journal of Advertising, 29*(2), 1–15.

Anderson, C., John, O. P., & Keltner, D. (2012). The personal sense of power. *Journal of Personality, 80*(2), 313–344. https://doi.org/10.1111/j.1467-6494.2011.00734.x

Baumeister, R. F., & Leary, M. R. (1995). The need to belong: Desire for interpersonal attachments as a fundamental human motivation. *Psychological Bulletin, 117*(3), 497–529. https://doi.org/10.1037/0033-2909.117.3.497

Beck, J. T., Rahinel, R., & Bleier, A. (2020). Company worth keeping: Personal control and preferences for brand leaders. *Journal of Consumer Research, 46*(5), 871–886. https://doi.org/10.1093/jcr/ucz040

Blocker, C., Zhang, J. Z., Hill, R. P., Roux, C., Corus, C., Hutton, M., Dorsey, J., & Minton, E. (2023). Rethinking scarcity and poverty: Building bridges for shared insight and impact. *Journal of Consumer Psychology, 33*(3), 489–509.

Braun, O. L., & Wicklund, R. A. (1989). Psychological antecedents of conspicuous consumption. *Journal of Economic Psychology,10*(2), 161–187.

Briñol, P., Petty, R. E., Valle, C., Rucker, D. D., & Becerra, A. (2007). The effects of message recipients' power before and after persuasion: A self-validation analysis. *Journal of Personality and Social Psychology, 93*(6), 1040–1053. https://doi.org/10.1037/0022-3514.93.6.1040

Cannon, C., Goldsmith, K., & Roux, C. (2019). A self-regulatory model of resource scarcity. *Journal of Consumer Psychology, 29*(1), 104–127. https://doi.org/10.1002/jcpy.1035

Carney, D. R., Cuddy, A. J. C., & Yap, A. J. (2015). Review and summary of research on the embodied effects of expansive (vs. contractive) nonverbal displays. *Psychological Science, 26*(5), 657–663. https://doi.org/10.1177/0956797614566855

Charles, K. K., Hurst, E., & Roussanov, N. (2009). Conspicuous consumption and race. *The Quarterly Journal of Economics, 124*(2), 425–467.

Chen, C. Y., Lee, L., & Yap, A. J. (2017a). Control deprivation motivates acquisition of utilitarian products. *Journal of Consumer Research, 43*(6), 1031–1047. https://doi.org/10.1093/jcr/ucw068

Chen, C. Y., Lee, L., & Yap, A. J. (2017b). Control deprivation motivates acquisition of utilitarian products. *Journal of Consumer Research, 43*(6), 1031–1047. https://doi.org/10.1093/jcr/ucw068

Cialdini, R. B., Trost, M. R., & Newsom, J. T. (1995). Preference for consistency: The development of a valid measure and the discovery of surprising behavioral implications. *Journal of Personality and Social Psychology, 69*(2), 318–328. https://doi.org/10.1037/0022-3514.69.2.318

Corcoran, K., & Mussweiler, T. (2010). The cognitive miser's perspective: Social comparison as a heuristic in self-judgements. *European Review of Social Psychology, 21*(1), 78–113.

Crawford, C., & Krebs, D. L. (2013). *Handbook of evolutionary psychology: Ideas, issues, and applications*. Psychology Press.

Curran, T., & Hill, A. P. (2019). Perfectionism is increasing over time: A meta-analysis of birth cohort differences from 1989 to 2016. *Psychological Bulletin, 145*(4), 410–429.

Cutright, K. M. (2012). The beauty of boundaries: When and why we seek structure in consumption. *Journal of Consumer Research*, *38*(5), 775–790. https://doi.org/10.1086/661563

Cutright, K. M., & Samper, A. (2014). Doing it the hard way: How low control drives preferences for high-effort products and services. *Journal of Consumer Research*, *41*(3), 730–745. https://doi.org/10.1086/677314

Dalton, A. N., & Huang, L. (2014). Motivated forgetting in response to social identity threat. *Journal of Consumer Research*, *40*(6), 1017–1038. https://doi.org/10.1086/674198

Dommer, S. L., & Swaminathan, V. (2013). Explaining the endowment effect through ownership: The role of identity, gender, and self-threat. *Journal of Consumer Research*, *39*(5), 1034–1050. https://doi.org/10.1086/666737

Duclos, R., Wan, E. W., & Jiang, Y. (2013a). Show me the honey! Effects of social exclusion on financial risk-taking. *Journal of Consumer Research*, *40*(1), 122–135. https://doi.org/10.1086/668900

Duclos, R., Wan, E. W., & Jiang, Y. (2013b). Show me the honey! Effects of social exclusion on financial risk-taking. *Journal of Consumer Research*, *40*(1), 122–135. https://doi.org/10.1086/668900

Eisenberger, N. I., Lieberman, M. D., & Williams, K. D. (2003). Does rejection hurt? An fMRI study of social exclusion. *Science*, *302*(5643), 290–292.

Fan, L., Li, X., & Jiang, Y. (2019). Room for opportunity: Resource scarcity increases attractiveness of range marketing offers. *Journal of Consumer Research*, *46*(1), 82–98. https://doi.org/10.1093/jcr/ucy059

Ferraro, R., Shiv, B., & Bettman, J. R. (2005). Let us eat and drink, for tomorrow we shall die: Effects of mortality salience and self-esteem on self-regulation in consumer choice. *Journal of Consumer Research*, *32*(1), 65–75. https://academic.oup.com/jcr/article/32/1/65/1796371

Fioravanti, G., Bocci Benucci, S., Ceragioli, G., & Casale, S. (2022). How exposure to beauty ideals on social networking sites influences body image: A systematic review of experimental studies. *Adolescent Research Review*, 7(3), 419–458. https://doi.org/10.1007/s40894-022-00179-4

Firat, A. F. (1991). *The consumer in postmodernity*. ACR North American Advances.

Friesen, J. P., Kay, A. C., Eibach, R. P., & Galinsky, A. D. (2014). Seeking structure in social organization: Compensatory control and the psychological advantages of hierarchy. *Journal of Personality and Social Psychology*, *106*(4), 590.

Gao, L., Wheeler, S. C., & Shiv, B. (2009). The "shaken self": Product choices as a means of restoring self-view confidence. *Journal of Consumer Research*, *36*(1), 29–38. https://doi.org/10.1086/596028

Gollwitzer, P. M., Wicklund, R. A., & Hilton, J. L. (1982). Admission of failure and symbolic self-completion: Extending Lewinian theory. *Journal of Personality and Social Psychology*, 43(2), 358.

Greenberg, J., Pyszczynski, T., & Solomon, S. (1986). The causes and consequences of a need for self-esteem: A terror management theory. *Public Self and Private Self*, 189–212.

Han, D., Duhachek, A., & Rucker, D. D. (2015). Distinct threats, common remedies: How consumers cope with psychological threat. *Journal of Consumer Psychology*, *25*(4), 531–545.

Heatherton, T. E., & Baumeister, R. F. (1991). Binge eating as escape from self-awareness. *Psychological Bulletin*, *110*(1), 86.

Heine, S. J., Proulx, T., & Vohs, K. D. (2006). The meaning maintenance model: On the coherence of social motivations. *Personality and Social Psychology Review*, *10*(2), 88–110.

Hubler, S. (2001). Americans fend off sorrow with laden fork and spoon; people are craving sweets, getting together for potlucks, canning goods, baking pies, and carbo loading (and therefore exercising). *Los Angeles Times*.

Jia, Y., & Wyer, R. S. (2022). The effect of control deprivation on consumers' adoption of no-pain, no-gain principle. *International Journal of Research in Marketing*, In press. https://doi.org/10.1016/j.ijresmar.2021.12.003

Kamakura, W. A., & Yuxing Du, R. (2012). How economic contractions and expansions affect expenditure patterns. *Journal of Consumer Research*, *39*(2), 229–247.

Kasser, T., & Sheldon, K. M. (2000). Of wealth and death: Materialism, mortality salience, and consumption behavior. *Science*, *11*(4), 348–351.

Kay, A. C., Gaucher, D., McGregor, I., & Nash, K. (2010). Religious belief as compensatory control. *Personality and Social Psychology Review*, *14*(1), 37–48. https://doi.org/10.1177/1088868309353750

Keltner, D., Gruenfeld, D. H., & Anderson, C. (2003). Power, approach, and inhibition. *Psychological Review*, *110*(2), 265.

Kim, J., Pai, J., Whitson, J., & Lee, S. (2020). A relational account of powerlessness: The role of the attachment system in consumer inaction. *Association for Consumer Research*, *48*. http://www.acrwebsite.org/volumes/2662310/volumes/v48/NA-48http://www.copyright.com/.

Kim, S., & Rucker, D. D. (2012). Bracing for the psychological storm: Proactive versus reactive compensatory consumption. *Journal of Consumer Research*, *39*(4), 815–830. https://doi.org/10.1086/665832

Kraut, R., Patterson, M., Lundmark, V., Kiesler, S., Mukophadhyay, T., & Scherlis, W. (1998). Internet paradox: A social technology that reduces social involvement and psychological well-being? *American Psychologist*, *53*(9), 1017.

Kwang, T., & Swann, W. B. (2010). Do people embrace praise even when they feel unworthy? A review of critical tests of self-enhancement versus self-verification. *Personality and Social Psychology Review*, *14*(3), 263–280. https://doi.org/10.1177/1088868310365876

Lambert, A. J., Eadeh, F. R., Peak, S. A., Scherer, L. D., Schott, J. P., & Slochower, J. M. (2014). Toward a greater understanding of the emotional dynamics of the mortality salience manipulation: Revisiting the "affect-free" claim of terror management research. *Journal of Personality and Social Psychology*, *106*(5), 655–678. https://doi.org/10.1037/a0036353

Landau, M. J., Kay, A. C., & Whitson, J. A. (2015). Compensatory control and the appeal of a structured world. *Psychological Bulletin*, *141*(3), 694–722. https://doi.org/10.1037/a0038703

Lisjak, M., Bonezzi, A., Kim, S., & Rucker, D. D. (2015). Perils of compensatory consumption: Within-domain compensation undermines subsequent self-regulation. *Journal of Consumer Research*, *41*(5), 1186–1203. https://doi.org/10.1086/678902

Loveland, K. E., Smeesters, D., & Mandel, N. (2010). Still preoccupied with 1995: The need to belong and preference for nostalgic products. *Journal of Consumer Research*, *37*(3), 393–408. https://doi.org/10.1086/653043

Mandel, N., & Heine, S. J. (1999). Terror management and marketing: He who dies with the most toys wins. *ACR North American Advances*.

Mandel, N., Rucker, D. D., Levav, J., & Galinsky, A. D. (2017). The compensatory consumer behavior model: How self-discrepancies drive consumer behavior. *Journal of Consumer Psychology*, *27*(1), 133–146. https://doi.org/10.1016/j.jcps.2016.05.003

Mandel, N., & Smeesters, D. (2008). The sweet escape: Effects of mortality salience on consumption quantities for high- And low-self-esteem consumers. *Journal of Consumer Research*, *35*(2), 309–323. https://doi.org/10.1086/587626

Mead, N. L., Baumeister, R. F., Stillman, T. F., Rawn, C. D., & Vohs, K. D. (2011). Social exclusion causes people to spend and consume strategically in the service of affiliation. *Journal of Consumer Research*, *37*(5), 902–919. https://doi.org/10.1086/656667

Mehta, R., & Zhu, M. (2016). Creating when you have less: The impact of resource scarcity on product use creativity. *Journal of Consumer Research*, *42*(5), 767–782. https://doi.org/10.1093/jcr/ucv051

Morrison, K. R., & Johnson, C. S. (2011). When what you have is who you are: Self-uncertainty leads individualists to see themselves in their possessions. *Personality and Social Psychology Bulletin*, *37*(5), 639–651. https://doi.org/10.1177/0146167211403158

Mukherjee, A. (2018). *The internet trap: Five costs of living online*. University of Toronto Press.

Mukherjee, A., & Dubé, L. (2012). Mixing emotions: The use of humor in fear advertising. *Journal of Consumer Behaviour, 11*(2), 147–161.

Mussweiler, T., Rüter, K., & Epstude, K. (2004). The ups and downs of social comparison: Mechanisms of assimilation and contrast. *Journal of Personality and Social Psychology*, *87*(6), 832–844. https://doi.org/10.1037/0022-3514.87.6.832

Packard, G., & Wooten, D. B. (2013). Compensatory knowledge signaling in consumer word-of-mouth. *Journal of Consumer Psychology*, *23*(4), 434–450. https://doi.org/10.1016/j.jcps.2013.05.002

Paley, A., Tully, S. M., & Sharma, E. (2019). Too constrained to converse: The effect of financial constraints on word of mouth. *Journal of Consumer Research*, *45*(5), 889–905. https://doi.org/10.1093/jcr/ucy040

Park, L. E., & Maner, J. K. (2009). Does self-threat promote social connection? The role of self-esteem and contingencies of self-worth. *Journal of Personality and Social Psychology*, *96*(1), 203–217. https://doi.org/10.1037/a0013933

Pitesa, M., & Thau, S. (2014). A lack of material resources causes harsher moral judgments. *Psychological Science*, *25*(3), 702–710. https://doi.org/10.1177/0956797613514092

Pittman, M., & Reich, B. (2016). Social media and loneliness: Why an Instagram picture may be worth more than a thousand Twitter words. *Computers in Human Behavior*, *62*, 155–167.

Popelnukha, A., Weng, Q., Ali, A., & Atamba, C. (2021). When do low-power customers complain? The joint effects of chronic sense of personal power and complaint success on complaining intentions. *Journal of Consumer Behaviour, 20*(1), 101–118. https://doi.org/10.1002/cb.1859

Raghunathan, R., & Trope, Y. (2002). Walking the tightrope between feeling good and being accurate: Mood as a resource in processing persuasive messages. *Journal of Personality and Social Psychology, 83*(3), 510–525. https://doi.org/10.1037/0022-3514.83.3.510

Randles, D., Heine, S. J., & Santos, N. (2013). The common pain of surrealism and death: Acetaminophen reduces compensatory affirmation following meaning threats. *Psychological Science, 24*(6), 966–973. https://doi.org/10.1177/0956797612464786

Richins, M. L. (1991). Social comparison and the idealized images of advertising. *Journal of Consumer Research, 18*(1), 71–83, https://www.jstor.org/stable/2489486

Rose Markus, H., & Kitayama, S. (1991). Culture and the self: Implications for cognition, emotion, and motivation. *Psychological Review, 98*(2), 224.

Roux, C., Goldsmith, K., & Bonezzi, A. (2015). On the psychology of scarcity: When reminders of resource scarcity promote selfish (and generous) behavior. *Journal of Consumer Research, 42*(4), 615–631. https://doi.org/10.1093/jcr/ucv048

Roy, A., & Mukherjee, A. (2023). The effect of perceived control on local consumption. *Psychology & Marketing*. https://doi.org/10.1002/mar.21834

Rucker, D. D., & Galinsky, A. D. (2008). Desire to acquire: Powerlessness and compensatory consumption. *Journal of Consumer Research, 35*(2), 257–267. https://doi.org/10.1086/588569

Rucker, D. D., Galinsky, A. D., & Dubois, D. (2012). Power and consumer behavior: How power shapes who and what consumers value. *Journal of Consumer Psychology, 22*(3), 352–368. https://doi.org/10.1016/j.jcps.2011.06.001

Schlosser, A. E. (2005). Posting versus lurking: Communicating in a multiple audience context. *Journal of Consumer Research*, 32(2), 260–265.

Schouten, J. W. (1991). Selves in transition: Symbolic consumption in personal rites of passage and identity reconstruction. *Journal of Consumer Research, 17*(4), 412–425. https://about.jstor.org/terms

Sharma, E., & Alter, A. L. (2012). Financial deprivation prompts consumers to seek scarce goods. *Journal of Consumer Research, 39*(3), 545–560. https://doi.org/10.1086/664038

Simon, H. A. (1986). Rationality in psychology and economics. *Journal of Business, 59*(4), 209–224.

Smith, P. K., & Trope, Y. (2006). You focus on the forest when you're in charge of the trees: Power priming and abstract information processing. *Journal of Personality and Social Psychology, 90*(4), 578–596. https://doi.org/10.1037/0022-3514.90.4.578

Spassova, G., & Lee, A. Y. (2013). Looking into the future: A match between self-view and temporal distance. *Journal of Consumer Research, 40*(1), 159–171. https://doi.org/10.1086/669145

Spence, J. T. (1984). Gender identity and its implications for the concepts of masculinity and femininity. *Nebraska Symposium on Motivation, 32*, 59–95.

Srivastava, J., & Raghubir, P. (2002). Debiasing using decomposition: The case of memory-based credit card expense estimates. *Journal of Consumer Psychology, 12*(3), 253–264.

Statista. (2023). https://www.statista.com/topics/1164/social-networks/#topicOverview

Steele, C. M., Spencer, S. J., & Aronson, J. (2002). Contending with group image: The psychology of stereotype and social identity threat. In Mark P. Zanna (Eds.), *Advances in experimental social psychology* (Vol. 34, pp. 379–440). Academic Press.

Stone, J., Wiegand, A. W., Cooper, J., & Aronson, E. (1997). When exemplification fails: Hypocrisy and the motive for self-integrity. *Journal of Personality and Social Psychology*, *72*(1), 54.

Tangney, J. P., Boone, A. L., & Baumeister, R. F. (2018). High self-control predicts good adjustment, less pathology, better grades, and interpersonal success. *Self-Regulation and Self-Control*, 173–212. https://doi.org/10.4324/9781315175775

Tesser, A., & Cornell, D. P. (1991). On the confluence of self processes. *Journal of Experimental Social Psychology*, *27*(6), 501–526. https://doi.org/10.1016/0022-1031(91)90023-Y

Valenzuela, S., Correa, T., & Gil de Zuniga, H. (2018). Ties, likes, and tweets: Using strong and weak ties to explain differences in protest participation across Facebook and Twitter use. *Political Communication*, *35*(1), 117–134.

Valkenburg, P., Beyens, I., Pouwels, J. L., Van Driel, I. I., & Keijsers, L. (2021). Social media use and adolescents' self-esteem: Heading for a person-specific media effects paradigm. *Journal of Communication*, *71*(1), 56–78. https://doi.org/10.1093/joc/jqaa039

Walls, H. L. (2018). Wicked problems and a 'wicked' solution. *Global Health*, *14*, 34. https://doi.org/10.1186/s12992-018-0353-x

Wang, C. S., Whitson, J. A., & Menon, T. (2012). Culture, control, and illusory pattern perception. *Social Psychological and Personality Science*, *3*(5), 630–638. https://doi.org/10.1177/1948550611433056

Whalen, P. J. (1998). Fear, vigilance, and ambiguity: Initial neuroimaging studies of the human amygdala. *Current Directions in Psychological Science*, *7*(6), 177–188.

White, G. L., & Leung, S. (2002). American tastes move upscale, forcing manufacturers to adjust. *Wall Street Journal*.

White, K., & Argo, J. J. (2009). Social identity threat and consumer preferences. *Journal of Consumer Psychology*, *19*(3), 313–325.

Whitson, J. A., & Galinsky, A. D. (2008). Lacking control increases illusory pattern perception. *Science*, *322*(5898), 115–117. https://doi.org/10.1126/science.1159845

Willer, R., Conlon, B., Rogalin, C. L., & Wojnowicz, M. T. (2013). Overdoing gender: A test of the masculine overcompensation thesis. *American Journal of Sociology*, *118*(4), 980–1022. https://doi.org/10.1086/668417

Yu, S., & Blader, S. L. (2020). Why does social class affect subjective well-being? The role of status and power. *Personality and Social Psychology Bulletin*, *46*(3), 331–348. https://doi.org/10.1177/0146167219853841

Yunger, J. L., Carver, P. R., & Perry, D. G. (2004). Does gender identity influence children's psychological well-being? *Developmental Psychology*, *40*(4), 572–582. https://doi.org/10.1037/0012-1649.40.4.572

Zheng, A., Duff, B. R. L., Vargas, P., & Yao, M. Z. (2020). Self-Presentation on social media: When self-enhancement confronts self-verification. *Journal of*

Interactive Advertising, *20*(3), 289–302. https://doi.org/10.1080/15252019.2020.1841048

Zhu, M., & Ratner, R. K. (2015). Scarcity polarizes preferences: The impact on choice among multiple items in a product class. *Journal of Marketing Research*, *52*(1), 13–26.

6

THE DARK SIDE OF INSTAGRAM OF FOOD

The Duality of Food-Related Social Media Posting

Paula C. Peter, Monica Mendini, Anjala Krishen, and Qin Zeng

Introduction: Social Media and Food

Instagram is one of the most popular social media platforms in the world, accounting for roughly one billion monthly active users. By 2025, Instagram is predicted to have 1.44 billion monthly active users or approximately 31 percent of global internet users. The United States currently has 143 million users (as of January 2023), many of whom are college students (Stout, 2021). Overall, 57 percent of Gen-Z consumers active on social media use Instagram and spend an average of five hours per week on the platform. Instagram is most popular in the age group of 25–34 years old; interestingly, data from December 2021 show that in the United States roughly a third of all users belonged to this age group (Statista, 2023). For the youngest consumers, spending time on Instagram has become ubiquitous in their daily lives.

Time invested in Instagram does not come without consequences, especially from a mental health standpoint. Research suggests that time spent on social media has been connected to negative mood (Fardouly et al., 2015), loneliness, depression, and mental health problems (Hunt et al., 2018). In particular, passive social media use (such as browsing other people's profiles without posting on their own) has been linked to negative behaviors. When viewing others' profiles which show appealing photos (e.g., of vacations, luxury products, social events, etc.), social media users might feel envy and loneliness (Krasnova et al., 2013) and experience the fear of missing out (FOMO) (Bui et al., 2022). Research also highlights that sometimes when the use of Instagram is frequent, individuals experience

DOI: 10.4324/9781003410058-9

sadness (#instasad), which is directly associated with greater depressive symptoms (Lup et al., 2015). In addition, especially considering adolescent females (even if not exclusively), emotional investment in social networking has been linked to disturbances related to body image (Meier & Gray, 2014), eating disorders (Holland & Tiggemann, 2017), a more depressive mood, a generally lower level of self-esteem, and poor body image (Tiggemann & Zaccardo, 2018). Several other studies show that higher social media usage among adolescents is often associated with higher risks of engaging in eating disorders (Marks et al., 2020; Wilksch et al., 2020). Previous research emphasizes that when female users spend too much time on social media, this can have an even greater negative effect on their eating behaviors (Tiggemann & Slater, 2013; Hendrickse et al., 2017; Holland & Tiggemann, 2017). As Instagram allows its users to apply a range of enhanced filters to beautify photos, people can present themselves online in distorted versions in comparison with their actual appearance (Chua & Chang, 2016); this emphasizes unrealistic goals, social comparison (e.g., jealousy for others' lives, fear of being left alone; Yang et al., 2018), lowers self-esteem (Cornelis & Peter, 2017), and creates anxiety (Jelenchick et al., 2013). In general, Instagram can contribute to beauty standards that are unrealistic and to issues related to body image, since users often present themselves with very favorable images, often by using photo editing tools. Exposure to idealized images of perfect bodies on Instagram might lead to negative body image perceptions and disordered eating behaviors or obesity-related diseases (Kozinets et al., 2017) among the youngest users (Chatzopoulou et al., 2020).

On the other hand, the Instagram platform has been linked to emotions such as happiness and satisfaction (e.g., Berezan et al., 2018; Cohen et al., 2019; Pittman & Reich, 2016; Slater et al., 2017; Tobin & Chulpaiboon, 2016; Voorveld et al., 2018) because of its hedonic (pleasure oriented) nature, wherein individuals are encouraged to view, post, and share content that triggers positive emotions (e.g., Casaló et al., 2017; Mendini et al., 2022a; Sheldon & Bryant, 2016). As emphasized by Voorveld and colleagues (2018), if compared to other social media sites, experiences on Instagram create the lowest possible number of negative emotions. Various researchers argue that Instagram usage is strongly connected to lower loneliness (Yang, 2016) and discontent (Leung, 2013). Further, spending time on social media platforms has been linked to belongingness (Nadkarni & Hofmann, 2012), care for others (Berezan et al., 2018; Krishen et al., 2016; Sheldon et al., 2011), the ability to externalize memories (Lee et al., 2015; Sheldon & Bryant, 2016), and gratitude (e.g., Koay et al., 2020; Mendini et al., 2022a; Renshaw & Hindman, 2017). When individuals post gratitude-related images on Instagram, exposure to such pictures can allow them to cultivate gratitude or engage in altruistic behaviors (e.g., donate to charities, Mendini et al., 2022a). Social media platforms can be used as a self-regulation tool that can support the maintenance of health-promoting behaviors (Zhou & Krishnan, 2019). Social media also creates a sense of community; users can share advice and tips and can support each other during the course of their virtual experiences. This mutual virtual support can be extremely beneficial for individuals who do not possess a strong support system in their offline lives, such as families or close friends (Zhou & Krishnan, 2019). Table 6.1 provides an illustration of the duality of Instagram.

Instagram is nowadays seen as an important instrument of communication and promotion, not just by brands or companies, but also by organizations interested in social marketing and consumer well-being. Nonprofit corporations have joined the social media bandwagon as a way to offer tailored and engaged content with the promise of being more effective and helping consumers help themselves. However, research associated with the negative effects of social media emphasizes its detrimental consequences on mental health mainly from mindless consumption of this medium. In the context of food decision-making, many people eat while distracted by posts, and this can in turn decrease satiety and increase calorie intake (see Spence et al., 2016, for a review). Moreover, those who consume food images often like to scroll food pages, experiencing a hypnotic and addictive feeling of pleasure (McDonnell, 2016) and continuous exposure to unrealistic body images might lead to eating disorders (Tiggemann & Slater, 2013; Hendrickse et al., 2017; Holland & Tiggemann, 2017).

Considering the marketing of food, research suggests how unhealthy food options on social media and Instagram might lead to poor food decision-making and obesity (e.g., Vassallo et al., 2018). Energy-dense, nutrient-poor (EDNP, Vassallo et al., 2018) foods and beverages are

TABLE 6.1 Negatives and Positives of Instagram on Mental Health

Negatives	*Positives*
Negative mood	Positive mood
Loneliness	Sense of belonging
Sadness	Happiness/joy
Depression/anxiety	Gratitude
Envy	Inspiration/care
Low self-esteem/poor body image	Satisfaction
Mental health problems	Lower loneliness/discontent
Obsession with self (e.g., eating disorders)	Altruistic behavior (e.g., charity donations)

prevalent on Instagram and food companies claim that their presence is in order to inform first about their brands and products, with healthier options included. However, research seems to show the negative implications of that with obesity and poor food decision-making continuously on the rise. As suggested by Vassallo and colleagues (2018), research is needed regarding the key elements that should be considered when promoting (healthy) food on Instagram. Because of its prevalence and popularity, consumers might rely on Instagram to hope for behavioral changes (e.g., adoption of healthier diets). Research on the positives does suggest that Instagram can be a powerful mechanism to generate community building and support. However, this claim is questionable considering that scant research has been done on the role of Instagram in promoting behavioral change for the better. Introducing healthier options on Instagram might not be as effective as previously believed to be the case.

This is problematic as the platform is widely used by marketers and young adults. Introducing healthier options in consumers' lifestyles when the consumers are the vulnerable ones (e.g., obese consumers) might be challenged by the current nature of Instagram that offers images and content that suits the behavioral characteristics of the target audience. Instagram posts reflect the current state in terms of attitude, interests, and behaviors and might not help when change is desired.

Instagram of Food

When individuals consume food, they have multiple goals. On the one hand, they are searching for ingredients and functional elements of products, and on the other hand, they are looking for the emotional values—such as affection, comfort, and pleasure—that the food is delivering to them (Block et al., 2011). In general, their culinary adventures likely include looking to increase their relationships with food, or food well-being, "a positive psychological, physical, emotional, and social relationship with food" (Block et al., 2011, p. 5). The idea of food well-being can be strongly linked to the pleasure experience they can derive while consuming food.

Instagram might offer the opportunity to nudge and build on persuasive design toward food well-being. Sticking to healthy diet guidelines is challenging (Hansen & Thomsen, 2018) since food pleasure is often not considered. Promoting a holistic approach to food and health (i.e., considering both nutrition and pleasure) may be more effective than simply promoting specific guidelines based on nutritional content for healthy food consumption. This is in line with an understanding of the experiential pleasure of food as the satisfaction and delight consumers receive from experiencing food (Batat et al., 2019).

On Instagram, food-related posts have particularly gained traction among Gen-Z individuals, and its usage has seen a surge in popularity amongst the 18–24 years old age group, with users reportedly checking the platform a minimum of five times a day (Djafarova et al., 2021; Wilson et al., 2019; Pilař et al., 2021). As an image-oriented social media platform, Gen-Z consumers seek enjoyment when viewing visually captivating images of different foods and recipes. The platform emphasizes the role of aesthetics and pleasure and has become a prominent source for individuals worldwide to look for culinary inspiration and/or to share pictures of their meals (Yang, 2019).

Instagram has a strong focus on food visualization culture. On the platform, food is primarily used for visual consumption rather than digestion, which in turn implies that the sense of sight is more relevant than the one of taste (Mendini et al., 2019; Walsh & Baker, 2020). Seeing food pictures or real food activates the same gustatory system (Simmons et al., 2005) since the human brain is able to infer taste and consumption reward—including energy content in the same manner (Toepel et al., 2009; van der Laan et al., 2011). The idea of foodtography (Coary & Poor, 2016), or Foodstagram, is becoming a prominent and widespread phenomenon on Instagram, wherein mostly Gen-Z consumers create food content by taking and sharing photos of their meals, whether they are followers, friends, or family (Andersen et al., 2021). Throughout this process, users create food diaries and autobiographical memories, to celebrate special occasions, or to share creations such as new plates or recipes (Coary & Poor, 2016).

Hashtags on Instagram play a crucial role when browsing for images and linking users who share similar interests (Ye et al., 2018). Hashtags are methods by which people tag and search for specific content on Instagram. Recently, it is very common to notice Gen-Z consumers engaging in culinary adventures that involve taking pictures of food, their meals, and immediately posting them on their social media accounts with the appropriate hashtag/s. The correct hashtags increase visibility, may allow for more followers and stimulate higher levels of engagement, and could help start a conversation or community around a specific topic. Hashtag/s might also serve as part of the digital personal branding a consumer might want to portray.

Hashtags serve as an instrument individuals can use to search for and filter information that is relevant to their beliefs, thoughts, or interests. By using hashtags, individuals can look for information that is pertinent to their goals. For example, someone who is trying to consume healthier food choices and needs inspiration might look for #healthyfood in order to facilitate the adoption of a healthier diet. On the opposite side, someone who is looking for indulgent foods might use the very popular hashtag

#foodporn as a way to be exposed to indulgent food images. Consumers assume that Instagram, through its artificial intelligence (AI) algorithm, will deliver relevant and personalized results based on their interests, attitudes, and behaviors, together with current trends. By showing the most relevant and popular posts associated with the searched hashtag (e.g., #healthyfood), the consumer will discover content relevant to him/her and potentially connect with networks of communities that share similar interests and behaviors.

From a theoretical standpoint, research on social media often refers to *selective exposure* (see Stroud, 2018, for a review) as the tendency of individuals to seek out and engage with information and content that is consistent with existing interests, attitudes, and behaviors. Selective exposure is not unique to social media and Instagram; instead, it is a psychological mechanism (bias) that social media and Instagram capitalize on in order to maintain interest in their platforms. Social media platforms, such as Instagram, prioritize pleasure in the user experience in order to make sure the users stay engaged.

According to the *Selective Exposure Self Affect Management (SESAM) model* (Knobloch-Westerwick, 2015), engagement may largely be driven by pleasure in consuming food images and may not help vulnerable consumers (i.e., low health-conscious) who might be motivated or driven by the need to change their dietary habits. Our chapter offers a first look at key limitations related to Instagram as an agent of change where consumption is largely driven by (aesthetic) pleasure. With a focus on low health-conscious versus high health-conscious consumers, we explore the role of different food hashtags on the pleasure experienced on Instagram in order to better understand how current interests, attitudes, and behaviors (low health-conscious vs. high health-conscious) might impact the effectiveness of different food hashtags on the pleasure experienced on the platform.

Selective Exposure and Instagram

Social media platforms are based on algorithms that tend to show content to individuals based on their previous engagement patterns. If a person looks for and engages more frequently with unhealthy eating content (e.g., unhealthy food), he/she is more likely to be shown such content, which in turn might lead to negative health behaviors and vice versa (Friedman et al., 2022). This emphasizes the complex relationship between food-related content on social media and individuals' existing attitudes, interests, and behaviors related to food and eating.

A theory that considers both the cognitive and affective components of selective exposure is the *SESAM* (Knobloch-Westerwick, 2015). SESAM proposes that individuals selectively expose themselves to information that confirms their preexisting feelings and attitudes while avoiding or minimizing exposure to information that challenges their beliefs. It is a theoretical framework that seeks to explain how people selectively expose themselves to certain information in order to manage their emotions and maintain a positive self-image (Knobloch-Westerwick, 2015). This behavior is driven by the desire to manage one's affective state, including emotions such as anxiety, guilt, or pleasure (Jang, 2014). SESAM acknowledges social media's potential negative effects in terms of the creation of echo chambers (Albarracin, 2022) where existing beliefs and biases are reinforced with the ability to evaluate alternative perspectives and gather a diverse range of information becomes limited. Ultimately, echo chambers can impede the development of critical thinking and impede societal progress (Albarracin et al., 2022).

According to the SESAM, people have a natural tendency to seek out information that confirms their existing beliefs and attitudes while avoiding information that contradicts them (Jang, 2014). The model suggests that this behavior is driven by two primary motivations: self-management and affect management. Self-management refers to the desire to maintain a consistent self-concept or self-image. People are motivated to seek out information that supports their beliefs and attitudes because it helps them feel more confident and secure in their self-concept. They may avoid information that challenges their beliefs and attitudes because it threatens their self-concept and creates feelings of uncertainty or insecurity. Affect management refers to the desire to regulate one's emotions.

People are motivated to seek out information that elicits positive emotions and avoid information that elicits negative emotions (Wilson, 2019). Wilson et al. (2019) investigated how selective exposure to images of healthy or unhealthy food on social media affects subsequent eating intentions and behaviors. Their research suggests that existing eating habits predict selective exposure to either healthy or unhealthy food imagery, which in turn influences food choices and eating intentions. Specifically, those who engaged in healthier eating habits were more likely to select healthy food postings, whereas those with less healthy eating habits were more likely to choose unhealthy food postings. Furthermore, viewing healthy or unhealthy food postings reinforced healthful or harmful eating intentions and behaviors. However, the study did not find support for the idea that individuals' motivations for self-improvement by aligning their behavior with expert recommendations drove selective exposure. Instead, individuals appeared to strive for self-consistency, and existing health behaviors shaped their selective exposure to health-relevant messages, which then reinforced ongoing behaviors—for better or worse, as it worked for both healthful and harmful behaviors. Moreover, Hansen and Thomsen (2018) conducted a survey study with a sample of 718 participants and found that an individual's existing attitude toward eating can influence how they define and perceive healthy eating, and this, in turn, can affect their dietary quality.

On Instagram, we hypothesize, according to SESAM, that selective exposure manifests through the AI algorithm as individuals search for images or content via hashtags. The intent of Instagram is to keep individuals engaged on the platform by addressing the search for a specific topic (e.g., healthy food) with content that allows for the maintenance of a consistent self-concept or self-image (a self-management component of SESAM) and by providing a positive experience (affect component of SESAM). No study to our knowledge has actually tested for hashtag-driven exposure offered by the social media platform (Instagram) to particular food-related images on food pleasure. Most of the studies conducted have been experimental or observational in nature with food images manipulated (instead of naturally generated by the social media algorithm). With a first empirical study, we explore the role of the most prominent food-related hashtags considering food pleasure between high health-conscious and low health-conscious consumers.

Exploratory Study

Our study investigates the effects of six of the most popular (over 1 million posts) scalable food-related hashtags as of November 2022: #food, #foodporn, #foodie, #foodstagram, #healthyfood, and #instafood on food pleasure experienced by health conscious versus non-health-conscious consumers. A recent study found hashtag scalability was the second most influential factor in determining the usefulness of information on Instagram, implying that it should be treated as a critical construct in user-related information processing on social networking sites (Lee et al., 2021).

Instagram, as a virtual platform used for visual storytelling, is primarily supposed to create pleasure, and more specifically in our context, pleasurable food experiences. Simpson and Weiner (1989, p. 1031) define pleasure as "the condition of consciousness or sensation induced by the enjoyment or anticipation of what is felt or viewed as good or desirable, including enjoyment, delight, and gratification. The opposite of pain." Today, food is a great source of pleasure (Alba & Williams, 2013), where satisfaction is defined by physical and emotional experiences that define many childhood memories.

Naylor and colleagues (2009, p. 223) define health consciousness as an "individual difference variable that assesses the degree to which a person plays an active role in maintaining their health." This is equivalent to arguing that health consciousness encourages consumers to maintain, increase, or sustain their well-being by focusing on preventive behaviors and health (Jayanti & Burns, 1998; Michaelidou & Hassan, 2008).

Mai and Hoffmann (2015) explore the relationship between health consciousness and taste preferences and test whether increasing health consciousness can reduce the impact of taste on food decisions. Health consciousness is defined as an individual's tendency to proactively maintain their physical well-being through preventive measures and healthcare (Howlett et al., 2009). It is considered a motivational factor that encourages individuals to take action to enhance or maintain their health. Health-conscious people are vigilant about their health status and are willing to take steps to improve it. Since health consciousness operates at a cognitive level, it can affect how consumers perceive the healthiness of food through labeling, and we add Instagram posts.

Sample and Procedures

This study employed a cross-sectional online survey to collect data from a convenience sample of 358 Gen-Z undergraduate students from a university in the United States.

Gen-Z, or post-millennials, includes individuals who are born between 1995 and 2015; they are part of the demographic cohort succeeding millennials. Gen-Z consumers are considered the first digital native generation, familiar with smartphones and social media, and willing to accept disruptive technology innovation. According to extant research (e.g., Mendini et al., 2022b; Mendini & Peter, 2018), Gen-Zs are particularly receptive to cause marketing, corporate social responsibility, and, in general, sustainable activities. Compared to previous generations, this consumer segment demands and embraces more sustainable product options (Granskog et al., 2020). This set of consumers is also willing to pay more for practices that enhance individual and societal well-being. In general, Gen-Z consumers are therefore very keen on healthy and sustainable (food) choices.

As an incentive, participants received extra course credit. The study received approval from the Institutional Review Board (IRB). Following the elimination of questionnaires with incomplete responses, the final sample consisted of n = 309 Gen-Z participants who have an Instagram account and regularly use it (average of 60 minutes a day). Nearly 42% identified as male and 58% as female. The average age was M = 21 years. In terms of procedure, subjects were invited to participate in an extra-credit opportunity for a large introductory marketing course. Subjects were asked to access their Instagram account and were randomly assigned to one of the six most prominent hashtags (over 1 million posts) related to food: #food, #foodporn, #foodstagram, #instafood, #foodie, and #healthyfood. Overall, the Instagram algorithm is designed to provide users with a personalized experience that reflects their attitudes, interests, and behaviors on the platform. The algorithm aims to surface the most relevant and engaging content for each user, helping to keep them engaged and active on the platform. By assigning subjects to a particular hashtag, we rely on Instagram as a social media platform providing the most salient food images for the Gen-Z consumer participating in our study. Once assigned to a particular hashtag, subjects were prompted to take a screenshot with at least 10 pictures, excluding videos and reels. A set of questions followed.

Measures

To measure health consciousness, a seven-item scale adapted from Hong's scale was used (Hong, 2009). The items were scored on a 7-point Likert scale ranging from "strongly disagree" to "strongly agree," and included the items in Table 6.2 (Cronbach's alpha.854). The score of the seven items was composited and averaged and grouped into two groups based on their average score: low health consciousness (score 0 to 5.5, n = 150) and high health consciousness (score 5.51 to 7, n = 159). According to Pilař and

TABLE 6.2 Constructs and Measurement Items

Construct	*Measurement Items*
Health consciousness (adapted from Hong, 2009)	I reflect about my health a lot.
	I'm very self-conscious about my health.
	I'm generally attentive to my inner feelings about my health.
	I'm constantly examining my health.
	I'm alert to changes in my health.
	I'm usually aware of my health.
	I'm aware of the state of my health as I go through the day.
Perceived pleasure	Eating the food in the screenshot you took would be pleasurable.
	You would enjoy eating the food in the screenshot you took.
	The food in the screenshot you took would be satisfying.
	The food in the screenshot you took would taste good.

colleagues (2021), with the improvement in health-conscious among the young generation, more and more young users engage with healthy food subjects on social media (Pilař et al., 2021) and that explains the skewness toward a higher number. The perceived pleasure was measured using 4 items (Cronbach's alpha.932) developed by the authors considering the literature on food well-being. Table 6.2 reports the constructs and measurement items.

Results

Without differentiating among the hashtags, low health-conscious (Lhc) consumers seem to experience less pleasure than high health-conscious (Hhc) consumers in processing the food images on Instagram ($M_{Lhc} = 5.57$ vs. $M_{Hhc} = 5.85$, $F = 6.424$, $p = .02$). The magnitude of the difference is not dramatic but still significant, indicating that for both groups Instagram of food, in general, provides pleasure, the intent of Instagram in order to guarantee continuous engagement, but with low health-conscious consumers experiencing less.

This seems to suggest the complexity related to pleasure experienced on Instagram where it is not just about tastiness but hedonic consumption defined as "the multisensory, fantasy, and emotive aspects of one's experience with products" (Hirschman & Holbrook, 1982, p. 92). More recently, Batat et al. (2019, p. 393) introduced the notion of experiential pleasure of food, defined as "the enduring cognitive (satisfaction) and emotional (i.e., delightful) value consumers gain from savoring the multisensory, communal, and cultural meaning in food experiences." The authors find "experiential food pleasure core factors," which are food: aestheticism, socialization, sharing, storytelling, memory and nostalgia, symbolism, and taste and sensation (Batat et al., 2019). Social networking platforms, and in particular Instagram, with the prevalence of images, highlight the prominence of the experiential and hedonic side of food consumption. Young consumers, particularly those born in Gen-Z, value emotional experiences with food that go beyond the gustatory aspect (Mendini et al., 2021, 2019) where hedonic (vs. functional) consumption takes precedence.

Considering the different hashtags, we investigated the relationship between the individual's level of health consciousness and perceived food pleasure between low health-conscious versus high health-conscious consumers. Considering time on Instagram as a covariate, the composite measure of food pleasure as a dependent variable, and health consciousness as our dependent variable, an ANOVA was run for each hashtag separately. The results reveal a significant difference between low health-conscious and high health-conscious consumers considering the hashtag #healthyfood

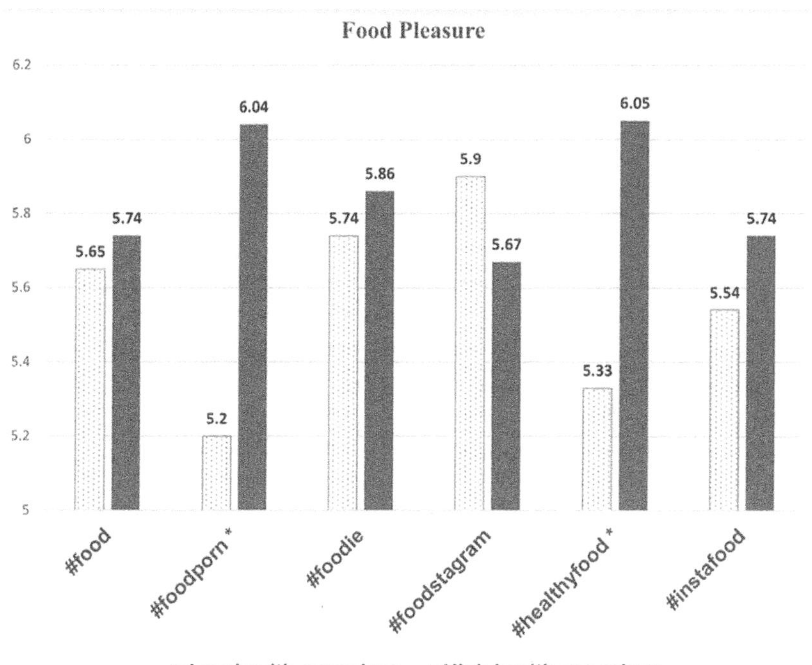

FIGURE 6.1 Food pleasure by low/high health consciousness by hashtags.

(M_{Lhc} = 5.33 vs. M_{Hhc} = 6.05, F = 6.709, p = .012) and #foodporn (M_{Lhc} = 5.2 vs. M_{Hhc} = 6.04, F = 15.535, p < .001). Specifically, individuals in the low health-conscious group exhibited lower food pleasure under the hashtags #healthyfood and #foodporn compared to the high health-conscious consumers. Figure 6.1 reports all the means of food pleasure for the different hashtags with an asterisk next to the hashtag with a significant (p < .05) difference.

The results suggest that low health-conscious individuals do experience less pleasure than high health-conscious individuals on Instagram, especially when processing #healthyfood and #foodporn. Looking at #healthyfood, it is possible that the images of food that low health-conscious consumers get exposed to are less appealing in terms of visual pleasure (e.g., greasier for low health-conscious and more colorful for high health-conscious consumers). Another explanation might be that highly health-conscious consumers feel supported (therefore higher levels of pleasure) in their lifestyle by the "healthy" term mentioned in the hashtag while low health-conscious might not ("healthy" might feel intimidating and not pleasurable). These potential explanations are not tested in our study but call for further investigation.

Interestingly, #foodporn is the hashtag that registers the lowest pleasure score for low health-conscious consumers while is at the top of the pleasure score for high health-conscious consumers. This is surprising considering the fact that low health-conscious consumers are expected to get exposed to food that is more tasty than high health-conscious consumers. The assumption here is that unhealthy equals more pleasurable according to the tasty and unhealthy intuition (Raghunathan et al., 2006). Unfortunately, our study does not account for the evaluation of tastiness but only pleasure.

The pleasure difference experienced by low versus high health-conscious consumers under these particular hashtags reveals how pleasure (Alba & Williams, 2013) is the core of food well-being (Block et al., 2011) and how low health-conscious consumers might be at a disadvantage in terms of what they are exposed to on Instagram, despite their potential interest in healthier options. Low health-conscious consumers might get exposed to more visceral (vs. epicurean) food experiences on Instagram (e.g. Dubé & Lebel, 2003; Loewenstein, 1996; Duncker, 1941; Cornil & Chandon, 2016a, 2016b) such as more greasy and high-calorie meals, less aesthetically pleasing food plating, and less creative culinary creations. Sugary and indulgent meals might prevail over healthy, beautiful, and creative meals as they appear to them on Instagram.

This underlines the potential limitations of Instagram in terms of promoting healthy options to low health-conscious consumers. Providing the hashtags #healthyfood or #foodporn might not be as effective as previously thought, considering the attitudes, interests, and behaviors of low health-conscious consumers. Of interest, #instafood reveals a potential opposite effect (even if not significant) where pleasure is higher for low health-conscious consumers (vs. high health-conscious consumers). Low health-conscious consumers might expect Instagram to deliver decadent and pleasurable food without the specificity provided by the other hashtags. Overall, these preliminary results underline how food images on Instagram do indeed provide pleasure but might have a differential effect if a person is low versus high health-conscious. The Instagram algorithm driving the exposure to different food images might help the ones who want the support and reinforcement (the positive side of Instagram) in their current behavior (high health-conscious consumers) but not the ones who are looking for change or need it the most (low health-conscious consumers).

Discussion and Solutions

Instagram is considered to be one of the most influential social networks among the younger generations, Gen-Z, generating more sales and higher engagement rates than all other platforms (Casaló et al., 2021). Our results reveal how Instagram might be good at reinforcing existing attitudes and behaviors but not necessarily at creating behavioral shifts considering pleasure as a motivator for adoption and maintenance of a healthy diet. This may explain why health organizations struggle to engage with unhealthy consumers on platforms such as Instagram, despite promoting healthy eating information. As Klassen et al. (2018) argue, even though health organizations have started to promote healthy eating information on Instagram, they still struggle to achieve significant success in reaching and engaging with Gen-Z audiences on the platform. Specifically, low health-conscious individuals may not get exposed to the most persuasive healthy content on social media. Our study suggests that being low versus high health conscious is an important determinant of what individuals are exposed to in terms of Instagram food.

According to our study, individuals in the high health-conscious group exhibit greater food pleasure overall and toward food under the images of #foodporn and #healthyfood. This could be explained by research that suggests that health-conscious people are more knowledgeable in evaluating information about food, and often form their food choices on health factors (Mai & Hoffmann, 2015) and images they get exposed to reflect that. However, this enriching experience toward healthy food might not emerge for low health-conscious individuals who might get exposed to less enticing and less visually appealing food images.

On the other side, considering highly health-conscious individuals, Seal et al. (2022) suggest that focusing too much on the visual appeal of healthy foods could contribute to disordered eating behaviors or unrealistic expectations around food. According to Seal et al. (2022), participants reported feeling guilty after being exposed to health-focused content on social media, especially among women, which might lead, according to our findings, to eating disorders (e.g., anorexia) among women. Moreover, considering #foodporn, research suggests that individuals who consume food pornography may experience a hypnotic and addictive feeling, similar to a typical consumer of human sexual pornography. McDonnell (2016) explains that while each photo brings pleasure, individuals might never be satisfied and always crave more. This might be problematic considering our findings regarding pleasure experienced with food images on Instagram, for both high health-conscious and low health-conscious consumers.

Overall, our findings highlight the importance of a *mindful approach* to the use of Instagram. In a world that is fast-paced and where resources seem to be more and more scarce, our study suggests the dangers of Instagram in terms of selective exposure. Fischer et al. (2008) found that individuals with depleted self-regulation resources are more likely to exhibit a stronger tendency for confirmatory information processing, which can lead to biased decision-making. The authors suggest that individuals should be aware of their own self-regulation resources and take steps to replenish them when necessary, in order to avoid confirmatory information processing tendencies. Studies also show that higher social media usage is associated with a higher risk of eating disorders among adolescents (Marks et al., 2020; Wilksch et al., 2020).

Furthermore, distracted eating while using screens has been linked to decreased satiety and increased caloric intake (Spence et al., 2016). Additionally, previous research suggests that the more time female users spend on social media, the more negative the effects on eating behaviors (Tiggemann & Slater, 2013; Hendrickse et al., 2017; Holland & Tiggemann, 2017). It is important that Gen-Z consumers learn to engage in mindful use of social media and Instagram, which means consciousness in terms of time spent on the platform and understanding of how Instagram works (positives, such as support and reinforcement of good behaviors, and negatives, such as echo chambers).

Instagram does not have the power to change someone's behavior, bypassing their preexisting attitudes, interests, and behaviors. However, it can support the willingness to change according to the literature if the individual actively seeks change. An *active search* compared to a passive scroll might be advised on Instagram if the goal is to look for community support. Research reveals that exposure to new "healthy" communities on the platform can help individuals discover new ideas and find fitting support systems for their healthy eating goals (Chung et al., 2017). For example, in a study conducted by Chatzopoulou and colleagues (2020), the authors showed that a group of individuals had unhealthy diets with excessive sugar and calorie intake, as well as harmful drinking habits prior to joining a fitness community on Instagram. However, after joining the fitness community on Instagram, they received help and learned about healthy food choices which enabled them to stay fit and avoid gaining weight.

Individuals as well as policymakers and schools need to focus more on teaching both the benefits and dangers of Instagram. Social media/Instagram literacy should be promoted at an early age in school and the education should be reinforced at the community college and university levels, especially when individuals have to learn to manage their time (how much time am I going to allow myself on social media/Instagram?) and make independent decisions (what am I going to eat tonight?). For example, a joint program between universities and policymakers could be established where professors who teach digital communication show students how different social media platforms operate and can be useful (or not) for behavioral change.

Considering food well-being (Block et al., 2011), healthy eating habits can and should be developed offline first in educational campaigns that are affiliated with schools and within health-related contexts such as doctor's office settings. Increasing the degree of consumer health consciousness, that is, increasing the degree to which consumers are interested in their health, is paramount for consumer well-being (Mai & Hoffmann, 2015). Research finds that, by curbing indulgent food-eating habits and reducing emotional eating tendencies, social marketing efforts can promote long-term intergenerational health benefits (Bui et al., 2023). In combination with this research, our findings suggest that culinary-related brands can utilize hashtags as a mechanism to promote healthy eating habits with educational campaigns, and ultimately promote the well-being of their social media user base. When individuals are satisfied with their social media experiences, they tend to develop positive attitudes toward social media (Krishen et al., 2019); however, this can be a potential problem for those who have self-regulatory issues and could fall prone to social media addiction (Wang et al., 2018). Social media addiction can also be related to the individual experience of FOMO, and potentially lead to depression, anxiety, and loneliness (Berezan et al., 2020; Bui et al., 2022). Individuals can break addictive behavioral patterns by practicing mindfulness and shifting their focus from virtual to physical space (Berezan et al., 2019). In fact, as discussed in Chan et al. (2022), social media consumers can move from FOMO to the joy of missing out (JOMO) by self-regulating their usage of popular channels such as Instagram. Viewing food-related posts on Instagram should not become a conduit for unhealthy eating habits and social media addiction. Instead, finding everyday pleasure in the posts can promote subjective well-being for social media users, especially when they are not prone to addiction or negative health behaviors.

Conclusion, Limitations, and Future Research

As other research highlights, social media analysis is needed in order to identify users' experiences, values, and attitudes toward food, which can be used in strategic management, business marketing, and health policy, and provide valuable insights into consumer behavior related to food choices (Pilař et al., 2021). Our study suggests that using the popular hashtags #healthyfood and #foodporn as tools for promoting healthy eating on Instagram has potential drawbacks and limitations. Such hashtags are not effective in the same way for everyone. A targeted approach needs to consider different hashtags and interventions early, holistically, and offline first. It is important to note that our insights are limited to the nature of the exploratory study we conducted.

This study relies on 309 Instagram users between the ages of 19 and 26, who are predominantly undergraduate students. Future studies with larger and more diverse samples could help to increase the generalizability of the results. Another limitation of this study is that the data collection method was self-reported through an online survey, which may be subject to response biases. Participants may have provided socially desirable responses, particularly when it comes to questions about their health consciousness. Furthermore, this study only focused on hashtags and pleasure. Even though according to a recent study by Lee et al. (2021), hashtags are a critical factor in users' information processing on social networking sites such as Instagram, our study did not explore the effects of other factors, such as captions, or comments. Therefore, future studies could investigate the impact of these other factors on the pleasure experienced by processing food images on Instagram. In addition, future studies could explore food picture differences according to the different hashtags (e.g., food category, colors, natural vs. processed, plating, aesthetic cues) and contextual effects (time of the day) to see potential differences in perception of pleasure.

Our results emphasize the holistic pleasure associated with healthy (#healthyfood) but also savory (#foodporn) food consumption. Culture is a determinant of food perceptions (e.g., some countries emphasize a more holistic approach to food than others, such as, Italy vs. USA), along with exposure (e.g., an individual who is raised in an environment where fried and seasoned food is considered delicious might perceive healthier alternatives as less tasty in comparison). Personal preferences and taste also play a role where certain textures and cooking modes might be preferred (e.g., grilled vs. fried). Finally, limited exposure, knowledge, and preparation might hinder the ability to perceive healthy options as tasty (e.g., learning new recipes when individuals approach veganism).

Lastly, while this study provided insights into pleasure experienced on Instagram, it did not investigate the direct link to behavioral outcomes such as intent to engage in a healthier diet. Future research should explore the underlying factors defining pleasure on Instagram and how that drives people to seek out and engage with food-related content on social media, particularly Instagram. Specifically, future studies could examine the role of visual elements, such as color, texture, and composition, in eliciting positive emotions toward food content.

The color of a food product influences the sense of taste of it. When a color does not match our expectations, we can perceive a food as being less tasty and with flavors we are not attracted to (Konica Minolta, 2018). For example, if we take pictures of fruits and vegetables, the color of the items determines how we perceive their freshness. In general, green is the color associated with being fresh, healthy, natural, well-balanced food, organic or vegetarian, and is now a symbol of health and well-being. It is in fact often associated with feelings of cheerfulness and relaxation. Future research can check whether the predominance of some colors in Instagram hashtags (e.g., #healthyfood: predominance of green) can be a driver in emphasizing the health-consciousness or the pleasure experienced by consumers on the platform. In addition, the texture or the context in which the food is presented online (e.g., the plate, the packaging) is relevant in an attempt to communicate healthiness and tastiness. Research showed in fact how marketers can promote the sales of healthy baby carrots by presenting them as snack food (McGray, 2011).

Moreover, future studies could explore how different types of food content, such as healthy versus unhealthy food, may impact participants' engagement experience on the platform differently. Future research could focus on investigating the impact of food-related content on individuals with different cultural backgrounds, age groups, and genders. Finally, longitudinal studies could be conducted to examine changes in participants' attitudes toward food pleasure over time and assess the long-term impact of exposure to different types of food content on individuals' dietary behaviors and overall health outcomes.

A key objective of the application of the SESAM model in this research was to shed light on the complex interactions between social media, attitudes, and behaviors, highlighting both the positive and negative impacts of Instagram on food-related behaviors and attitudes (Cinelli, 2020; Bastos et al., 2018; Del Vicario, 2016; Bakshy, 2015; An et al., 2013). Understanding users' attitudes regarding sharing visual content and the impact of the SESAM model on Instagram is important to gain valuable insights into young people's behavior toward food (Wilson et al., 2019). Future studies should explore the complexity of the relationship between food-related content on social media and individuals' attitudes, interests, and behaviors related to food and eating. Therefore, it is important to further investigate how food images on social media affect young people's attitudes toward food, particularly in terms of pleasure and satisfaction, and whether an individual's level of health-consciousness moderates this attitude.

References

Alba, J. W., & Williams, E. F. (2013). Pleasure principles: A review of research on hedonic consumption. *Journal of Consumer Psychology*, *23*(1), 2–18.

Albarracin, M., Demekas, D., Ramstead, M. J., & Heins, C. (2022). Epistemic communities under active inference. *Entropy*, *24*(4), 476.

An, J., Quercia, D., & Crowcroft, J. (2013, May). Fragmented social media: A look into selective exposure to political news. In *Proceedings of the 22nd international conference on world wide web* (pp. 51–52). Association for Computing Machinery.

Andersen, T., Byrne, D. V., & Wang, Q. J. (2021). How digital food affects our analog lives: The impact of food photography on healthy eating behavior. *Frontiers in Psychology*, *12*, 634261.

Bakshy, E., Messing, S., & Adamic, L. A. (2015). Exposure to ideologically diverse news and opinion on Facebook. *Science*, *348*(6239), 1130–1132.

Bastos, M., Mercea, D., & Baronchelli, A. (2018). The geographic embedding of online echo chambers: Evidence from the Brexit campaign. *PLoS One*, *13*(11), e0206841.

Batat, W., Peter, P. C., Moscato, E. M., Castro, I. A., Chan, S., Chugani, S., & Muldrow, A. (2019). The experiential pleasure of food: A savoring journey to food well-being. *Journal of Business Research*, *100*, 392–399.

Berezan, O., Krishen, A. S., Agarwal, S., & Kachroo, P. (2018). The pursuit of virtual happiness: Exploring the social media experience across generations. *Journal of Business Research*, *89*, 455–461.

Berezan, O., Krishen, A. S., Agarwal, S., & Kachroo, P. (2020). Exploring loneliness and social networking: Recipes for hedonic well-being on Facebook. *Journal of Business Research*, *115*, 258–265.

Berezan, O., Krishen, A. S., & Jenveja, A. N. U. J. (2019). Loneliness and social media: The interplay of physical and virtual social space. *Marketing and Humanity: Discourses in the Real World*, 49–68.

Block, L. G., Grier, S. A., Childers, T. L., Davis, B., Ebert, J. E., Kumanyika, S., Laczniak, R. N., Machin, J. E., Motley, C. M., Peracchio, L., Pettigrew, S., Scott, M., & Bieshaar, M. N. G. (2011). From nutrients to nurturance: A conceptual introduction to food well-being. *Journal of Public Policy & Marketing*, *30*(1), 5–13.

Bui, M., Krishen, A., & Kemp, E. (2023). It's a force of habit: Influences of emotional eating on indulgent tendencies. *Journal of Consumer Marketing*, *40*(4), 445–457.

Bui, M., Krishen, A. S., Anlamlier, E., & Berezan, O. (2022). Fear of missing out in the digital age: The role of social media satisfaction and advertising engagement. *Psychology & Marketing*, *39*(4), 683–693.

Casaló, L. V., Flavián, C., & Ibáñez-Sánchez, S. (2017). Understanding consumer interaction on instagram: The role of satisfaction, hedonism, and content characteristics. *Cyberpsychology, Behavior, and Social Networking*, *20*(6), 369–375.

Casaló, L. V., Flavián, C., & Ibáñez-Sánchez, S. (2021). Be creative, my friend! Engaging users on Instagram by promoting positive emotions. *Journal of Business Research*, *130*, 416–425.

Chan, S. S., Van Solt, M., Cruz, R. E., Philp, M., Bahl, S., Serin, N., Amaral, N. B., Schindler, R., Bartosiak, A., Kumar, S., & Canbulut, M. (2022). Social media and mindfulness: From the fear of missing out (FOMO) to the joy of missing out (JOMO). *Journal of Consumer Affairs*, *56*(3), 1312–1331.

Chatzopoulou, E., Filieri, R., & Dogruyol, S. A. (2020). Instagram and body image: Motivation to conform to the "Instabod" and consequences on young male wellbeing. *Journal of Consumer Affairs*, *54*(4), 1270–1297.

Chua, T. H. H., & Chang, L. (2016). Follow me and like my beautiful selfies: Singapore teenage girls' engagement in self-presentation and peer comparison on social media. *Computers in Human Behavior*, *55*, 190–197.

Chung, C. F., Agapie, E., Schroeder, J., Mishra, S., Fogarty, J., & Munson, S. A. (2017, May). When personal tracking becomes social: Examining the use of Instagram for healthy eating. In *Proceedings of the 2017 CHI conference on human factors in computing systems* (pp. 1674–1687). National Institutes of Health.

Cinelli, M., Brugnoli, E., Schmidt, A. L., Zollo, F., Quattrociocchi, W., & Scala, A. (2020). Selective exposure shapes the Facebook news diet. *PLoS One*, *15*(3), e0229129.

Coary, S., & Poor, M. (2016). How consumer-generated images shape important consumption outcomes in the food domain. *Journal of Consumer Marketing*, *33*(1), 1–8.

Cohen, R., Fardouly, J., Newton-John, T., & Slater, A. (2019). # BoPo on Instagram: An experimental investigation of the effects of viewing body positive content on young women's mood and body image. *New Media & Society*, *21*(7), 1546–1564.

Cornelis, E., & Peter, P. C. (2017). The real campaign: The role of authenticity in the effectiveness of advertising disclaimers in digitally enhanced images. *Journal of Business Research*, *77*, 102–112.

Cornil, Y., & Chandon, P. (2016a). Pleasure as a substitute for size: How multisensory imagery can make people happier with smaller food portions. *Journal of Marketing Research*, *53*(5), 847–864.

Cornil, Y., & Chandon, P. (2016b). Pleasure as an ally of healthy eating? Contrasting visceral and Epicurean eating pleasure and their association with portion size preferences and wellbeing. *Appetite*, *104*, 52–59.

Del Vicario, M., Vivaldo, G., Bessi, A., Zollo, F., Scala, A., Caldarelli, G., & Quattrociocchi, W. (2016). Echo chambers: Emotional contagion and group polarization on facebook. *Scientific Reports*, *6*(1), 37825.

Djafarova, E., & Bowes, T. (2021). 'Instagram made Me buy it': Generation Z impulse purchases in fashion industry. *Journal of Retailing and Consumer Services*, *59*, 102345.

Dubé, L., & Lebel, J. (2003). The categorical structure of pleasure. *Cognition and Emotion*, *17*(2), 263–297.

Duncker, K. (1941). On pleasure, emotion, and striving. *Philosophy and Phenomenological Research*, *1*(4), 391–430.

Fardouly, J., Diedrichs, P. C., Vartanian, L. R., & Halliwell, E. (2015). Social comparisons on social media: The impact of Facebook on young women's body image concerns and mood. *Body Image*, *13*, 38–45.

Fischer, P., Greitemeyer, T., & Frey, D. (2008). Self-regulation and selective exposure: The impact of depleted self-regulation resources on confirmatory information processing. *Journal of Personality and Social Psychology*, *94*(3), 382.

Friedman, V. J., Wright, C. J., Molenaar, A., McCaffrey, T., Brennan, L., & Lim, M. S. (2022). The use of social media as a persuasive platform to facilitate nutrition and health behavior change in young adults: Web-based conversation study. *Journal of Medical Internet Research*, *24*(5), e28063.

Granskog, A., Lee, L., Magnus, K. H., & Sawers, C. (2020). *Survey: Consumer sentiment on sustainability in fashion* (p. 17). McKinsey & Company.

Hansen, T., & Thomsen, T. U. (2018). The influence of consumers' interest in healthy eating, definitions of healthy eating, and personal values on perceived dietary quality. *Food Policy*, *80*, 55–67.

Hendrickse, J., Arpan, L. M., Clayton, R. B., & Ridgway, J. L. (2017). Instagram and college women's body image: Investigating the roles of appearance-related comparisons and intrasexual competition. *Computers in Human Behavior*, *74*, 92–100.

Hirschman, E. C., & Holbrook, M. B. (1982). Hedonic consumption: Emerging concepts, methods and propositions. *Journal of Marketing*, *46*(3), 92–101.

Holland, G., & Tiggemann, M. (2017). "Strong beats skinny every time": Disordered eating and compulsive exercise in women who post fitspiration on Instagram. *International Journal of Eating Disorders*, *50*(1), 76–79.

Hong, H. (2009). Scale development for measuring health consciousness: Re-conceptualization. *that Matters to the Practice*, 212.

Howlett, E. A., Burton, S., Bates, K., & Huggins, K. (2009). Coming to a restaurant near you? Potential consumer responses to nutrition information disclosure on menus. *Journal of Consumer Research*, *36*(3), 494–503.

Hunt, M. G., Marx, R., Lipson, C., & Young, J. (2018). No more FOMO: Limiting social media decreases loneliness and depression. *Journal of Social and Clinical Psychology*, *37*(10), 751–768.

Jang, S. M. (2014). Seeking congruency or incongruency online? Examining selective exposure to four controversial science issues. *Science Communication*, *36*(2), 143–167.

Jayanti, R. K., & Burns, A. C. (1998). The antecedents of preventive health care behavior: An empirical study. *Journal of the Academy of Marketing Science*, *26*(1), 6–15.

Jelenchick, L. A., Eickhoff, J. C., & Moreno, M. A. (2013). "Facebook depression?" Social networking site use and depression in older adolescents. *Journal of Adolescent Health*, *52*(1), 128–130.

Klassen, K. M., Borleis, E. S., Brennan, L., Reid, M., McCaffrey, T. A., & Lim, M. S. (2018). What people "like": Analysis of social media strategies used by food industry brands, lifestyle brands, and health promotion organizations on Facebook and Instagram. *Journal of Medical Internet Rsearch*, *20*(6), e10227.

Knobloch-Westerwick, S. (2015). The selective exposure self-and affect-management (SESAM) model: Applications in the realms of race, politics, and health. *Communication Research*, *42*(7), 959–985.

Koay, S. H., Ng, A. T., Tham, S. K., & Tan, C. S. (2020). Gratitude intervention on Instagram: An experimental study. *Psychological Studies*, *65*, 168–173.

Konica Minolta. (2018). *How color affects your perception of food.* Retrieved June 22, 2023, from https://sensing.konicaminolta.us/blog/how-color-affects-your-perception-of-food/

Kozinets, R., Patterson, A., & Ashman, R. (2017). Networks of desire: How technology increases our passion to consume. *Journal of Consumer Research*, *43*(5), 659–682.

Krasnova, H., Wenninger, H., Widjaja, T., & Buxmann, P. (2013). *Envy on Facebook: A hidden threat to users' life satisfaction?* [IDEAS Working Paper Series from RePEc].

Krishen, A. S., Berezan, O., Agarwal, S., & Kachroo, P. (2016). The generation of virtual needs: Recipes for satisfaction in social media networking. *Journal of Business Research*, *69*(11), 5248–5254.

Krishen, A. S., Berezan, O., & Raab, C. (2019). Feelings and functionality in social networking communities: A regulatory focus perspective. *Psychology & Marketing*, *36*(7), 675–686.

Lee, E., Lee, J. A., Moon, J. H., & Sung, Y. (2015). Pictures speak louder than words: Motivations for using Instagram. *Cyberpsychology, Behavior, and Social Networking*, *18*(9), 552–556.

Lee, H. M., Kang, J. W., & Namkung, Y. (2021). Instagram users' information acceptance process for food-content. *Sustainability*, *13*(5), 2638.

Leung, L. (2013). Generational differences in content generation in social media: The roles of the gratifications sought and of narcissism. *Computers in Human Behavior*, *29*(3), 997–1006.

Loewenstein, G. (1996). Out of control: Visceral influences on behavior. *Organizational Behavior and Human Decision Processes*, *65*(3), 272–292.

Lup, K., Trub, L., & Rosenthal, L. (2015). Instagram# instasad?: Exploring associations among instagram use, depressive symptoms, negative social comparison, and strangers followed. *Cyberpsychology, Behavior, and Social Networking*, *18*(5), 247–252.

Mai, R., & Hoffmann, S. (2015). How to combat the unhealthy=tasty intuition: The influencing role of health consciousness. *Journal of Public Policy & Marketing*, *34*(1), 63–83.

Marks, R. J., De Foe, A., & Collett, J. (2020). The pursuit of wellness: Social media, body image and eating disorders. *Children and Youth Services Review*, *119*, 105659.

McDonnell, E. M. (2016). Food porn: The conspicuous consumption of food in the age of digital reproduction. In *Food, media and contemporary culture: The edible image* (pp. 239–265). Palgrave Macmillan.

McGray, D. (2011). *How carrots became the new junk food*. Retrieved June 22, 2023, from www.fastcompany.com/739774/how-carrots-became-new-junk-food

Meier, E. P., & Gray, J. (2014). Facebook photo activity associated with body image disturbance in adolescent girls. *Cyberpsychology, Behavior and Social Networking*, *17*(4), 199–206.

Mendini, M., Batat, W., & Peter, P. C. (2021). Designing luxurious food experiences for millennials and post-millennials. In *Developing successful global strategies for marketing luxury brands* (pp. 261–273). IGI Global.

Mendini, M., & Peter, P. C. (2018). Chapter eleven marketing for social change. In *Marketing and humanity: Discourses in the real world* (p. 206).

Mendini, M., Peter, P. C., Honea, H., and Grasso, M. (2022a). The new ethical consumer: The coming consumer mandate for inclusive and innovative luxury fashion practices that support social well-being. In *The rise of positive luxury* (pp. 22–38), Routledge, https://doi.org/10.4324/9781003163732

Mendini, M., Peter, P. C., & Maione, S. (2022b). The potential positive effects of time spent on Instagram on consumers' gratitude, altruism, and willingness to donate. *Journal of Business Research*, *143*, 16–26.

Mendini, M., Pizzetti, M., & Peter, P. C. (2019). Social food pleasure: When sharing offline, online and for society promotes pleasurable and healthy food experiences and well-being. *Qualitative Market Research: An International Journal*, *22*(4), 544–556.

Michaelidou, N., & Hassan, L. M. (2008). The role of health consciousness, food safety concern and ethical identity on attitudes and intentions towards organic food. *International Journal of Consumer Studies*, *32*(2), 163–170.

Nadkarni, A., & Hofmann, S. G. (2012). Why do people use Facebook? *Personality and Individual Differences*, *52*(3), 243–249.

Naylor, R. W., Droms, C. M., & Haws, K. L. (2009). Eating with a purpose: Consumer response to functional food health claims in conflicting versus complementary information environments. *Journal of Public Policy & Marketing*, *28*(2), 221–233.

Pilař, L., Stanislavská, L. K., Kvasnička, R., Hartman, R., & Tichá, I. (2021). Healthy food on instagram social network: Vegan, homemade and clean eating. *Nutrients*, *13*(6), 1991.

Pittman, M., & Reich, B. (2016). Social media and loneliness: Why an Instagram picture may be worth more than a thousand Twitter words. *Computers in Human Behavior*, *62*, 155–167.

Raghunathan, R., Naylor, R. W., & Hoyer, W. D. (2006). The unhealthy=tasty intuition and its effects on taste inferences, enjoyment, and choice of food products. *Journal of Marketing*, *70*(4), 170–184.

Renshaw, T. L., & Hindman, M. L. (2017). Expressing gratitude via instant communication technology: A randomized controlled trial targeting college students' mental health. *Mental Health & Prevention*, *7*, 37–44.

Seal, A., Gavaravarapu, S. M., & Konapur, A. (2022). Can foodporn prime healthy eating? Thinking beyond digital gazing and satiety. *European Journal of Clinical Nutrition*, 1–4.

Sheldon, K. M., Abad, N., & Hinsch, C. (2011). A two-process view of Facebook use and relatedness need-satisfaction: Disconnection drives use, and connection rewards it. *Journal of Personality and Social Psychology*, *100*(4), 766.

Sheldon, P., & Bryant, K. (2016). Instagram: Motives for its use and relationship to narcissism and contextual age. *Computers in Human Behavior*, *58*, 89–97.

Simmons, W. K., Martin, A., & Barsalou, L. W. (2005). Pictures of appetizing foods activate gustatory cortices for taste and reward. *Cerebral Cortex*, *15*(10), 1602–1608.

Simpson, J. A., & Weiner, E. S. (1989). *The Oxford English dictionary*. Oxford University Press.

Slater, A., Varsani, N., & Diedrichs, P. C. (2017). # fitspo or# loveyourself? The impact of fitspiration and self-compassion Instagram images on women's body image, self-compassion, and mood. *Body Image*, *22*, 87–96.

Spence, C., Okajima, K., Cheok, A. D., Petit, O., & Michel, C. (2016). Eating with our eyes: From visual hunger to digital satiation. *Brain and Cognition*, *110*, 53–63.

Statista. (2023). *Instagram—statistics and facts*. Retrieved June 6, 2023, from https://www.statista.com/topics/1882/instagram/#topicOverview

Stout, D. (2021). *Social media statistics 2021: Top networks by the numbers*. Retrieved June 6, 2023, from https://dustinstout.com/social-media-statistics/#instagram-stats

Stroud, N. J. (2018, January 11). Selective exposure theories. In K. Kenski & K. H. Jamieson (Eds.), *The Oxford handbook of political communication* (Online ed.). Oxford Handbooks, Oxford Academic. (Original work published 2017)

Tiggemann, M., & Slater, A. (2013). NetGirls: The internet, Facebook, and body image concern in adolescent girls. *International Journal of Eating Disorders, 46*(6), 630–633.

Tiggemann, M., & Zaccardo, M. (2018). 'Strong is the new skinny': A content analysis of# fitspiration images on Instagram. *Journal of Health Psychology, 23*(8), 1003–1011.

Tobin, S. J., & Chulpaiboon, P. (2016). The role of social connection in satisfaction with Instagram photographs. *Translational Issues in Psychological Science, 2*(3), 303.

Toepel, U., Knebel, J. F., Hudry, J., le Coutre, J., & Murray, M. M. (2009). The brain tracks the energetic value in food images. *Neuroimage, 44*(3), 967–974.

van der Laan, L. N., De Ridder, D. T., Viergever, M. A., & Smeets, P. A. (2011). The first taste is always with the eyes: A meta-analysis on the neural correlates of processing visual food cues. *Neuroimage, 55*(1), 296–303.

Vassallo, A. J., Kelly, B., Zhang, L., Wang, Z., Young, S., & Freeman, B. (2018). Junk food marketing on Instagram: Content analysis. *JMIR Public Health and Surveillance, 4*(2), e9594.

Voorveld, H. A., Van Noort, G., Muntinga, D. G., & Bronner, F. (2018). Engagement with social media and social media advertising: The differentiating role of platform type. *Journal of Advertising, 47*(1), 38–54.

Walsh, M. J., & Baker, S. A. (2020). Clean eating and Instagram: Purity, defilement, and the idealization of food. *Food, Culture & Society, 23*(5), 570–588.

Wang, P., Wang, X., Wu, Y., Xie, X., Wang, X., Zhao, F., Ouyang, M., & Lei, L. (2018). Social networking sites addiction and adolescent depression: A moderated mediation model of rumination and self-esteem. *Personality and Individual Differences, 127*, 162–167.

Wilksch, S. M., O'Shea, A., Ho, P., Byrne, S., & Wade, T. D. (2020). The relationship between social media use and disordered eating in young adolescents. *International Journal of Eating Disorders, 53*(1), 96–106.

Wilson, B., Knobloch-Westerwick, S., & Robinson, M. J. (2019). Picture yourself healthy—how users select mediated images to shape health intentions and behaviors. *Health Communication, 34*(8), 838–847.

Yang, C. C. (2016). Instagram use, loneliness, and social comparison orientation: Interact and browse on social media, but don't compare. *Cyberpsychology, Behavior, and Social Networking, 19*(12), 703–708.

Yang, C. C., Holden, S. M., Carter, M. D., & Webb, J. J. (2018). Social media social comparison and identity distress at the college transition: A dual-path model. *Journal of Adolescence, 69*, 92–102.

Yang, S. (2019). *Aesthetics of food: The role of visual framing strategies for influence building on Instagram*. Rochester Institute of Technology.

Ye, Z., Hashim, N. H., Baghirov, F., & Murphy, J. (2018). Gender differences in Instagram hashtag use. *Journal of Hospitality Marketing & Management, 27*(4), 386–404.

Zhou, X., & Krishnan, A. (2019). What predicts exercise maintenance and well-being? Examining the influence of health-related psychographic factors and social media communication. *Health Communication, 34*(6), 589–597.

PART 4

Privacy, Artificial Intelligence, and Vulnerable Children on Social Media

While the previous part focused on some specific issues relating to body image, self-esteem, eating disorders, and negative self-discrepancies, we shift to the final part (Part 4) of this book. Part 4 is broad, as it is about the dark side of privacy issues and consumer data securities or lack thereof. We end with privacy because it is something that every single social media user (or internet user for that matter) should care about and know some solutions to best manage their personal or financial information to best protect themselves and their families. Chapter 7 by Sifaoui, Eastin, Wilcox, and Doorey is one of the first to focus on why and how aspects of artificial intelligence algorithms in social media can be harmful. In their review chapter, they offer some solutions as to how to best protect your consumer data in the age of AI.

7. The Dark Side of Consumer Privacy in the Age of Artificial Intelligence

Asma Sifaoui, Matthew S. Eastin, Gary B. Wilcox, and Alexandra M. Doorey

Related to privacy solutions, many have advocated for regulations, reforms, or laws to protect consumers in the era of social media and artificial intelligence. Thus, this problem and solution-oriented book concludes with a summary of relevant laws and regulations that can help protect some of our most vulnerable people—children, and by default the parents who want to protect their children against some of the harmful or adult-oriented social media content. In Chapter 8, Brown, Pounders, and Wilcox

DOI: 10.4324/9781003410058-10

examine a case study with respect to privacy for children and social media. They note specific laws and regulations as solutions.

8. Examining the Issues of Social Media, Children, and Privacy: A Case Study

   Madison K. Brown, Kathrynn R. Pounders, and Gary B. Wilcox

7

THE DARK SIDE OF CONSUMER PRIVACY IN THE AGE OF ARTIFICIAL INTELLIGENCE

Asma Sifaoui, Matthew S. Eastin, Gary B. Wilcox, and Alexandra M. Doorey

Introduction: The Privacy Problem with Social Media and Artificial Intelligence

Since the birth of the big data era age, the sharing, collection, and use of personal data has grown exponentially, with a huge amount of personal data constantly being collected from a number of new and evolving sources. For marketers and companies, the value of this consumer data lies in the ability to better understand consumers' wants, needs, and behavioral histories. Such enables marketers a more nuanced understanding of audiences, segmentation opportunities, and even individual consumers. However, amid the alluring promises of data analytics and personalization, the pervasive gathering and use of personal data in marketing raises significant concerns. These concerns are mainly related to consumers' worry about the misuse of their personal and intimate information as well as the unauthorized secondary use of that information by other parties. Indeed, consumers are increasingly concerned about the risks associated with sharing their data overtly and covertly with organizations. These risks can be related to dataveillance and the issues that arise from continually monitoring an individual's behavior. As such, the art and science of profiling individuals bring new privacy challenges to consumers, organizations, and regulators.

Implementations of consumer insights acquired from data-driven marketing practices are utilized to engage consumers and form stronger relationships that serve the needs of both marketers and consumers. Mobile and wearable devices are enhancing consumers' "digital presence" by allowing interactions with emerging technologies in innovative ways. As consumers

DOI: 10.4324/9781003410058-11

become uber connected, these technologies are becoming effective of giving targeted, communications via geo-location, behavior monitoring, and even health information. With more detail and sophistication, sensors found in wearable devices and mobile technologies even have the ability to provide a better understanding of consumer's feelings and emotions.

With the proliferation of advanced tools that collect, process, and share information, marketers and advertisers have taken advantage to better reach their audiences through advanced targeting. While personalization of advertising messages is not a new phenomenon, the use of data analytics and artificial intelligence has allowed for a level of precision that was previously not possible. Business models are adapting to include these new efficiencies, with behavioral marketing and predictive analytics becoming more accurate. This strategic shift toward personalization allows marketers to customize content and delivery for specific consumers and ultimately achieve greater efficiencies (Adomavicius & Tuzhilin, 2005, p. 83). In exchange for personalized services and information, consumers face a tradeoff where they give up their privacy to have access to the benefits of personalization. (Tezinde et al., 2002; Chellappa & Sin, 2005; Awad & Krishnan, 2006; Xu et al., 2011).

Carefully constructed profiles based on individual needs and preferences allow marketers to communicate with consumers with highly relevant messages often at the precise point of purchase. However, beneath the tailored consumer experiences lies a darker side of the vast and precise collection of personal data. The meticulous construction of consumer profiles gives organizations access to an intimate array of an individual's life. Moving further into the shadows of this is the overwhelming collection and flow of this information to different parties. In most instances, it is hard to pinpoint what party has what and for what purpose the data is used.

Mobile technology, as well as the big data revolution it helps to drive, has brought about a need for a new way of thinking and new methods of managing data in order to overcome the dark side of technology and artificial intelligence (AI). The lack of a comprehensive privacy framework in the United States amplifies the challenges faced by consumers in managing their privacy. There is an overwhelming gap between the existing technological and organizational practices and relevant consumers' literacy. This includes pervasive data collection and consumers who are not equipped to meaningfully review and negotiate the terms of privacy policies. The way in which businesses and government regulators in the United States handle the possession, gathering, and utilization of consumers' data is gaining attention from the public, highlighting the need to reconsider policies and self-regulatory principles. Consumer groups and privacy advocates have demanded mechanisms that can adequately manage the access, movement, and dissemination of personal information, particularly data streams accessed from personal devices such as smartphones, tablets, and wearables.

However, the industry has failed to regulate itself and breaks boundaries of individual expectations and the implicit social contracts with consumers (Dutta & Bilbao-Osorio, 2014). With the increased tensions regarding privacy, as advocated by policymakers and activists, marketers are starting to recognize the importance of privacy and data practices to consumers. By actively addressing consumer worries regarding data collection, usage, and individual control of information, marketers, and organizations can strengthen their reputations and business models by enforcing measures that protect the security and privacy of users' data.

The absence of such frameworks can lead to a chaotic ecosystem that relies on the extortion of personal data in exchange for these services and products offered by businesses, which results in an unbalance of power between the different parties. The power of organizations translated into commodifying consumer data favors the creation of a monopolistic environment where consumers lose their ability to choose and control. That is, in an age of increased reliance on digital media, the definition of privacy expectations can become blurred. How can consumers, marketers, and regulators define these expectations today?

Organization of the Chapter

This chapter examines the changing nature of consumer data and information acquisition as it intersects with consumer privacy and security. The following sections provide an up-to-date perspective of emerging technology and privacy issues within social media, wearable and mobile devices. A discussion of the use of big data to facilitate personalized marketing is followed by a mobile usage and marketing technologies update. The next section discusses the integrated future of mobile technology, wearables, and personalized health data. Following that discussion, privacy and security issues raised by technology use is explored. The chapter concludes with recommendations for future regulation relating to consumer privacy and security.

The Dark Side of Digital Behavioral Marketing

A concern that consumers have for their mental health is that the digital revolution has brought serious privacy issues and fears. Marketers and advertisers have long relied on personalized messages to connect with their target audiences, but today's consumers feel like they are constantly monitored, tracked, targeted, and being "sold to." With the widespread adoption of advanced profiling and tracking technologies, the personalization of persuasive messages has become increasingly tailored and precise. The technique enabling this level of personalization is referred to as "online behavioral advertising." This is defined as "the practice of monitoring people's online behavior and using the collected information to show people individually targeted advertisements" (Boerman et al., 2017, p. 363). Marketers today have access to a wide range of consumer data, including personal identifiers, demographics, lifestyle, interests and preferences, shopping behavior, and real-time location data (Phelps et al., 2000; Unni & Harmon, 2007; White et al., 2008). In fact, real-time location data allows for hyper-localized marketing efforts that can be customized based on a consumer's current location (Jai et al., 2013; Lambrecht & Tucker, 2013). The aggregation of these data enables the creation of a very detailed consumer profile that helps marketers to personalize online behavioral messages to individuals and reach them at the right time with the right medium. By analyzing behavior patterns and preferences, marketers can create highly targeted campaigns that are more likely to resonate with their intended audience.

This technique has also benefited from the advances in machine learning and data analytics. Indeed, the emergence of AI and machine learning has revolutionized the advertising industry (Li, 2019; Rodgers, 2021). These technologies have enabled the rise of data-driven advertising such as computational advertising. Computational advertising is defined as a "broad, data-driven advertising approach facilitated by enhanced computing capabilities, mathematical models/algorithms, and technology infrastructure to create and deliver messages and monitor/surveil an individual's behaviors"(Huh & Malthouse, 2020, p. 1). In fact, computational advertising relies heavily on the collection, mining, and aggregation of granular-level data (Helberger et al., 2020).

As marketers gain access to an ever-expanding array of consumer data, organizations can leverage this information to enhance and guide managerial decision-making (Shah & Murthi, 2021). The advanced tools in analyzing these data have also shaped how marketers are using and analyzing the information gathered making predictions and inferences about consumers even more accurate. Modeling consumers' behavior uses factors such as psychometric characteristics (Kastanakis & Voyer, 2012) to personalize the persuasive message at an individual level. Finally, armed with collected behavioral data and a comprehensive understanding of market dynamics, companies can use sophisticated data modeling techniques (Sivarajah et al., 2017; Vlačić et al., 2021) and strategies based on AI (Ma & Sun, 2020; Ordenes & Silipo, 2021) to maximize the impact of their marketing activities.

Marketing interest in behavioral targeting is vast (Li, 2019; Rodgers, 2021). The Federal Trade Commission (FTC) showed that Acxiom, a major data broker, had more than 3,000 data points on every adult in the U.S. (FTC, 2014b). The FTC's report highlighted the data collection practices conducted by the company, which served as a reference point for understanding the challenges around consumer privacy and regulation within the online advertising industry. In numerous cases, data aggregators and brokers operate without engaging directly with users or the apps they are using, which means that consumers are unaware of how companies are monetizing their personal information.

The opportunity for marketers in the big data revolution is perhaps not "big data," but individual models of consumers' personal "little data" worlds. The implications for advertisers and businesses are expanding, as technology continues to fuel the "application economy." The market's momentum to innovate, appeal to consumer interests, and upend current business models requires that the (marketing) industry views privacy and security as a competitive differentiator and apparatus of trust for individuals and organizations (Espinel, 2015, p. 33).

Mobile Technology and Marketing

The ubiquity of mobile innovations allows marketers to observe and reach consumers more rapidly with hyper-targeted, personalized messages. The explosive growth in smartphone and smart device ownership over the past several years has fueled a shifting focus to mobile in the digital market space. Today, 85% of American adults own a smartphone, up from just 35% in 2011 (Greenwood, 2022b). American's time spent with mobile devices has grown and consumers continue to spend more time and attention on mobile technology, transitioning activities from desktops and laptops to smartphones and other mobile devices for shopping purposes (Kukar-Kinney et al., 2022; Orimoloye et al., 2022). In fact, according to a recent study, the daily average screen time on phones, excluding phone calls, has witnessed a notable rise, reaching a total of 4 hours and 30 minutes as of April 2022 (Statista, 2023a). Projections suggest that this duration is anticipated to reach 4 hours and 39 minutes by 2024 (Statista, 2023a). The ongoing growth of digital platforms, the rising popularity of digital audio formats like podcasts, as well as the steady implementation of 5G technology, which enhances the advertising potential of virtual reality and augmented reality, are expected to contribute positively to mobile ad revenues throughout 2023.

According to the U.S. Mobile App Report, digital media usage has grown by 49% with mobile application use having increased by 90% and contributing to 77% of the growth in digital media consumption (IAB, 2023). In fact, 87% of smartphone users spend their mobile time on apps, with the average mobile user globally spending 5.01 hours daily on social apps in 2022 (Statista, 2023a). Personal mobile technologies and the applications, connectivity, and ubiquity they provide have become an everyday essential for almost every consumer.

Mobile advertising is defined as "any paid message communication by mobile media with the intent to influence the attitude, intentions, and behavior of those addressed by the commercial messages" (Mir, 2011, p. 3). Expenditures on mobile ads have increased rapidly and is predicted to continue. Mobile ad revenues gain a greater share of marketing budgets; according to the 2022 IAB Internet Advertising Revenue Report, ad revenues reached a record high of $154.1 billion in 2021. Due to the time people spend with their phones, mobile ads have proven to be successful. The ability to offer messages and special offers to consumers in real time and via location information allows for messages to be received in close proximity to the point of purchase, making these messages quite relevant. Furthermore, less ad clutter on mobile platforms may also help explain to mobile advertising effectiveness.

The blurring of physical and digital worlds will continue to offer marketers the opportunity to create digital experiences for consumers. According to Statista, there is strong growth in mobile commerce, with mobile retail e-commerce spending in the United States surpassing 387 billion U.S. dollars in 2022 (Topic: Mobile Commerce in the United States, 2023b). Brands recognize the potential of this emerging market space, with 98% of marketers affirming they believe offline and online marketing is merging and ranking digital commerce as the top area of investment for marketing. As a result, marketing budgets are addressing innovation, and senior management at agencies expect that marketing's responsibility will increase, with e-commerce and innovation being the main growth areas (Gartner, 2021).

The Future of Mobile Commerce

Mobile technology with targeted access to consumers will be a fundamental component in the integration of information into the big data world. Data collected from mobile technology will become a central focus of government agencies, business models, industries, and privacy policies. As a result, it is crucial to address questions of information privacy and protection for individuals' personal data in these varying contexts, with a specific focus on consumers' information sensitivities to the types of data captured as well as their privacy preferences.

Legal, technical, and self-regulatory policies have emerged in response to concerns about collection and processing of personal data and the sending of unsolicited marketing communications to mobile users (Milberg et al., 1995; Cranor, 2005; Solove, 2006; FTC, 2010; Dutta & Bilbao-Osorio, 2014). However, the effectiveness of such policies in ensuring protection to mobile users while encouraging a free-market economy has not been established. Furthermore, the current state of mobile online behavior tracking, and data collection has not been adequately examined in detail at either the industry or consumer level. As both federal and industry self-regulation have fallen behind the pace of mobile device proliferation, there exists the potential for exploitation of consumer information and consumer privacy.

The increased interest in wearable technology using mobile health and fitness tracking technology will keep bringing brands new opportunities to establish themselves competitively and communicate with consumers. The health ecosystem, including mobile health tracking technology, stands at a crossroads. Health and biometric data can be used in several key applications to bring consumer benefits and enhance user experience. But, with the mobile and wearable market unregulated, the capture and redistribution of health information may heighten consumers' information sensitivities and privacy concerns. As consumers incorporate digital technologies into their lives, the information gained introduces opportunities to gain access to personal data for marketing purposes. Moreover, the quantity and breadth of personal information being collected are shocking.

According to the Finances Online Report, in 2021, individuals created 2.5 quintillion bytes of data every day, and by 2025, global data creation is expected to grow to more than 180 zettabytes (Andre, 2023). The rise of "big data" attributed to the proliferation of information-sensing technologies, radio-frequency identification readers, surveillance cameras, microphones, and wireless sensor networks (Eastin et al., 2016). McKinsey defines big data as "datasets so large that typical database software tools are unable to capture, store, manage, and analyze them" (Manyika et al., 2011, p. 1).

Further, mobile technology and the targeted, specific, and constant access to consumers that it permits will be a central contributor to the big data universe. While total traffic over IP networks is projected to increase by a compound annual growth rate (CAGR) of 24% from 2021 to 2026 (Gitnux, 2023), mobile traffic is growing at a CAGR of 27.9% over 2022–2030 (Yahoo Finances, 2023). As a result, data collected from mobile devices will be a focus of marketers, businesses, and regulators as they seek out tactics for their campaigns.

Marketers now have the ability to aggregate multiple information sources to build personal profiles about consumers, which can be used to narrowly target profitable audience segments with personalized marketing communications (Vesanen, 2007). The alleged value of data-driven marketing for consumers is that they receive highly relevant, personalized messages based on their individual behaviors, interests, and preferences, often at the precise point of need.

However, multiple studies have found that many individuals are concerned about the amount of personal data being collected (particularly within sensitive contexts), via search engines, websites, mobile devices, and data aggregators. Research shows that consumers often experience unease regarding the extensive collection and processing of their data for advertising purposes. Such data harvesting poses a threat to their privacy (Segijn & Van Ooijen, 2022) and autonomy (Solove, 2007; Büchi et al., 2022). Furthermore, this led to a rise in skepticism among many users regarding technology and the utilization of their personal data for persuasive purposes (Smit et al., 2014). Moreover, 91% of Americans feel they have lost control over their personal information online and express a consistent lack of confidence about the privacy of their data (Rainie, 2016). This reaction is supported by research showing that consumers are turning to technologies that allow them to skip tracking, encrypt communications, block ads, and register on do-not-track lists (Lerman, 2014).

Information privacy and the protection of personal data are human rights (Schwartz & Solove, 2011). "Personally identifiable information" (PII) delineates the legal threshold condition for the loss of anonymity or privacy. PII refers to any information that can be used to identify someone. In the United States, there is no comprehensive definition of what PII is. Instead, each state has its own set of laws and regulations that regulate consumer data and privacy. This also includes their unique definition of PII. Some states have specific statutes or data breach notification laws that outline the types of information considered PII. The lack of a comprehensive definition of what constitutes a PII amplifies the challenges of privacy concerns among consumers, technology companies, organizations, and regulators. An array of online profiles, pin numbers, access codes, behaviors, and mobile location records all establish concrete links between social and technological concepts of identity (Wessels, 2012).

Today's consumer is no longer anonymous since almost every form of communication and behavior produces data that can be captured, aggregated, and analyzed (Zwick & Dholakia, 2004; Buckingham, 2008; Wessels, 2012; Eastin et al., 2016). Information collected for one purpose can be readily retrieved for another, and the possible association between aggregated data about a consumer makes nearly every point of accessible data personally identifiable. On July 11, 2022, the FTC shared concerns regarding collecting sensitive information on consumers and reiterated its commitment to "fully enforcing the law against illegal use and sharing of highly sensitive data" (FTC, 2022). In their statement, the federal agency highlighted the abundance of sensitive information that is being collected from devices that consumers are using on a daily basis. In fact, smartphones, wearable fitness trackers, "smart home" devices, and even the web browsers consumers routinely use have the capability to track or infer private information about consumers. These data points can pose immeasurable threats to personal privacy. However, the situation becomes even more invasive when these connected devices and technology companies collect, aggregate, and profit from this data. Health data more precisely pose more challenges regarding safeguarding the privacy and security of even more personalized and intimate information about consumers.

Most scholars agree the practice of personalized advertising involves proactively tailoring marketing messages and delivery platforms to reach individual consumers based on their preferences and personal information while maintaining the principles of mass message marketing (Chellappa & Sin, 2005; Dolnicar & Jordaan, 2007; Teradata, 2015). The collection of intimate data about consumers will only proliferate with technological innovations. From consumers' exact geographical location to their voices using AI assistants to their health data captured by wearable devices, the amount and depth of personal information available to companies is expected to grow and thus will make targeting consumers more precise than ever before. Advertisers employ sophisticated technologies that track individual consumers' characteristics, preferences, and behaviors in real time to construct individual-specific profiles and deliver custom messages (Schwartz & Solove, 2011). Successful personalized advertising hinges upon marketers' ability to acquire and process consumer information and personal data, as well as consumers' willingness to use personalization services (Chellappa & Sin, 2005). If consumers get fed up with their loss of privacy, some may simply not use the technologies if they can. This emerging digitally targeted world offers extraordinary opportunities for advertisers and organizations to immediately analyze messaging effectiveness (Dutta & Bilbao-Osorio, 2014). Marketers with the greatest ability to collect and process the most comprehensive constellations of consumer data will lead the market by having the most complete and precise understanding of their audiences (Dutta & Bilbao-Osorio, 2014; Teradata, 2015).

Although consumer awareness of the personalized advertising ecosystem remains relatively low, data-driven marketing is a massive and quickly expanding business. As companies continue to place greater emphasis on the tracking and collection of consumer behavioral information, the business has grown exponentially. The 2022 IAB Internet Advertising Revenue Report reveals that targeted digital advertising revenues in the United States hit $209.7 billion in 2021. This number demonstrates a growth of

10.8% year-over-year between 2021 and 2022. Despite expectations of a slowdown in advertising revenues following the growth observed post-COVID-19, the internet advertising industry in the United States demonstrated resilience by achieving an overall revenue increase of $20.4 billion compared to 2021. This achievement is noteworthy considering the prevailing high inflation rates and economic uncertainty during 2022. Additionally, with the introduction of new regulations at the state level that aim to regulate privacy and consumer data, it is becoming clear that the industry needs to adapt and evolve beyond the traditional methods of data collection and analysis.

Wearables and the New Health Economy

Even though double-digit growth for smartphones has ended, smartphone and mobile internet users will continue to increase. As of 2022, there were 307 million smartphone users in the United States, which represents 85% of American adults (Zippia, 2023). For the wearable category, a report by Vicert showed that in 2019, the number of connected wearable health devices reached $722 million. This number demonstrated significant growth as compared to $325 million in 2016. Furthermore, it is anticipated that the number of connected wearables will surpass $1 billion after 2022. More specifically, the wearable market is expected to expand significantly, with a projected market size of $265.4 billion by 2026. This represents a CAGR of 18%. In particular, the market showed a remarkable growth rate of 41.51% from 2021 to 2022 (Markets & Markets, 2023).

Computing has seen a transition from PCs and laptops to mobile devices, including smartphones and tablets, causing the industry to shift to a point where consumer interaction with the Internet is moving closer to the body and becoming more personal (Kaul & Wheelock, 2015). The development of smart devices and wearables, and the rapid growth of sensors, will provide devices with more context of the physical world, enabling them to work autonomously to support consumer insights. Wearable computing is proliferating and is undoubtedly revolutionizing human interaction with technology.

The wearables market encompasses many devices, applications, and use cases. Wearable devices include a combination of device types, which are worn or attached to the body to serve a specific function or provide a utility (Barnes, 2014; Hulkower, 2015a, 2015b; eMarketer, 2015). These devices allow consumers to track their health and fitness behaviors while monitoring their vitals and biometric information, providing users an understanding of their bodies. These advantages are generating growing interest among consumers, making the wearables market the fastest-growing tech sector

(Salesforce Research, 2015). According to a Gartner, Inc. report, global consumer expenditure on wearable devices reached a total of $81.5 billion in 2021, reflecting a notable increase of 18.1% compared to the $69 billion recorded in 2020. This surge in spending can be attributed to consumers' heightened awareness of health, well-being, and lifestyle changes. Furthermore, as outlined, the report notes that the United States is experiencing substantial growth in the wearable device sector, with the adoption rate among U.S. consumers rising from 9% to 33% within a four-year period leading up to 2021.

With a large total addressable market, manufacturers are quickly developing new products that are more attractive to consumers and thus escalating their demand. The Deloitte 2021 Connectivity and Mobile Trends survey showed that 58% of U.S. households own a smartwatch or fitness tracker. The report also shows that since the onset of the COVID-19 pandemic, approximately 14% of customers in the United States have made purchases of these fitness devices (Deloitte Insights, 2022). Consumers are mainly using these devices for step counting, monitoring workout performance, tracking their heart health, and assessing sleep quality. Amazingly, in the fourth quarter of 2022, 139 million wearables were shipped globally, which demonstrates an important increase compared to past years (Statista, 2023a). Additionally, 492 million units of wearables, including smartwatches, fitness monitors, smart wearables, head-mounted displays, and various other devices, were sold in 2022 alone (Statista, 2023a).

This two-way device integration where data from the smartwatch or smart wearable is simultaneously transmitted and analyzed on the smartphone creates enhanced and more adaptive user experiences and will continue to grow in importance for brands (Nudd, 2015). Notably, mobile health technologies collect far more sensitive information about the individual than other online and mobile applications, as many health-tracking devices collect data continuously over prolonged periods of time (Avancha, Baxi & Kotz, 2012). An apparent dichotomy between privacy attitudes and privacy behaviors is receiving mounting attention from social media (Barnes, 2006), online commerce (Awad & Krishnan, 2006), and smartphones (Sutanto et al., 2013). This phenomenon has been termed broadly as the "privacy paradox" or "personalization-privacy paradox" when data privacy considerations are in the context of consumer targeting for personalized marketing.

Smartphone integration and health data. Product designers are driving the adoption of technologies that interpret different sensing inputs, facilitate faster connectivity between devices and mobile payments, detect location, and enable context awareness. Wearable devices that stream data about consumers and their environment in real-time and sensors in smartphone applications that detect location and movement are contributing substantially to the big data universe. Phone-based personal health data is being generated more frequently, with consumers tracking data on smartphones and wearable devices, including vitals such as heart rate and blood pressure, glucose and hydration levels, pedometer and accelerometer information, sleep metrics, stress levels, and weight. Most of these tools enable users to record their behaviors, including physical activity and exercise, diet and nutrition, medications and prescriptions taken, and clinical data (Kaul & Wheelock, 2015).

Despite potential dark side issues, Americans see some hope for these tools and wearables. According to the Vicert report (Petrovic, 2022), there is vast consumer interest in receiving health information from new health-sensing technologies. In fact, 30% of U.S. adults use wearable technology for healthcare reasons, as of 2020. Moreover, 92% of smartwatch users use them for health and fitness reasons. The report also suggests that nearly 50% of users rely on this technology daily, with more than 80% being willing to share their results with their care provider.

Consumer Privacy and Security with Artificial Intelligence and Social Media

The constant collection of personal information on consumers raises concerns regarding privacy and security. The magnitude of the data collected and shared with different parties (e.g., partners, publishers, and data brokers) creates challenges for consumers to understand the risks associated with using these technologies. Within this complex network of parties sharing and aggregating data, important questions should be asked: Who has control over this ecosystem, and who has the power to actually protect consumer data?

Marketers and organizations collecting personal and behavioral information about consumers online claim that consumers are willing to share personal data despite privacy risks in exchange for the value offered by personalized offers and services (Culnan, 1993; Culnan & Armstrong, 1999; Tezinde et al., 2002; Chellappa & Sin, 2005). The proliferation of these techniques related to the collection, processing, and use of that information and the complexity of the ecosystem that surrounds these techniques make it difficult for consumers to fully understand the risks involved and make informed decisions about their data. These risks include the jeopardy of privacy, security breaches, and potential misuse of personal information by third parties. Indeed, technology companies and the legal structure that manages and regulates privacy in the United States are based on the idea that consumers are able to control these privacy risks.

This paradigm is referred to as the privacy self-management (Solove, 2012). This framework has shaped how privacy is being regulated today. In 1999, Schwartz raised these concerns about the effectiveness of consent obtained through privacy notices. He noted that it is unlikely for consumers to be informed or give voluntarily their consent. He argued that these notices often go unnoticed, use ambiguous legal language, and fail to provide meaningful choices for consumers. These challenges include the discrepancy between the privacy policies shared by organizations and those of third parties with whom they share data. Furthermore, the frequent changes in privacy policies without adequate notice, as well as the complex nature of user data flows within the digital advertising space often remain incomprehensible to consumers.

According to Richards (2021), privacy as control suffers from many deficiencies including the idea that privacy-self management brings many problems such as the overwhelming definition of control that affords users the "option" or many "options" to control their privacy. Here, users fall into the trap of agreeing to terms and conditions for example while not really knowing what they are agreeing to. The fact that the responsibility of control is given to the users to choose what to do can be problematic when the ecosystem of tech companies makes it harder for consumers to read these lengthy terms and notices and makes it even harder for users to comprehend the implications of this "notice and choice." The observations made by these scholars highlight the limitations and shortcomings of the current framework that aims to protect individuals' privacy.

Privacy as a social contract is based on mutual and beneficial agreements between the involved parties regarding the use and sharing of information. This concept argues that privacy expectations are better managed when all parties involved have a clear understanding of their rights and responsibilities. Our own research (Sifaoui et al., 2023) has looked at empirically measuring this concept by providing a framework that integrates consumers' literacy and the efficacy of social contracts. More specifically, it is argued that consumers' understanding of social contracts can be measured by assessing their knowledge of data sharing practices of the involved parties. This new outlook considers the individual differences between consumers and their relationships with organizations. This approach acknowledges consumers' literacy in shaping their attitudes and their behaviors toward disclosing their information, and their usage of digital media. Simply, older ideas of privacy including hiding behind various state and federal laws to boost profits are no longer applicable in today's new world. Transparency between organizations, policymakers, and consumers will be required so that consumers have an elevated literacy related to social contracts that span across current and future digital platforms.

Health data is one of the most sensitive types of personal information and has usually been protected with much more stringent regulatory regimes and controls. However, as noted earlier, health and fitness applications collect and transmit sometimes sensitive personal information about users' health details to third parties. The settlement in FTC vs. Flo (2022) highlights the increased role of the federal agency in protecting health information from apps (Federal Trade Commission, 2022). Indeed, the FTC accused Flo, a menstrual tracking app, of violating its promise of securing sensitive health information collected about their users. It is alleged that the company shared such data with third parties that provided marketing and analytics services to the app including big tech organizations such as Facebook and Google, thus violating consumer privacy.

The information shared included device model or language setting; consumer-specific identifiers including username, email address, and a string of identifiers; unique device IDs, MAC address or IMEI; unique third-party-specific identifiers; and personal consumer information including exercise routine, symptom searches, dietary habits, zip code geolocation, and gender (Federal Trade Commission, 2014a). The FTC also identified third-party ad servicing that received information from four health apps including the same unique identifiers that were transmitted to the third parties. Yet, disagreement exists between groups of researchers and practitioners regarding how to view and address consumer privacy concerns in the face of data-driven marketing, especially where health data is involved. On one hand, marketers assume that consumers are becoming accustomed to being tracked and that living a public life is the new default for internet-connected users (Sayre & Horne, 2000; Mitchell et al., 2014; Rainie & Anderson, 2014; Madden & Rainie, 2015). From a legal standpoint, the voluntariness of sharing information is part of this "give and take" equation where consumers consent to the trade-offs based on the "notice and choice."

On the other hand, scholars, practitioners, and policymakers assert that if marketers fail to adequately address privacy concerns, consumer distrust toward technology and the services offered may hinder innovation and limit its use and acceptance (Mottl, 2015). They posit that by addressing the existing concerns of users regarding privacy, security, and data practices, as well as by increasing consumer literacy and informing users about the usage of their personal information, consumers will gain a stronger sense of assurance regarding data protection and will increase their ability to manage their privacy effectively. In fact, according to a report by Dentsu (2019), more than 64% of the people surveyed believe the main cause of distrusting technology companies is the mishandling of personal information. Furthermore, the report showed that eight out of ten people would stop doing business with an organization that misused their data.

Research on consumer attitudes, opinions, and behaviors regarding the privacy of their personal data from wearable technologies has established that consumers are concerned about the breadth and quality of personal information being collected (Ackerman, 2013; Kavassalis et al., 2003; Lee & Benbasat, 2003; Watson et al., 2002). A study examining consumers' sentiments about data collected for marketing purposes, reported that 91% of individuals do not want marketers selling their information, even if they are compensated. In addition, two-thirds feel that it should be illegal for companies to collect or use such data without getting prior consent.

Consumers are increasingly adopting technologies that allow them to elude tracking, block online and mobile ads (PageFair, 2015), and register on do-not-track lists (Davis, 2015). Cranor (2005) identified three central areas of consumers' information privacy concerns, including the type of data collected, how data will be used, and whether or not the data will be shared. Over the years, privacy laws and regulations have been developed to address these concerns and provide individuals with control over their data. The General Data Protection Regulation (GDPR) in Europe and the California Consumer Privacy Act (CCPA) as well as its amended version, the California Privacy Rights Acts that went into effect in January 2023, are examples of such laws.

These regulations require companies to be transparent about what data they collect, how it is used, and who it is shared with. They also give individuals the right to access their data, request its deletion, and opt out of its collection. Research also demonstrates, however, that consumers generally lack awareness and knowledge about what personal data is being collected and by whom, as well as how it is being shared and used (Turow et al., 2023; Turow et al., 2005). Large percentages of American consumers hold inaccurate assumptions about the collection and use of their personal information and "overestimate the extent to which the government protects them from certain forms of data collection" (Turow et al., 2015, p. 16).

Unfortunately, on mobile devices and in mobile computing contexts, users exercise less caution than in other computing environments despite the more personal and pervasive information generated from these technologies (Mitchell et al., 2014).

Recent research has looked at the understanding of consumers regarding the interactions they have with technology companies. Illustrating the digital contracts they sign routinely as social contracts, a new outlook on the relationship between consumers and technology companies has emerged.

These social contracts should be seen as a mutual agreement between consumers and companies where the responsibilities and expectations of both parties are clearly stated and outlined. This perspective looks at the literacy of consumers in regard to these contracts that they are forming with different tech companies, highlighting the importance of the active role that consumers should be playing in these relationships.

As technological advancements continue to proliferate, it becomes crucial for organizations to fulfill their part of the social contract and prioritize the privacy and security of their users' information. With the abundance of information available, the need to better safeguard it and increase the transparency of data practices will continue to be a pressing issue.

Conclusions and Solutions: Future Research Agenda

The omnipresence of mobile devices makes it easier for marketers to track consumers' online behavior and even easier to collect intimate information such as location data, patterns, and biometric information. This level of surveillance amplifies concerns about privacy and consent. The challenge with this accessibility to consumer data is the purpose for which it is being used when it falls between the hands of parties that can use it against consumers' best interests. When data harvesting can be used to profile individuals for either manipulating them as in the case of Cambridge Analytica or infringing on their personal boundaries such as in the case of Clearview AI, or selling geographical data to law enforcement, consumers become nothing more than "data pawns" in a new economy where human privacy rights are up for sale to the highest bidder.

The evolving landscape of privacy regulations and consumers' increased concerns require a proactive approach from all these stakeholders. Prioritizing data privacy, embracing transparency, and respecting individual choices will be crucial in building trust, meeting consumer expectations, and fostering a sustainable and responsible data ecosystem. To navigate this complex landscape, it is important to strengthen privacy frameworks and establish clear guidelines for data collection, storage, and usage. While more states are strengthening their privacy frameworks such as California, Virginia, Colorado, and Connecticut, the lack of an overarching federal framework that provides consistent standards for data protection and usage across industries is still lacking. It is here that consumer understanding and trust will emerge as key concepts in the growth and acceptance of big data collection practices and hyper-personalized messaging.

Today, consumers need to be part of these conversations and should play a role in shaping the development of ethical and responsible data practices. Increasing consumer literacy and efficacy in privacy management should be a priority for regulators and organizations. Firms need to adjust their methods to meet consumers' privacy expectations, or at the very least, a threshold of understanding. Creating a mechanism such as real-time data feedback channels between consumers and organizations will enhance privacy concerns and organizational awareness, thus better serving users' needs.

To develop comprehensive, flexible policies and self-regulatory mechanisms that reduce privacy concerns while facilitating the growth of mobile and digital marketing, a clearer understanding of consumers' perceived risks involved with data disclosure is necessary, particularly when considering information about commerce and health-related activities.

Identifying the changing conditions where consumers welcome ad personalization and data-driven messaging strategies requires ongoing, continual research as new technologies emerge, devices become more connected, and privacy perceptions evolve. By prioritizing responsible data collection and analysis practices, advertisers can leverage the power of data to create more personalized and effective marketing campaigns while also maintaining consumer trust. Such a research agenda would allow researchers to develop policy recommendations for the industry to consider before stringent government regulations potentially restrict growth. Collaboration between practitioners and policymakers is crucial. It will help ensure that regulations are fair and effective, while also allowing for innovation and growth in the marketing industry.

References

Ackerman, L. (2013). *Mobile health and fitness applications and information privacy*. Privacy Rights Clearinghouse.

Adomavicius, G., & Tuzhilin, A. (2005). Personalization technologies: A process-oriented perspective. *Communications of the ACM*, *48*(10), 83–90.

Andre, L. (2023, May 16). *Fifty-three important statistics about how much data is created every day*. https://financesonline.com/how-much-data-is-created-every-day/

Avancha, S., Baxi, A., & Kotz, D. (2012). Privacy in mobile technology for personal healthcare. *ACM Computing Surveys (CSUR)*, *45*(1), 3.

Awad, N. F., & Krishnan, M. S. (2006). The personalization privacy paradox: An empirical evaluation of information transparency and the willingness to be profiled online for personalization. *MIS Quarterly*, 13–28.

Barnes, K. (2014). *Health wearables: Early days, PricewaterhouseCoopers (PwC) health research institute and consumer intelligence series* (pp. 2–11). Price Waterhouse Cooper.

Barnes, S. B. (2006). A privacy paradox: Social networking in the United States. *First Monday*, *11*(9).

Boerman, S. C., Kruikemeier, S., & Zuiderveen Borgesius, F. J. (2017). Online behavioral advertising: A literature review and research agenda. *Journal of Advertising*, *46*(3), 363–376.

Büchi, M., Festic, N., & Latzer, M. (2022). The chilling effects of digital dataveillance: A theoretical model and an empirical research agenda. *Big Data & Society*, *9*(1), https://doi.org/10.1177/20539517211065368.

Buckingham, D. (2008). Introducing identity. *Youth, Identity, and Digital Media*, *1*.

Chellappa, R. K., & Sin, R. G. (2005). Personalization versus privacy: An empirical examination of the online consumer's dilemma. *Information Technology and Management*, 6(2–3), 181–202.

Cranor, L. F. (2005). Privacy policies and privacy preferences. *Security and Usability*, 447–472.

Culnan, M. (1993). How did they get my name?: An exploratory investigation of consumer attitudes toward secondary information use. *MIS Quarterly*, *17*(3), 341–363.

Culnan, M., & Armstrong, P. (1999). Information privacy concerns, procedural fairness, and impersonal trust: An empirical investigation. *Organizational Science*, *10*(1), 104–115.

Davis, W. (2015, October 7). Lawmakers call for stronger do-not-track standards. *Mediapost Policy Blog*. http://www.mediapost.com/publications/article/259971/lawmakers-call-for-stronger-do-not-track- standards.html.

Deloitte Insights. (2022). *Connectivity and mobile trends study* (3rd ed.). https://www2.deloitte.com/us/en/insights/industry/telecommunications/connectivity-mobile-trends-survey.html

Dentsu. (2019, April). *Human needs in a digital world*. https://www.dentsu.com/us/en/our-latest-thinking/society/digital-society-index-2019-human-needs-in-a-digital-world

Dolnicar, S., & Jordaan, Y. (2007). A market-oriented approach to responsibly managing information privacy concerns in direct marketing. *Journal of Advertising*, *26*(2), 123–149.

Dutta, S., & Bilbao-Osorio, B. (2014). The global information technology report 2014—rewards and risks of big data. *INSEAD and World Economic Forum*, 35–93.

Eastin, M. S., Brinson, N. H., Doorey, A., & Wilcox, G. (2016). Living in a big data world: Predicting mobile commerce activity through privacy concerns. *Computers in Human Behavior*, *58*, 214–220.

eMarketer. (2015, October). *Cross-device marketing roundup*. https://www.emarketer.com/public_media/docs/eMarketer_Cross_Device_Marketing_Roundup.pdf

Espinel, V. (2015, September 1). *Deep shift: Technology tipping points and societal impact*. http://www3.weforum.org/docs/WEF_GAC15_Technological_Tipping_Points_report_2015.pdf

Federal Trade Commission. (2010, December). *Protecting consumer privacy in an era of rapid change: A proposed framework for businesses and policymakers* (pp. 72–119).

Federal Trade Commission. (2014a). *Spring privacy series: Consumer generated and controlled health data*. https://www.ftc.gov/system/files/documents/public_events/195411/2014_05_07_consumer-generated-controlled-health-data-final-transcript.pdf

Federal Trade Commission. (2014b). *Data brokers: A call for transparency and accountability*. https://www.ftc.gov/system/files/documents/reports/data-brokers-call-transparency-accountability-report-federal-trade-commission-may-2014/140527databrokerreport.pdf

Federal Trade Commission. (2022, September 6). Location, health, and other sensitive information: FTC committed to fully enforcing the law against illegal use and sharing of highly sensitive data. *Federal Trade Commission*. https://www.ftc.gov/business-guidance/blog/2022/07/location-health-and-other-sensitive-information-ftc-committed-fully-enforcing-law-against-illegal

FTC vs. Flo. (2022). https://www.ftc.gov/news-events/news/press-releases/2021/06/ftc-finalizes-order-flo-health-fertility-tracking-app-shared-sensitive-health-data-facebook-google

Gartner. (2021, January 11). *Gartner forecasts global spending on wearable devices to total $81.5 B*. https://www.gartner.com/en/newsroom/press-releases/2021-01-11-gartner-forecasts-global-spending-on-wearable-devices-to-total-81-5-billion-in-2021

Gitnux. (2023). *Internet traffic statistics and trends in 2023*. https://blog.gitnux.com/internet-traffic-statistics/

Greenwood, S. (2022b, May 11). Mobile technology and home broadband 2021. *Pew Research Center: Internet, Science & Tech*. https://www.pewresearch.org/internet/2021/06/03/mobile-technology-and-home-broadband-2021/

Helberger, N., Huh, J., Milne, G., Strycharz, J., & Sundaram, H. (2020). Macro and exogenous factors in computational advertising: Key issues and new research directions. *Journal of Advertising*, *49*(4), 377–393.

Huh, J., & Malthouse, E. C. (2020). Advancing computational advertising: Conceptualization of the field and future directions. *Journal of Advertising*, *49*(4), 367–376.

Hulkower, B. (2015a, July). Mobile advertising and shopping—US. *Mintel Oxygen Database*.

Hulkower, B. (2015b, December). Wearable technology—US. *Mintel Oxygen Database*.

IAB. (2023, April 20). *Interactive advertising Bureau insights*. https://www.iab.com/insights/internet-advertising-revenue-report-full-year-2022/

Jai, T. M. C., Burns, L. D., & King, N. J. (2013). The effect of behavioral tracking practices on consumers' shopping evaluations and repurchase intention toward trusted online retailers. *Computers in Human Behavior*, *29*(3), 901–909.

Kastanakis, M., & Voyer, B. (2012). Cultural effects on perception and cognition: Integrating recent findings and reviewing implications for consumer research. *ACR North American Advances*.

Kaul, A., & Wheelock, C. (2015). Wearables: 10 trends to watch. *Tractica LLC*, 3–11. https://www.tractica.com/wp-content/uploads/2015/08/WP-WD10T-15-Tractica.pdf

Kavassalis, P., Spyropoulou, N., Drossos, D., Mitrokostas, E., Gikas, G., & Hatzistamatiou, A. (2003). Mobile permission marketing: Framing the market inquiry. *International Journal of Electronic Commerce*, *8*(1), 55–79.

Kukar-Kinney, M., Scheinbaum, A. C., Orimoloye, L. O., Carlson, J. R., & He, H. (2022). A model of online shopping cart abandonment: Evidence from e-tail clickstream data. *Journal of the Academy of Marketing Science*, *50*(5), 961–980.

Lambrecht, A., & Tucker, C. (2013). When does retargeting work? Information specificity in online advertising. *Journal of Marketing Research*, *50*(5), 561–576.

Lee, Y. E., & Benbasat, I. (2003). Interface design for mobile commerce. *Communications of the ACM*, *46*(12), 48–52.

Lerman, K. (2014). *Beyond the bulls-eye: Building meaningful relationships in the age of big data*. https://www.communispace.com/uploadedfiles/researchinsights/best_practices/bestpractices_beyondthebullseye_buildingrelationshipsintheageofbigdata.pdf.

Li, H. (2019). Special section introduction: Artificial intelligence and advertising. *Journal of Advertising*, *48*(4), 333–337.

Ma, L., & Sun, B. (2020). Machine learning and AI in marketing–connecting computing power to human insights. *International Journal of Research in Marketing*, *37*(3), 481–504.

Madden, M., & Rainie, L. (2015, May 20). Americans' attitudes about privacy, security and surveillance. *Pew Internet & American Life Project*. http://www.pewinternet.org/files/2015/05/Privacy-and-Security-Attitudes-5.19.15_FINAL.pdf

Manyika, J., Chui, M., Brown, B., Bughin, J., Dobbs, R., Roxburgh, C., & Hung Byers, A. (2011, May). Big Data: The next frontier for innovation, competition and productivity. *McKinsey Global Institute Report*. http://www.mckinsey.com/insights/business_technology/big_data_the_next_frontier_for_ innovation/

MarketsandMarkets. (2023, July 5). *Wearable technology market size, future outlook and emerging trends*. https://www.marketsandmarkets.com/Market-Reports/wearable-electronics-market-983.html

Milberg, S. J., Burke, S. J., Smith, H. J., & Kallman, E. A. (1995). Values, personal information privacy, and regulatory approaches. *Communications of the ACM*, *38*(12), 65–74.

Mir, I. (2011). Consumer attitude towards m-advertising acceptance: A cross-sectional study. *Journal of Internet Banking & Commerce*, *16*(1), 1–22.

Mitchell, M., Wang, A. I. A., & Reiher, P. (2014). *Mobile usage patterns and privacy implications*. http://www.cs.fsu.edu/~awang/papers/permoby2015.pdf

Mottl, J. (2015, August 11). *Consumers remain wary over safety of health wearables, wellness apps*. http://www.fiercemobilehealthcare.com/story/consumers-remain-wary-over-safety-health-wearables-wellness-apps/2015-08-11

Nudd, T. (2015, January 2). *How brands can use biometric data in ways that go far beyond fitness*. http://www.adweek.com/news/advertising-branding/how-brands-can-use-biometric-data-ways-go-far-beyond-fitness-165108

Ordenes, F. V., & Silipo, R. (2021). Machine learning for marketing on the KNIME Hub: The development of a live repository for marketing applications. *Journal of Business Research*, *137*, 393–410.

Orimoloye, L. O., Scheinbaum, A. C., Kukar-Kinney, M., Ma, T., Sung, M. C., & Johnson, J. (2022). Differential effects of device modalities and exposure to online reviews on online purchasing: A field study. *Journal of Advertising*, *51*(4), 430–439.

PageFair. (2015). *The 2015 ad blocking report*. https://blog.pagefair.com/2015/ad-blocking-report/

Petrovic, V. (2022, November 30). Wearable healthcare technology statistics. *Vicert*. https://vicert.com/blog/wearable-healthcare-technology-statistics/

Phelps, J., Nowak, G., & Ferrell, E. (2000). Privacy concerns and consumer willingness to provide personal information. *Journal of Public Policy & Marketing*, *19*(1), 27–41.

Rainie, L., & Anderson, J. (2014, December 18). Digital life in 2025: The future of privacy. *Pew Internet & American Life Project*. http://www.pewinternet.org/files/2014/12/PI_FutureofPrivacy_121814_pdf1.pdf

Rainie, L., & Duggan, M. (2016, January 14). Privacy and information sharing. *Pew Internet & American Life Project*. http://www.pewinternet.org/files/2016/01/PI_2016.01.14_Privacy-and-Info-Sharing_FINAL.pdf

Richards, N. (2021). *Why privacy matters*. Oxford University Press.

Rodgers, S. (2021). Themed issue introduction: Promises and perils of artificial intelligence and advertising. *Journal of Advertising*, *50*(1), 1–10.

Salesforce Research. (2015). *State of wearables report: Putting wearables to work, insights on wearable technology in business*. https://secure.sfdcstatic.com/assets/pdf/misc/StateOfWearablesReport.pdf

Sayre, S., & Horne, D. (2000). Trading secrets for savings: How concerned are consumers about club cards as a privacy threat? *Advances in Consumer Research*, *27*(1).

Schwartz, P. M., & Solove, D. J. (2011). PII problem: Privacy and a new concept of personally identifiable information. *New York University Law Review*, *86*, 1814.

Segijn, C. M., & Van Ooijen, I. (2022). Differences in consumer knowledge and perceptions of personalized advertising: Comparing online behavioural advertising and synced advertising. *Journal of Marketing Communications*, *28*(2), 207–226.

Shah, D., & Murthi, B. P. S. (2021). Marketing in a data-driven digital world: Implications for the role and scope of marketing. *Journal of Business Research*, *125*, 772–779.

Sifaoui, A., Bright, L. F., & Eastin, M. S. (2023). "Failure to notice or noticing the failure": Defining the social contract literacy, a novel approach to understanding users' literacy of digital contracts. *International Communication Association*.

Sivarajah, U., Kamal, M. M., Irani, Z., & Weerakkody, V. (2017). Critical analysis of Big Data challenges and analytical methods. *Journal of Business Research*, *70*, 263–286.

Smit, E. G., Van Noort, G., & Voorveld, H. A. (2014). Understanding online behavioural advertising: User knowledge, privacy concerns and online coping behaviour in Europe. *Computers in Human Behavior*, *32*, 15–22.

Solove, D. J. (2006). A taxonomy of privacy. In *University of Pennsylvania law review* (pp. 477–564). University of Pennsylvania.

Solove, D. J. (2007). I've got nothing to hide and other misunderstandings of privacy. *San Diego Law Review*, *44*, 745.

Solove, D. J. (2012). Introduction: Privacy self-management and the consent dilemma. *Harvard Law Review*, *126*, 1880.

Statista. (2023a, March 6). *Daily time spent on mobile phones in the U.S. 2019–2024*. https://www.statista.com/statistics/1045353/mobile-device-daily-usage-time-in-the-us/

Statista. (2023b, March 9). *Mobile commerce in the United States*. https://www.statista.com/topics/1185/mobile-commerce/#topicOverview

Sutanto, J., Palme, E., Tan, C. H., & Phang, C. W. (2013). Addressing the personalization-privacy paradox: An empirical assessment from a field experiment on smartphone users. *Mis Quarterly*, *37*(4), 1141–1164.

Teradata. (2015). *Global data-driven marketing survey: Progressing toward true individualization*. http://applications.teradata.com/DDM-Survey/welcome/.ashx

Tezinde, T., Smith, B., & Murphy, J. (2002). Getting permission: Exploring factors affecting permission marketing. *Journal of Interactive Marketing*, *16*(4), 28–36.

Tractica LLC. (2015). *Emerging interface technologies for mobile devices*. https://www.tractica.com/research/emerging-interface-technologies-for-mobile-devices/

Turow, J., Feldman, L., & Meltzer, K. (2005). Open to exploitation: America's shoppers online and offline. *A Report from the Annenberg Public Policy Center of the University of Pennsylvania*. http://repository.upenn.edu/asc_papers/35

Turow, J., Hennessy, M., & Draper, N. (2015). *The tradeoff fallacy: How marketers are misrepresenting American consumers and opening them up to exploitation*. The Annenberg School for Communication, University of Pennsylvania. https://www.asc.upenn.edu/sites/default/files/TradeoffFallacy_1.pdf

Turow, J., Lelkes, Y., Draper, N. A., & Waldman, A. E. (2023). Americans can't consent to companies' use of their data. *International Journal of Communication*, *17*, 4796–4817.

Unni, R., & Harmon, R. (2007). Perceived effectiveness of push vs. pull mobile location based advertising. *Journal of Interactive Advertising*, *7*(2), 28–40.

Vesanen, J. (2007). What is personalization? A conceptual framework. *European Journal of Marketing*, *41*, 409–418.

Vlačić, B., Corbo, L., e Silva, S. C., & Dabić, M. (2021). The evolving role of artificial intelligence in marketing: A review and research agenda. *Journal of Business Research*, *128*, 187–203.

Watson, R. T., Pitt, L. F., Berthon, P., & Zinkhan, G. M. (2002). U-commerce: Expanding the universe of marketing. *Journal of the Academy of Marketing Science*, *30*(4), 333–347.

Wessels, B. (2012). Identification and the practices of identity and privacy in everyday digital communication. *New Media & Society*. https://doi.org/10.1177/1461444812450679.

White, T. B., Zahay, D. L., Thorbjørnsen, H., & Shavitt, S. (2008). Getting too personal: Reactance to highly personalized email solicitations. *Marketing Letters*, *19*, 39–50.

Xu, H., Luo, X. R., Carroll, J. M., & Rosson, M. B. (2011). The personalization privacy paradox: An exploratory study of decision-making process for location-aware marketing. *Decision Support Systems*, *51*(1), 42–52.

Yahoo Finance. (2023, May 18). *Mobile data traffic global market 2022–2030: Rise in smartphone connection speeds to drive growth*. https://rb.gy/t1icc

Zippia. (2023, March 2). 25+ Incredible US smartphone industry statistics 2023: How many Americans have smartphones. *Zippia.com*. https://www.zippia.com/advice/us-smartphone-industry-statistics/

Zwick, D., & Dholakia, N. (2004). Whose identity is it anyway? Consumer representation in the age of database marketing. *Journal of Micromarketing*, *24*(1), 31–43.

8

EXAMINING THE ISSUES OF SOCIAL MEDIA, CHILDREN, AND PRIVACY

A Case Study

Madison K. Brown, Kathrynn R. Pounders, and Gary B. Wilcox

Introduction

The Privacy Problem: Children as Vulnerable Social Media Users

Billions of people use social media platforms every day, and social media is a predominant part of society from a variety of contexts, ranging from personal entertainment and connection to marketing and branding strategy. Despite the positive influences associated with using social media, in recent years, social media companies have come under fire for their mishandling of user data. Multiple companies have experienced data breaches, putting their customers in the uncomfortable position of having to rethink their relationship with these companies. The infamous Cambridge Analytica scandal was the catalyst for an outbreak of privacy concerns from social media users after nearly 87 million Facebook accounts had their private data exploited. Since then, social media and advertising companies have struggled to regain their user's trust and confidence that their personal data is being adequately protected.

While consumers have increasingly expressed concern for increased regulation of their private data, one significant stakeholder is often neglected in the conversation regarding online privacy concerns: children. In this chapter, the definition of a child refers "to an individual who is a minor, who is below legal age or the age of majority" (Cornell Law School Legal Information Institute, n.d.). The age of majority is 18 in most states (Cornell Law School Legal Information Institute, n.d.). Children are a consumer segment that is often forgotten when it comes to media and advertising

DOI: 10.4324/9781003410058-12

(Snyder, 2016). As vulnerable consumers, children are uniquely affected by targeted advertising practices on social media. It has been established that children of certain ages have difficulty distinguishing between personalized ads and regular social media content (Radesky et al., 2020, p. 2). Additionally, since children are not able to give contractual consent, they have an increased need for protection from social media platforms and advertisers. The purpose of this chapter is to explore the following research questions:

RQ1: What are the dark side issues related to social media, children, and privacy?
RQ2: What current laws and regulations are in place in the United States to protect consumers' private data as it relates to social media platforms?
RQ3: How has the European Union addressed issues related to social media and privacy?

This chapter is organized into five sections. Section 1 reviews ethical issues related to advertising and children and Section 2 discusses online privacy concerns. Section 3 provides an overview of current laws and regulations that impact children's privacy. Section 4 provides a case study focusing on Meta and the European Union's General Data Protection Regulation (GDPR). The chapter concludes with recommendations for future regulation relating to children's privacy and security in the United States. It ends with proposed solutions to the stated problems with respect to children as vulnerable consumers on social media.

Section 1: Concerns with Children and Advertising

Introduction

The relationship between children and advertising is complex. Although children have been exposed to advertising practices for decades, the primary medium of exposure to advertisements was television. Today, children experience millions of advertisements when using a variety of online platforms. Children are increasingly using social media apps, such as Instagram, TikTok, and YouTube, where they post and engage with content. Although 13 is the "minimum age to open an account on nearly every social media platform—TikTok, Instagram, X- formerly known as Twitter, Pinterest, Kik, YouTube, Snapchat, Facebook, and more—" they are easily bypassed (Graber, 2023). In fact, about 81% of parents in the United States allow their children under 11 years old to watch YouTube (De Veirman et al., 2019, p. 2). These platforms enable children to spread electronic word of mouth about their favorite brands and products. Advertisers welcome the increased presence of children online because "they are perceived as authentic and credible sources of information" (De Veirman et al., 2019, p. 5).

It has been long understood that children are unable to make the distinction between entertaining content and advertisements (Radesky et al., 2020, p. 2). Children's ability to critically think about or identify ads is undermined when they are "linked to rewards or embedded in trusted social networks or personalized digital platforms" (Radesky et al., 2020, p. 2). When children interact with content, their brain undergoes two key information processes. First, children must determine if the content in front of them is an ad or not. The second step, which is much more difficult, "involves the child's ability to recognize the persuasive intent of commercial messages, along with the capacity to apply that knowledge as a cognitive filter to moderate commercial influence" (Graff et al., 2012, p. 395). Brand placement appears to be a huge problem for children since this technique "embeds brands within an entertaining context, using subtle persuasion processes that distract attention away from the commercial message" (Owens et al., 2013, p. 203).

Research shows that young children, typically under the age of seven years, are slow to recognize the persuasive intent of advertisements (Radesky et al., 2020, p. 7). At this stage of their development, the "cognitive abilities, emotion regulation, and moral development" of children are still immature (De Veirman et al., 2019, p. 2). Children ages seven to eleven years old are only slightly better at discerning these practices, however, they "lack the abstract thinking skills that help individuals recognize advertising as a larger commercial concept" (Radesky et al., 2020, p. 2). It is not until children are around twelve years that they begin to identify television advertisements and their persuasive intent to influence behavior. Even as children begin to understand the persuasive intent, they are still vulnerable to advertising. Marketers have an easier time connecting with children because, at this stage of life, tweens are "still trying to figure out who they are, what they like, and who they want to be" (Holiday & Brinson, 2022, p. 77). This is why a common strategy in advertising that targets this age demographic reflects a "parasocial relationship with the brand spokesperson (e.g., Puma, Kylie Jenner)" and encourages tweens to consider products as extensions of their own identities (Holiday & Brinson, 2022, p. 78). A parasocial relationship in this scenario is defined as "the relationships consumers develop with media characters, making them important sources of information" (De Veirman et al., 2019, p. 3). Young children seek companionship with fun and likable characters so it is easy for them to form connections with social media characters, such as Tony the Tiger (De Veirman et al., 2019, p. 3). In turn, advertisers embed likable characters in children's movies or video games hoping that these parasocial relationships lead to the sale of endorsed products without children recognizing any persuasive intent.

Digital and Social Media Advertising

Children are spending more time than ever before engaging with nontraditional forms of media such as "the Internet, social media, user-created content, video games, mobile applications (apps), virtual or augmented reality, virtual assistants, and Internet-connected toys" (Radesky et al., 2020, p. 2). Children under eight years spend an average of one hour a day using mobile devices (Meyer et al., 2019, p. 32). The daily screen time for children aged 8–12 is an average of 5 hours and 33 minutes a day (Moyer, 2022). Additionally, advertisers spent approximately $343 billion on personalized social media advertisements in 2019 and are constantly increasing their ad budgets (Hayes et al., 2021, p. 16).

Ryan's World, a child influencer who has earned over 35.4 million subscribers by reviewing toys and products on YouTube, is a controversial illustration of the increased advertising presence on social media. Advertisers are utilizing child influencers, such as Ryan, who earned $22 million in 2018, because "in return for free promotional goods or payment, brands ask these influencers to endorse their products on their social media profiles" which reach millions of parents and children (De Veirman et al., 2019, p. 2). On social media, influencers include subtle advertisements in their usual, organic content. This format gives "their followers an insight into the brands they love and use in their daily life" without coming across as intrusive or pushy (De Veirman et al., 2019, p. 2). However, since children have yet to develop advertising literacy, they are unable to understand the persuasive intent of this sponsored content. These kids then can feel some mental health issues such as anxiety or negative emotions, such as feelings of inadequacy if they do not have so many or the right toys as these child influencers do. Kids simply cannot compute that these child influencers are in essence paid forms of communication intended to inform, persuade, or remind them (or their parents) to buy the items shown. Kids may also feel some jealousy and not understand these emotions. Some may even say that the parents are exploiting their children's names, images, and likenesses at risk of the child's current or future mental health.

Child advocacy groups have voiced their disapproval of this user-created content found on social media platforms and video-streaming services, such as TikTok, because of the "large amount of child-directed influencer marketing, [which is] often undisclosed" (Radesky et al., 2020, p. 2). Social media is a beacon for influencer marketing which is a "form of advertising when (1) influencers receive a compensation (free products or financial payment) and (2) advertisers have control over the content" (De Veirman et al., 2019, p. 2). Due to the seemingly authentic nature of this type of partnership, young social media users are most prone to follow influencers and make purchases based on influencer recommendations, as illustrated by Figure 8.1.

Children trust and look up to child influencers because of their shared interests and activities. As a result, child influencers are "perceived as very relatable and approachable, due to the highly personal content they post and the interactions they have with their followers" (De Veirman et al., 2019, p. 6). The content these influencers post provides their audience a glimpse into their lives so that they may be seen as peers. For example, Ryan's World does an excellent job of creating an online environment that fosters a friendly community for his subscribers. His content centers around "his daily routines, including the type of cereal he eats, the toys he plays with, and the places he goes to in his vlogs" (De Veirman et al., 2019, p. 6).

One significant issue with influencer marketing is that it allows brands to be integrated within content often without the influencer disclosing the commercial nature of their post. For example, an official complaint was filed with the Federal Trade Commission (FTC), accusing Ryan's World of deceiving children by promoting sponsored videos that imitate his organic content where even parents would struggle to identify the advertisement. The FTC prohibits this type of promotional content as endorsements must contain a "clear and conspicuous" disclosure that "is difficult to miss (i.e., easily noticeable) and easily understandable by ordinary consumers" (National Archives, 2023). This guideline is in place so that viewers are aware of the intent behind influencer reviews to make informed purchase decisions.

Another example of this new kind of advertising can be seen in games found in app stores. Gamified advertising rewards users for watching ads or buying products during the game. Children are more easily persuaded to consume content when engaging with "ad videos within gamified features, such as coin/token collection or ability to advance to the next level" (Meyer et al., 2019, p. 37). Their weak attention control and impulse inhibition only add to their susceptibility to "ads with highly salient (e.g., larger, sparkling) or novel features (e.g., hidden within a present) and may be less likely to wait for the X to appear to minimize a pop-up ad" (Meyer et al., 2019, p. 38). Further, free apps, which are more appealing to low-income children, have an increased prevalence of advertising and pop-up features that interrupt playing time (Meyer et al., 2019, p. 38). In sum, nontraditional forms of media are "inextricably connected with the

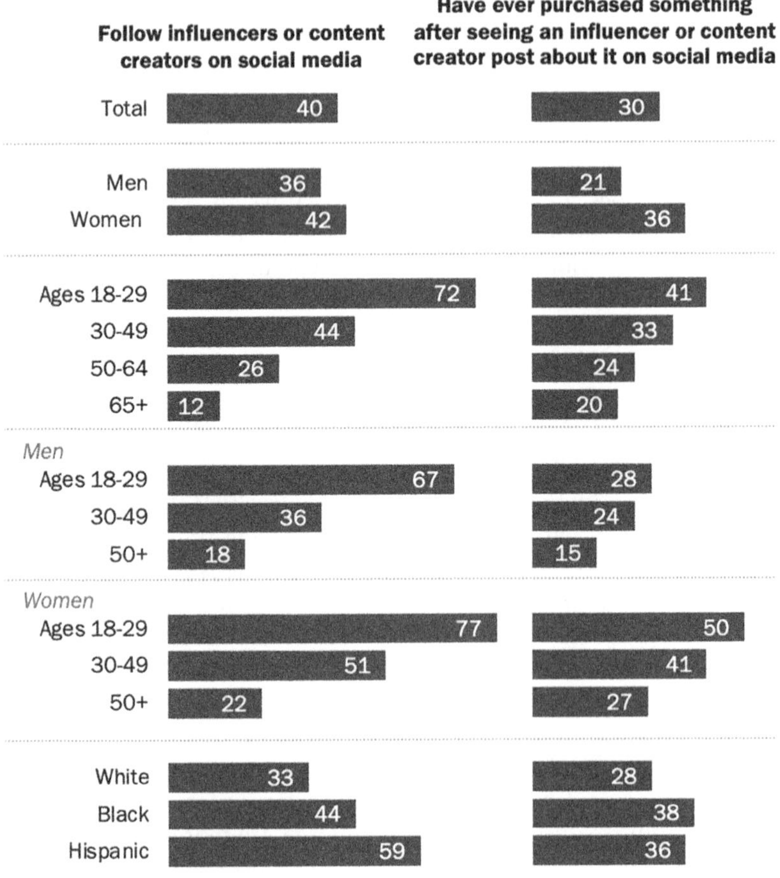

FIGURE 8.1 U.S. influencer marketing spend (2019–2024) (Oberlo).

Credit: For shopping, phones are common and influencers have become a factor—especially for young adults. Pew Research Center, Washington, D.C. (November 21, 2022)

entertainment itself (e.g., video game, licensed product, movie, or a television program) and often appears as part of the entertainment" (Owens et al., 2013, p. 197), making it difficult for children to discern the difference between advertising and content.

Personalization

Mobile and app platforms are consumed with personalized and embedded forms of advertising that complement interactive experiences (Meyer et al., 2019, p. 33). Personalization in advertising increases the rate at which consumers respond and interact online. Through this process, advertisers deliver personalized content to "individual homes based on identified viewers' online and location-based behaviors to present them with messages reflecting their interests, inclinations, and preferences" (Holiday & Brinson, 2022, p. 76). This method is more effective because it discourages consumers from turning away by presenting advertisements that are relevant and valuable to them. Although these messages look like traditional TV ads, addressable TV is so precise and sophisticated that it uses "data-mining techniques to find the most receptive eyes for each personalized message" (Holiday & Brinson, 2022, p. 77).

This type of advertising practice is harmful to children because they are even less able to recognize these ads. In the United States, children under the age of 13 are "somewhat protected from personalized advertising by the Children's Online Privacy Protection Act (COPPA), which limits data collection and behavioral targeting to young children" (Holiday & Brinson, 2022, p. 78). While television "advertising to young children in the United States has been regulated by the Federal Communications Commission since the 1970s," children are interacting more often with nontraditional forms which is more likely to cause an advanced level of harm (Meyer et al., 2019, p. 32). Although advertisers are not responsible for monitoring users' age restrictions on apps, they are aware that their ads are being pushed to this age demographic on these platforms. Children are being exploited by personalized ads on social media without consequence because these platforms are complex and largely unregulated.

Section 1 Conclusion

In summary, children have long been considered vulnerable consumers due to their cognitive inability to distinguish between entertaining content and advertisements (Radesky et al., 2020, p. 2). As brands and marketers continue to implement new strategies compatible with the

Internet, social media platforms, apps, and new technologies, children will continue to be increasingly exposed and potentially more vulnerable to advertisements. Personalized messaging and nontraditional media are under critical review as society debates whether this kind of content should be acceptable for children to interact with or if it should be better regulated to reduce potential harm. Children as online consumers have a complicated relationship with this new era of media because these platforms were not designed in ways that protect them from harm. The inadequate amount of legal protection intensifies the vulnerability of children and social media.

Section 2: Children and Privacy Concerns Online

Introduction

As we continue further into the twenty-first century, advertising on social media is rapidly changing and growing in complexity. Although most social media users have become accustomed to the personalized messaging seen online, increased concerns regarding the use and exploitation of private data are being voiced. Social media and other technology companies are struggling to determine the best way to address these privacy concerns without sacrificing the profit they earn by managing user data. While most people are focusing on how privacy issues impact the general consumer, children as an audience segment are often neglected as vulnerable consumers in the social media space

As discussed in the previous section, children are a vulnerable consumer group when it comes to advertising on social media. As children continue to navigate online apps, current advertising practices put them at risk for sharing sensitive information without their knowledge and potentially putting them in danger. This section serves to explore the privacy implications of advertising on social media as it relates to children. In this section, we first examine the relationship between advertising practices and private data, which is followed by a discussion of how major tech companies are responding to privacy concerns.

Advertising and Private Data

As children continue to engage with social media, they encounter a great risk of sharing private information online. Social media and other mobile apps require users to build online personas based on their real-life identities, preferences, and opinions. From the moment a child interacts online they begin to decide how much personal information they want to share with their friends and strangers. Although children see online activities as a source of fun and entertainment, advertisers have always viewed the Internet as a "mainstream commercial medium" (Montgomery et al., 2017, p. 2).

The ad industry uses big data to create new opportunities to track children's "behaviors and target them with personalized content and marketing messages based on individual profiles" (Montgomery et al., 2017, p. 1). Big data refers to "the data sets and analytical techniques in application that are so large and complex that they require advanced and unique data storage, management, analysis, and visualization technologies" (Montgomery et al., 2017, p. 2). Using technologies such as "cookies," which are pieces of code stored in web browsers, advertisers and marketers can track users as they move from site to site (Chen, 2021). Since the establishment of app stores, advertisers have used these invisible trackers to collect data about users' actions within apps and sell them to data brokers for more targeted messaging (Chen, 2021).

The more content children consume online the more likely advertisers will expand their data collection, tracking, and profiling techniques. Advances in technology and artificial intelligence make this process easier and quicker than ever. Advertisers can track users throughout the internet, regardless of what device they're using. Complex algorithms allow advertisers to personalize the user's experience, "alter what an individual sees in a newsfeed or other online content, and create advertising messages based on the user's interests, friends, and routine actions" (Montgomery et al., 2017, pp. 2–3). The prevalence of this data tracking has commanded approximately 50% of social media users to believe that they have little or no control over who can access their private information regarding online searches, as shown in Figure 8.2.

Based on these findings it can be determined that advertisers do not have to work too hard to access children's private data. As previously mentioned, social media relies on heavy disclosure of personal information, such as "hobbies, birthdates, and demographics" (Xie & Karan, 2019, p. 2). Any information, shared voluntarily or not, increases a privacy risk for children. While users can control how much personal information they share with their audience, advertisers rarely ask for permission before collecting users' data. Most children use the Internet daily and, perhaps unknown to their parents, many have social media accounts. Even though most social media platforms require users to be at least 13 years old, many kids find a way to access social media anyway.

Adults are also to blame for the exposure of minor's private information online. For instance, children are often present "in their parents' social media outlets, such as mommy blogs, which raises questions about whether children should be protected from their parents publishing intimate or private details of their lives without consent" (De Veirman et al.,

About half of Americans feel as if they have no control over who can access their online searches

% who say they feel ___ control over who can access the following types of their information

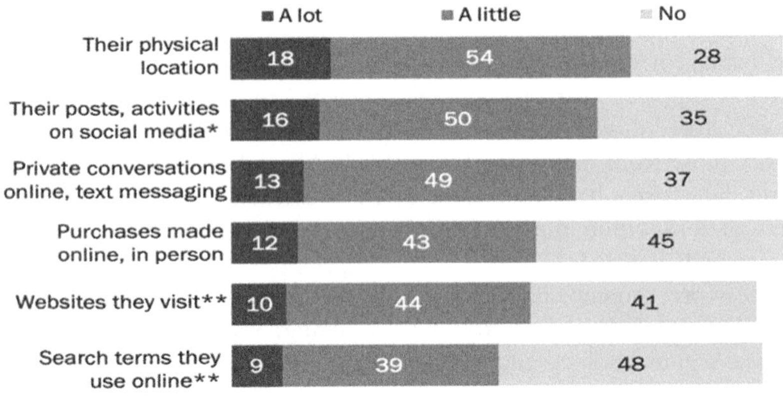

* Based on social media users.
** Based on internet users.
Note: Respondents were randomly assigned questions about how much control they feel they have over who can access different types of their information. Those who did not give an answer are not shown.
Source: Survey of U.S. adults conducted June 3-17, 2019.
"Americans and Privacy: Concerned, Confused and Feeling Lack of Control Over Their Personal Information"

PEW RESEARCH CENTER

FIGURE 8.2 How Americans feel about the control of their private data online (Pew Research Center, 2019).

Credit: Americans and privacy: concerned, confused and feeling lack of control over their personal information. Pew Research Center, Washington, D.C. (November 15, 2019)

2019, p. 11). Today the sharing of children's private information online has become the norm. From minors naively disclosing private details online to parents posting their children without legal consent, advertisers are given easy access to this consumer segment.

Company Responses to Privacy Concerns

Major tech companies have had to react to privacy concerns as consumers and the government have demanded a response. For example, in response to online privacy concerns, Apple and Google are beginning to rework their policies surrounding data collection (Chen, 2021). Specifically, Apple decided to implement tools into its products that block advertisers at the user's discretion. Google, which relies on digital ads, decided to "have it both ways by reinventing the system so it can continue aiming ads at people without exploiting access to their personal data" (Chen, 2021). However, these responses do not include actions to protect children—in fact, children are rarely part of the conversation.

Section 2 Conclusion

Advertisers and big technology companies are in a unique position where they have to address privacy concerns on a national stage if not an international stage. Social media users are speaking out against the use of cookies and other tracking technologies that store private data without their knowledge. As children continue to spend more time online, they are at an increased risk of disclosing sensitive information without knowledge of potential consequences.

Section 3: Laws and Regulations Relating to Children, Advertising, and Social Media

Introduction

The purpose of this section is to review and discuss the current laws and regulatory groups relating to children, advertising, private data, and social media. Although this chapter focuses on laws and potential social media regulations in the United States, it will also investigate regulations established by the European Union because they are more proactive in terms of tackling online privacy concerns. These findings will be used to infer how children could be better protected if laws and regulations were implemented to help ease privacy concerns on social media.

Current U.S. Regulatory Guidelines

The United States does not have a straightforward law or regulation to protect children's private data from advertising practices via social media. At time of this writing, the U.S. is considering a new federal bill called the Protecting Kids on Social Media Act (Fung, 2023). With this drafted bill, social media companies could be banned from allowing children under 13 years old make social media accounts or interact with other social media users; note however that kids would still be allowed to see content without having to log on (Fung, 2023).

Also, there are some existing guidelines that affect the privacy issues separately and allow one to infer what a potential, holistic law could look like. The FTC, the nation's consumer protection agency, has spent decades presiding over and giving guidance to numerous cases involving unfair and deceptive advertising practices. These guidelines pertain to the advertising industry as well as businesses that participate in advertising practices. When targeting children, there are certain "products and services you can't advertise to children, certain tactics you cannot use to market products or services that can be marketed to children, and certain restrictions and special opt-ins that must be met to market to children" as determined by the FTC (Knighton, 2022). A few of these guidelines are elaborated upon further in the text. They are based on precedents and general rulings the FTC has set throughout its history rather than explicit laws it enforces (Jennings & Engel, 2004):

1. **Limited unhealthy food marketing:** The United States considers child obesity to be a major problem, therefore, advertisers are required to restrict their promotion of "unhealthy, sugary or fatty foods to children" (Rampton, 2016). This rule only applies when specifically targeting children as an audience, "such as advertising a children's menu or children's toys or running ads on channels" likely to have youth viewership (Knighton, 2022). Advertisers attempt to avoid regulatory violations by choosing not to market to children directly, instead focusing on families and adults with the implication that children can consume the food as well. If children are targeted directly, then advertisers need to disclose both the healthy and unhealthy ingredients a product contains (Jennings & Engel, 2004).
2. **Mature content:** Although this should be obvious, it's important to note that it's the advertiser's responsibility to monitor their content on public platforms to ensure that it follows age-restricted guidelines. Advertisers cannot expose children to "nudity, sexual language, violence or other sensitive subjects via mobile advertisements" (Rampton, 2016). While advertisers should attempt to create child-friendly advertisements, if mature content is present then they can utilize "a legal-binding agreement that visitors to [their] site" must check before continuing to view the site (Knighton, 2022). This process provides proof that a business did not knowingly allow children to view their marketing content so that advertising regulations are not violated (Jennings & Engel, 2004).
3. **Data collection restrictions:** Due to the Children's Online Privacy Protection Rule (COPPA), which will be further discussed later in this chapter, advertisers cannot "collect personal data on anyone under the age of 13 in the United States" (Knighton, 2022). Although some data can be collected from teens aged 16 and above, this data is still limited to

information like their first name, state residence, and age. Information such as "addresses, last names, birthdates, and social security numbers" cannot be collected from children under the age of 18 (Rampton, 2016). The reason personal information is regulated is that data is very valuable to advertisers since "it informs businesses as to who their target audience should be and what tactics to use" (Knighton, 2022). Advertisers are prohibited from targeting children with marketing campaigns; therefore, this regulation includes restrictions on collecting their data.

4. **No contracts:** Minors, those under the age of 18, in the United States cannot legally enter a binding, contractual agreement. They cannot "be held financially responsible for services, making purchasing decisions or be held legally responsible for goods, services or purchases" (Rampton, 2016). Therefore, mobile applications that request users to agree to terms and conditions before accessing their service are considered invalid as it applies to minors. Although parents are expected to agree to these contracts on behalf of their children, the ease with which minors can bypass age restrictions online further complicates and discredits this regulation. This example is also demonstrative of the issues that relate to parents, children, and social media (Jennings & Engel, 2004).

Regulating Agencies and Social Media Law

The FTC's mission is to "create and enforce safeguards that protect the American consumer against unfair, deceptive, fraudulent, and otherwise harmful practices in the marketplace" (Knighton, 2022). This agency is tasked with enforcing advertising and marketing regulations and establishing fines when deemed necessary. When it comes to advertising practices, the FTC pays close attention to "advertisements that make claims which may be hard for even an adult consumer to evaluate" in addition to any content regarding health and safety (Knighton, 2022). The FTC's main consideration when determining if violations have occurred is the extent to which consumers could potentially be harmed or injured.

Although social media is still considered uncharted territory, the FTC has issued a few general guidelines that advertisers can reference. The FTC recommends that advertisers evaluate their social media ads with the same criteria they would for traditional platforms, such as broadcast television or websites. One of the main standards that the FTC enforces involves the disclosure of advertisements. The FTC states that if the disclosure is "required to prevent an ad from being misleading, such disclosure must appear in a clear and conspicuous manner" (American Bar Association, 2017). Further, if a disclosure is needed it is to appear in a location and use wording that an average consumer can understand. Although this guideline protects the general social media user, it further reinforces the idea that advertisements may be particularly difficult to identify, especially for children.

Another regulatory group that oversees advertising practices in the United States is the Children's Advertising Review Unit (CARU) of the Council of Better Business Bureaus. The CARU, which was formed in 1974, "looks after the children's section of the advertising industry's self-regulatory system" and frequently produces "Self-Regulatory Guidelines for Children's Advertising" (Knighton, 2022). Despite being a self-regulatory group and having no legally binding power, CARU's guidelines are compatible with the COPPA as it relates to the practice of collecting private data from children under the age of 13.

The FTC and CARU have provided very little direction on how to address advertising concerns specifically related to social media. Currently, social media as a platform is largely unregulated because federal laws and regulatory groups have not been able to keep up with the constant evolution and complexity of this medium. However, "social media law" is a growing area of law that seeks to address advertising, children, and privacy concerns. Social media law includes both civil and criminal considerations and covers a variety of legal concerns that relate to social media, such as "privacy, including the rights of both social media users and third parties . . . .; defamation; advertising law; and intellectual property (IP) law" (Winston & Strawn LLP, n.d.). This area of law focuses on consumer rights rather than protecting corporations.

Social media law is very new and vastly underdeveloped. Additionally, current advertising laws and guidelines authored by the FTC and CARU are not advanced enough to account for the needs of children as consumers, privacy concerns, and the complexity of social media as an uncharted platform. In recent years, there has been an increased call for lawmakers to create legislation that would better protect social media privacy, despite having achieved little success. As of now, there are "no national comprehensive social media privacy laws" but there are advertising laws and laws pertaining to children that can be applied to the larger issue at hand (FindLaw, 2018). In the next section, current laws relevant to protecting children's private data from harmful advertising practices via social media will be examined.

Current U.S. Laws and Regulations

Although no longer in effect as it was originally implemented, one of the most famous pieces of Congressional legislation that attempted to regulate the Internet was the **Communications Decency Act of 1996 (CDA).**

The CDA "was enacted as part of Title V of the Telecommunications Act of 1996, to regulate the internet and online communications" (Minc, n.d.). The legislation directly addressed children intending to prevent them from viewing "obscene or indecent" content online. Moreover, the CDA ruled "the knowing transmission of obscene messages to minors and transmission of material that depicted or described" organs involving sexual activities as a federal, criminal offense in the United States (Minc, n.d.).

The Communications Decency Act was an influential piece of legislation. Nevertheless, after a 1997 Supreme Court case ruled it unconstitutional, **Section 230** was salvaged. Section 230 of the Communications Decency Act is one of the most significant pieces of Internet legislation in the United States and is seen by many as the "twenty-six words that created the Internet" (Minc, n.d.). Under Section 230, third parties cannot sue internet service providers, such as Google and Facebook, for content found on their platforms. This law aims to protect technology and social media companies because it "shields companies that can host trillions of messages from being sued into oblivion by anyone who feels wronged by something someone else has posted—whether their complaint is legitimate or not" (Ortutay, 2023). Section 230 is often credited for the rapid evolution and growth of the Internet because it enabled internet companies to develop without the fear of being held liable for the content their users publish on their platforms.

Section 230 applies to the topic of this chapter because it "created a climate in which the Facebooks of the world came to believe that anything bad happening to their users was someone else's fault" (LoMonte, 2018). When it comes to interfering in matters occurring on their platforms, such as the collection of children's private data, it has been "rare to see a social media company pay consequences for its actions—or inactions—because of a broad immunity shield" spurred by Section 230. By creating a space where only the original creators of harmful content are liable, a precedent was established that protected internet companies from taking responsibility when issues arose. Additionally, for a long time, internet companies convinced Congress and users that the distribution of harmful content is so vast that companies like Facebook cannot possibly regulate and thus be responsible for those consequences. However, it's important to note that these companies can be held liable for "breaching promises made to customers in their terms of service" since this does not require treating the site as a publisher (LoMonte, 2018). This stipulation will be addressed later on in this chapter.

The next regulation we discuss is the COPPA. It sets specific requirements that operators of websites and online services that are directed to children must follow. The rule applies to operators that "have actual knowledge that they are collecting personal information online from a child under 13 years of age" (Vedova, n.d.). This law was enacted in 1998 but was updated in 2013 to reflect the rapid changes in technology and internet capabilities. The FTC oversees this law and administers violations that "can result in law enforcement actions, including civil penalties, so compliance counts" (Vedova, 2013). COPPA puts parents in control of the collection of children's data and aims to protect children's privacy and safety online.

Since social media platforms are considered "mobile apps that send or receive information online" it falls into the category of websites or online services (Vedova, 2013). This stipulation also applies to apps that deliver behaviorally targeted ads. The FTC has a variety of factors that determine whether or not an online service targets children under 13, such as "the subject matter of the site or service, visual and audio content, the use of animated characters or other child-oriented activities and incentives, the age of models, the presence of child celebrities or celebrities who appeal to kids, ads on the site or service that are directed to children, and other reliable evidence about the age of the actual or intended audience" (Vedova, 2013). Under COPPA, an online service "collects" data if personal information is submitted for use to the child-directed site or on behalf of another site. This includes collecting personal information through third parties like plug-ins, ad networks, or cookies. A child's personal information refers to their name, home address, email address, and phone number as well as more detailed data such as their social security number or "a photo, video, or audio file containing a child's image or voice" (Vedova, 2013).

For years, COPPA has been considered the most reliable source to ensure companies adhere to advertising regulations regarding children. The best way to comply with COPPA is to post a privacy policy on the homepage or wherever personal data is being collected by children. The privacy policy should "clearly and comprehensively describe how personal information collected online from kids under 13 is handled" (Vedova, 2013). A key component of this rule is the emphasis on parental rights and responsibilities to the child. Under COPPA, websites and online services are required to give parents direct notice of "information practices before collecting information from their kids" (Vedova, 2013). In addition, the privacy policy must tell parents that only necessary and relevant information will be collected. Under COPPA, parents have the right to "review their child's personal information, direct you to delete it, and refuse to allow any further collection or use of the child's information" (Vedova, 2013). The most interesting element of this rule is that parents can deny disclosure to third parties except if it's part of the service (i.e., on social media platforms).

The next regulation that is discussed is the updated **Self-Regulatory Guidelines for Children's Advertising** published by CARU. The new guidelines came into effect on January 1, 2022. Since 2014 was the last updated draft of CARU's guidelines, these changes "directly reflect the new online and digital focus of children's advertising that has blossomed over the past decade, with the changes addressing digital media, influencer marketing, and in-app and in-game advertising, among other updates" (Naydonov et al., 2022). Although the guidelines were updated, the core mission of CARU has stayed the same. CARU's goal is to protect children by advocating for "truthful and clear advertising that does not depict or promote inappropriate or unsafe behavior to children" (Naydonov et al., 2022). The regulatory group has a firm stance on the "special responsibility" advertisers have to protect "children who have limited knowledge, experience, sophistication, and maturity" (Naydonov et al., 2022)

The updated Self-Regulatory Guidelines for Children's Advertising provide changes that advertisers should keep in mind when targeting children with marketing practices. For targeted advertising, the term "children" has been broadened to refer to those under the age of 13 whereas previously the guidelines covered ages 12 and younger. The CARU has clarified the factors that determine when advertisements are "primarily directed" toward children to include: "(1) subject matter; (2) visual or audio content; (3) use of child-oriented animated characters, child-oriented activities, or incentives; (4) age of models; (5) presence of child celebrities who appeal to children; (6) language or other characteristics; (7) competent and reliable empirical evidence regarding audience compositions; and (8) evidence regarding the intended audience" (Naydonov et al., 2022).

The CARU also updated its guidelines to reflect the growing amount of time children are spending on smartphones. A new section has been added to concentrate on in-app advertising and purchases. As standard, the new guideline encourages advertisers to avoid deceptive, harmful, or manipulative advertising in mobile apps but extends to "[include] 'deceptive door openers' or 'social pressure or validation' to encourage ad viewing or in-app/in-game purchases" (Naydonov et al., 2022). The new rule states that digital advertisements must provide a clear, easy way for a child to dismiss or exit the ad. Lastly, this section establishes that mobile ads, applications, and games that require in-app "purchases must make it clear that the purchase involves real-world money" (Naydonov et al., 2022).

The CARU revised the definitions for some of the guideline's most commonly used wording. For instance, to better explain how information must be presented in advertising, the words "clear" and "conspicuous" were altered. "Clear" refers to words that are "easily understandable by ordinary children" and "conspicuous" means words "presented in a manner that is easily noticeable, i.e., difficult to miss, by ordinary children" (Naydonov et al., 2022). The updated guideline reinforces the idea that there should be increased transparency in advertising. The CARU confirmed that the appropriateness of disclosures will vary depending on the age of the target audience since there are various stages of brain development present for children 13 and under.

Although these rules are followed by most advertisers, the CARU is a self-regulating group so their guidelines are not legally binding. Nevertheless, the CARU "has the power to challenge advertisements that it believes violate its Children's Advertising Guidelines and issue a decision regarding that purported violation" (Naydonov et al., 2022). Those who ignore the CARU guidelines risk receiving attention from the FTC. As calls for advertising legislation become more frequent the CARU will likely be the main authority for evaluating guidelines.

Although this bill has yet to be passed by Congress, it's worth noting that lawmakers are attempting to make social media safer for children. In May of 2023, Senators Richard Blumenthal (D-CT) and Marsha Blackburn (R-TN) reintroduced the Kids Online Safety Act (KOSA) with slight alterations to the original 2022 version (Fraser, 2023). KOSA, a bipartisan bill aimed to combat the negative mental health problems that children and adolescents attribute in part to social media, has gained the support of nearly half of the Senate. This bill would require social media "platforms to affirmatively mitigate key, defined harms—depression and suicidal ideation, eating disorders, addiction, bullying, sexual exploitation, and the sale of illicit drugs to minors" (Fraser, 2023). Social media companies would have to address these harms by modifying their platforms' design and the type of content pushed to minors without approval. Parents are in favor of this bill because it provides "more tools to protect private information, disable addictive product features, allow minors to opt out of manipulative algorithmic recommendations, and, most importantly, enable the strongest safety settings by default" (Fraser, 2023). What makes KOSA so promising is that it holds "online platforms accountable through annual, independent auditing" (Fraser, 2023). KOSA has gained support from lawmakers across both party lines, including President Biden. However, Big Tech companies are fighting the bill due to their unwillingness to "to update their business models to prioritize health and wellbeing over profits and ad revenue" (Fraser, 2023).

In sum, parents and young people are calling for lawmakers to address this mental health emergency that children are experiencing due to the addictive and invasive nature of social media. Whether or not KOSA is passed, it seems that political leaders are finally ready to begin a serious conversation about social media concerns.

State Initiatives

Despite the lack of comprehensive privacy laws in the United States, the next few pages highlight five states that have consumer data privacy laws going into effect sometime in 2023. One of the most significant regulations and the one that sets the gold standard for digital privacy law in the United States is the **California Privacy Rights Act (CPRA)**, also known as Proposition 24. The CPRA is a ballot measure that was approved by California voters in November 2020. It amends the **California Consumer Privacy Act (CCPA)**, which was signed into law in 2018, and adds "new additional privacy protections that began on January 1, 2023" (State of California Office of the Attorney General, n.d.). The CPRA classifies personal information as anything that relates to or can be associated with a particular person or household. Sensitive personal information is related to things such as a user's social security, diverse license, precise geolocation, financial card, or genetic information (State of California Office of the Attorney General, n.d.).

Proposition 24 gives California residents more control over their personal data and how businesses use it. The CPRA gives California residents the right to know what personal information advertisers have collected from them and how they intend to use it. Under this law, California residents also have the right to ask for their data to be deleted, with exceptions. Users can also opt out of the sale or sharing of their personal data "including via a user-enabled global privacy control" (State of California Office of the Attorney General, n.d.). The CPRA gives users the right to correct any inaccurate information advertisers have about them, as well as the right to request that businesses use their sensitive data for a limited number of reasons. A key stipulation of this law states that businesses cannot require users to "waive these rights, and any contract provision that says [users must] waive these rights is unenforceable" (State of California Office of the Attorney General, n.d.).

Another law that went into effect on January 1, 2023, is the **Virginia Consumer Data Protection Act (VCDPA)**. The VCPA is the second law in the United States, after California, to enact consumer privacy legislation. Similar to the CPRA, this law gives consumers the right to access and delete their information from businesses both off and online. In addition, it "requires companies to conduct data protection assessments related to processing personal data for targeted advertising and sales purposes" (Bloomberg Law, n.d.). The law also has some restrictions about de-identified data, "or data modified to no longer directly identify individuals from whom the data were derived" (Bloomberg Law, n.d.). Interestingly, the VCDPA only applies to businesses that satisfy one of two thresholds, both focusing on the number of users that a company has access to. For the VCDPA to apply, advertisers must collect the personal data of at least 100,000 users in a year, as well as "the personal data of at least 25,000 consumers, while deriving over 50 percent of gross revenue from the sale of that data" (Bloomberg Law, n.d.).

The VCDPA has a few limitations and areas for confusion. First, the law focuses on people who conduct business in the state and develop products or services that target Virginia residents. However, the legislation fails to define what "target" means. The VCDPA also neglects to explain how the state will "enforce consumer requests to delete personal data that has been incorporated into an automated decision-making algorithm," which is an issue seen in most states' consumer privacy legislation (Bloomberg Law, n.d.). As for targeted advertising, the term "personal data" does not refer to "information that could be linked to a consumer's device" to authorize the exercise of cookies and IDFAs (Identifiers for Advertisers) (Bloomberg Law, n.d.). Most important to this chapter, the VCDPA mandates that businesses that collect children's data must comply with COPPA.

The next state that recently introduced a consumer privacy law is Colorado. The **Colorado Privacy Act (CPA)**, which went into effect on July 1, 2023, "gives consumers the right to know what personal information is being collected about them, why it is being collected, and how it will be used" (Secure Privacy, 2022). Furthermore, it gives consumers the right to oversee how their personal information is used, correct any inaccurate information, and delete it as desired. Essentially, the CPA gives consumers the right to opt out of the collection of their data as it's used for targeted advertising, personal data sales, or profiling (Secure Privacy, 2022). Consumers can request a copy of their personal data; however, they can only do this no more than twice a year.

The CPA considers "consumers" to be those operating as individuals which applies to the parents or guardians of children under the age of 13. It defines "personal data" as anything that can reasonably be traced back to an individual. It singles out the personal data of a known child to refer to "sensitive data" as well as other classifications, such as "racial or ethnic origin, religious beliefs, a mental or physical health condition or diagnosis" among others (Secure Privacy, 2022). To ensure that businesses comply with the CPA, they must "provide a clear and conspicuous notice informing consumers that they have the right to opt out of targeted advertising and sales of their personal data" as well as obtain user's consent before collecting sensitive data (Secure Privacy, 2022). The Colorado Attorney General's Office did not set a fine for each violation, however, detected deceptive trade practices under the CPA can call for up to a $20,000 fine per violation.

The **Connecticut Data Privacy Act (CTDPA)** is another law that went into effect on July 1, 2023. Like the other recently introduced consumer privacy laws, the CTDPA grants consumers new rights to their private data and explains how businesses must comply with the new regulations. The CTDPA gives consumers the right to know if a business has access to their private data, the right to access and delete said information, the right to correct false information, and the right to obtain a portable, technological copy of their private data (Stransky et al., 2022). The most notable consumer right given by this law is the right to opt out of the processing of their private data "to the extent it relates to targeted advertising, the sale of personal data, or certain types of profiling that have significant impact on the consumer" (Stransky et al., 2022). By 2025, Controllers are required to provide consumers with a mechanism that allows them to consent or opt out of the processing of their private data. The CTDPA refers to "Controllers" as businesses that process Connecticut residents' personal data and "Processors" as "the third-party service providers that assist Controllers in data processing activities" (Stransky et al., 2022). The term "targeted advertising" refers to the Controller's ability to create personalized advertisements based on the user's data that has been collected over time on one or many platforms.

The CTDPA also has classifications for what businesses this law applies to. For instance, only Controllers that produce goods or services in Connecticut and target that state's residents during the previous calendar year are expected to follow these regulations. These businesses must have either collected and processed the personal information of over 75,000 residents or "controlled or processed personal data of at least 25,000 consumers and derived over 25% of their gross revenue from the sale of personal data" (Stransky et al., 2022). Similar to other laws of the same category, the CTDPA requires that Controllers provide consumers with a reasonably clear and distinct privacy notice that speaks to their data processing intentions. This information should refer to "categories of personal data collected and processed, purposes of processing, categories of personal data shared with third parties, categories of recipients" (Stransky et al., 2022). Overall, the CTDPA takes a lot of cues from California and Virginia regarding consumer privacy rights.

The last consumer privacy law is the **Utah Consumer Privacy Act (UCPA)** which went into effect on December 31, 2023. The UCPA provides consumers with rights to their personal data. Consumers can access and delete the personal data that the Controller, or business, collected. Residents of Utah can also obtain a copy of their data in a "portable" format provided by the Controller. Lastly, consumers can opt out of the collection of their data via the disclosure by a Controller for practices such as targeted advertising. Controllers must respond to requests within 45 days, however, they can charge a fee for the second request for information made within a year (Berry et al., 2022).

Although similar to its predecessors, the UCPA is thought to have lighter obligations for businesses to adhere to. This law applies to businesses that target products or services to residents of the state, and "have annual revenues of at least $25 million" (Berry et al., 2022). In addition, for this law to apply, businesses must collect or process the personal data of at least 100,000 Utah residents or acquire "over 50 percent of gross revenue from the "sale" of personal data and control or process personal data of 25,000 or more consumers" (Berry et al., 2022). Controllers are still required to post privacy notices about the intended use of consumers' personal data, however, they only need to provide an opportunity to opt out of the use of sensitive information rather than a choice to opt-in to collect such data.

These five state laws have many similarities and differences. For instance, each state defines the "sale" of personal data a little differently. California, Colorado, and Connecticut refer to "sale" as something that requires financial and other valuable considerations (Jaeger, 2023). On the other hand, Virginia and Utah refer to a "sale" as "the exchange of personal data 'for monetary consideration by a controller to a third party'" (Jaeger, 2023). Therefore, it's unclear if cookie data used for targeting advertising practices would be applicable in this context. These state laws also vary in the function of universal opt-out mechanisms. California, Colorado, and Connecticut recognize universal opt-out rights for consumers instead of "having to make individual opt-out requests through each website" (Jaeger, 2023). By contrast, Virginia does not enforce this requirement and Utah does not address this condition. Overall, these five laws have attempted to provide guidelines for consumer privacy laws but have taken slightly different approaches.

While these five state laws center around private consumer data, Illinois has become the first state to sign a child labor law that specifically focuses on kids' influencers, social media apps, and privacy concerns. **S.B. 1782**, which goes into effect on July 1, 2024, "will entitle child influencers to a percentage of earnings based on how often they appear on video blogs or online content that generates at least 10 cents per view" (Savage, 2023). The content must be created in the state of Illinois and the child will have to be present in at least at least 30% of the content in a 30-day period. This law addresses the concern that many parents have created large followings on social media that earn profit based on the presence of their children without setting aside any of the profit for their children. S.B. 1782 ensures that child influencers, "which covers children under the age of 16 featured in monetized online platforms," will have access to a trust account containing gross earnings from their appearances once they turn 18, or else the child can sue (Savage, 2023).

The legislation intends to protect child influencers from having their private information exploited for monetary gain. For instance, controversial social media content posted by parents features "intimate details of their children's lives—grades, potty training, illnesses, misbehaviors, first periods—for countless strangers to view" (Savage, 2023). This seems like oversharing to some and could bring some unwanted bullying to the child, especially as this content tends to have a long-lasting digital footprint. And even later, when the child is an adult, they often do not have the account settings to delete the embarrassing or unwanted content. This type of content usually becomes the focus of many sponsorship deals which often brings in tens of thousands of dollars. Paid advertising on social media has become a new source of income for many families but it comes at the exploitation of children working in these digital environments. Unlike traditional entertainment settings, such as the movie and music industries, parents are not obligated to set aside earnings for their child stars. S.B. 1782 aims to rectify this problem by requiring parents to maintain records of their kids' appearances on monetized social media platforms.

Section 3 Conclusion

This section provides an overview of the current state of the country's regulations on privacy and social media. However, it is important to note that the majority of the laws just mentioned do not specifically include protection for children. These regulations, especially the five that go into effect in 2023, provide a solid foundation for the future of online data privacy and targeted advertising regulations. Additionally, S.B. 1782 offers insight into how other states might begin to protect child influencers online, paying close attention to privacy concerns and financial exploitation.

Section 4: Case Study

Meta and the GDPR

This section discusses Meta (parent company of Facebook, Instagram, and WhatsApp) and the European Union's General Data Protection Regulation (GDPR) as a case study that could be a potential model piece of legislation for protecting consumers' private information while using online platforms. Although this case study does specifically involve children, we include this case to demonstrate how social media companies can be held liable for the harm their platforms cause and believe that children could be better protected through similar government reactions that incorporate children.

In the last five years, Meta, which changed its name from Facebook in 2021 and became the parent company of Facebook, Instagram, and WhatsApp, has weathered a rocky relationship between the United States government and the European Union. Although Meta had previously been held in high esteem as an innovator of the digital world, the social media company soon fell into hot water regarding major privacy issues (Satariano, 2023a, 2023b). This public relations disaster started in 2018 with the infamous Cambridge Analytica scandal. For the first time, Meta CEO Mark Zuckerberg was brought in to testify in front of top officials on both sides of the Atlantic to address their privacy concerns (Watson, 2018).

In 2018 it was discovered that Cambridge Analytica, a British political data firm, collected the personal information of up to 87 million Facebook profiles. The firm, which was founded by Stephen K. Bannon and Robert Mercer, a wealthy Republican donor, hired Alexander Kogan, an outside researcher, to obtain the data. Their intent was to use Facebook data to "identify the personalities of individual American voters and influence their behavior" (Frenkel & Rosenberg, 2018). This psychographic modeling, a questionable method, was done in support of the 2016 Trump campaign. Through Kogan, Cambridge Analytica "paid users small sums to take a personality quiz and download an app, which would scrape some private information from their profiles and from those of their friends" (Frenkel & Rosenberg, 2018). This method was developed by data scientists at Cambridge University. It was supposed to reveal information about a user that even their close family would know, however, many debated the effectiveness of this method.

Although this technique was allowed at the time, Meta did not alert users that their data was being harvested, which violated laws in Britain and multiple states in the United States (i.e., states that currently enforce data privacy laws, such as the five previously mentioned). Kogan told Meta and the sampled "app's users that he was collecting information for academic purposes, not for a political data firm" with ties to Trump's 2016 campaign (Frenkel & Rosenberg, 2018). However, Meta did not attempt to question how this information was being used. This event occurred around the same time that the Facebook platform was accused of spreading fake news and Russian propaganda. At this time, the United States was investigating "how Russian actors infiltrated the platform by placing ads and posts to influence the 2016 election" (Frenkel & Kang, 2018). Additionally, a similar issue arose in England as British lawmakers were looking into how the Facebook app was influencing "fake news and Russian meddling in the country's referendum to leave the European Union" (Frenkel & Rosenberg,

2018). After numerous Congressional hearings and investigations by law enforcement, Meta admitted that its platform was used by outside forces to sway voters. Cambridge Analytica had harvested "millions of Facebook users through an app offering a personality test, then gave it to a service promising to use vague and sophisticated techniques to influence voters" (Duffy, 2022). Although these psychographic profiles were not generated by Meta itself, the technology company still failed to protect users' data and did not inform users of this issue once it became aware.

The Cambridge Analytica scandal exposed a major weakness in the design of the Facebook app. The social media company disclosed a "vulnerability in its search and account recovery functions that it said could have exposed "most" of its 2 billion users to having their public profile information harvested" (Frenkel & Kang, 2018). The application's search and account recovery function was designed so that anyone who had prior information about another user, such as a phone number or email address, could abuse the system by secretly harvesting their public profile information (Frenkel & Kang, 2018). To rectify the issue, Meta pledged to limit the types of data that outside businesses could collect from users. Additionally, outside businesses were prohibited from using the app to gather information related to users' religious and political beliefs. As a result, users now have the ability "to give permission before an app can collect information beyond their names and addresses" (Frenkel & Kang, 2018). Meta also agreed to "stop using third-party data from companies such as Experian and Acxiom to help supplement its own data for ad targeting" (Frenkel & Kang, 2018). In an effort to appease U.S. regulators and members of Congress, Meta agreed to implement new privacy policies that were easier for users to understand.

This scandal established the largest crisis Meta had experienced in its 14-year history and negatively affected the public opinion of policymakers and consumers. Senators were supporting calls for informing users about how their data is being shared and secured. Consumers demanded to know how the social media company planned to earn back their trust and reassure them that their data wasn't being misused. Although Meta deflected blame when the news first broke, as an executive tweeted that the information link was not a "data breach" since "no systems were infiltrated, no passwords or information were stolen or hacked," the company eventually acknowledged that it should have better-secured user data (Frenkel & Rosenberg, 2018).

However, this distinction made the situation appear worse for Meta. Since numerous companies have fallen victim to data breaches, especially around this time period, this reality would have fared better with public opinion. What happened with Cambridge Analytica, on the other hand, reflected the intended purpose of their app. The platform's systems were not infiltrated; rather this scandal reflected "Facebook's systems working as designed: data was amassed, data were extracted, and data was exploited" (Wong, 2019). Even after the crisis, phone numbers were used for non-security purposes. It was evident that the social media company did not have a true desire to address privacy concerns and was more worried about protecting its market share amid the controversy (Wong, 2019).

Nevertheless, Meta answered for their negligence with several monetary fines. For instance, the FTC and Meta agreed to a $5 billion settlement as a result of the Cambridge Analytica scandal and years of mishandling of privacy concerns. However, it is worth noting that although this fine was the largest in FTC history, it only accounts for about a month's worth of revenue for the social media company (Fung, 2019). Another aspect of the settlement required independent members of Meta's board to form a privacy oversight committee. The purpose of this committee is to ensure that Meta complies with FTC regulations or they'll "risk being held personally liable" (Fung, 2019). Additionally, outside assessments of Meta's privacy practices must be left to the auditor's own investigation instead of relying on materials from the company (Fung, 2019).

The same day, the FTC released news of their settlement, the Securities and Exchange Commission (SEC) announced its charges against Meta. The settlement required Meta to pay $100 million "for making misleading disclosures regarding the risk of misuse of Facebook user data" (The Securities and Exchange Commission, 2019). According to the SEC's press release on the matter, Meta had known about the Cambridge Analytica incident in 2015. Meta claimed that they had inquired about the data at the time, however, once Cambridge Analytica said that they were not using the data and had deleted it, Meta did not see a reason to investigate further (Watson, 2018). From 2015 to 2018, Meta spoke about the potential for user data misuse "as merely hypothetical when Facebook knew that a third-party developer had actually misused Facebook user data" (The Securities and Exchange Commission, 2019). The situation was made worse by the fact that Meta "had no specific policies or procedures in place to assess the results of their investigation for the purposes of making accurate disclosures in Facebook's public filings" (The Securities and Exchange Commission, 2019). This denial of wrongdoing and failure to implement a proper disclosure process led to the SEC issuing this monetary fine.

Meta also received criticism across the Atlantic. After the U.K.'s Information Commissioner's Office (ICO) investigated the company for its role in the use of social media data to advance political purposes, Meta agreed to pay about a $643,000 fine (Zialcita, 2019). The ICO determined that the Cambridge Analytica scandal reflected Meta's failure to keep their user's personal information secure, thus causing the company to breach data protection laws. The fine was issued after the social media company went through multiple rounds of appeals and more than a year of litigation with the ICO. Since the Cambridge Analytica data was collected in 2015, the ICO imposed the maximum possible penalty under the Data Protection Act 1998. Despite the monetary fine, it was agreed that Meta wouldn't have to admit any liability and could "retain documents disclosed during the appeal to use in its own investigation into Cambridge Analytica" (Zialcita, 2019). This is yet another example of laws or settlements attempting to protect social media companies rather than completely holding them accountable for the harm they cause consumers.

The last settlement came almost five years after the Cambridge Analytica scandal. Last December, Meta agreed to pay $725 million "to settle a longstanding class action lawsuit" regarding the Cambridge Analytica controversy (Duffy, 2022). This lawsuit was filed on behalf of Facebook users who were affected by third-party access to their data. An estimated "250 and 280 million people may be eligible for payments as part of the class action settlement" (Duffy, 2022). The lawsuit required hundreds of hours of depositions involving current and former Meta employees, as well as examining millions of pages of relevant documents. As part of the settlement, Meta did not have to admit any wrongdoings, similar to the ICO's ruling.

While Meta desperately tried to keep public approval in early 2018, the Cambridge Analytica scandal wasn't the only issue that the social media company was worried about. About a month after the world learned about the British data leak, the European Union implemented a landmark data privacy law and started an investigation into Meta's privacy practices. The European Union's GDPR set the standard for privacy protection policies worldwide. The GDPR "is a comprehensive data privacy law that applies to organizations that collect, store, or hold personal data belonging to data subjects in EU member states" (Pop, 2022). Like other definitions, the European Commission defines personal data as any information that identifies a specific individual. Organizations must comply with the GDPR if they operate, sell goods or services, or monitor the behavior of citizens within the EU. The GDPR has strict requirements for processing personal information, and violators of the law face "penalties as high as 4% of global annual revenues" (Browne, 2023).

The Irish Data Protection Commission's (DPC) investigation into Meta, which began the day the GDPR went into effect in 2018, ended at the beginning of 2023. As a result, "the Irish privacy regulator concluded [Meta's] advertising and data handling practices were in breach of EU privacy laws" (Browne, 2023). The case was about "how Meta receives legal permission from users to collect their data for personalized advertising" (Satariano, 2023). The main issue revolved around Meta's terms of service agreement that included language that essentially required users to allow the app access to their data to be used for personalized advertisements without providing alternative options. When downloading Meta platforms, such as Facebook, Instagram, WhatsApp, and Messenger, this lengthy statement must be accepted before users can enjoy the app's services. The ruling determined that "placing the legal consent within the terms of service essentially forced users to accept personalized ads," thus violating the GDPR (Satariano, 2023). Authority over this case was given to Ireland's data privacy board since it acts as Meta's main regulator and Dublin serves as the social media company's European headquarters.

This case represents a major setback for Meta regarding privacy regulations and has huge financial implications. The company was ordered to pay two fines amounting to about $414 million because of GDPR violations. Meta was given three months to comply with the verdict, however, Ireland's DPC didn't specify what this entails. The worst-case scenario for Meta would be to cease collecting users' data for personalized advertisements. The company would probably need to "re-engineer its service to silo off most data it collects from European users, or stop serving them entirely" (Schechner, 2021). If users are given the choice of whether they want their data collected for targeted promotions then Meta would likely lose a lot of its advertising business. User data, "such as what videos on Instagram prompt a person to stop scrolling, or what types of links a person clicks when browsing Facebook feeds," is extremely valuable to advertisers because it helps them gauge an individual's purchasing interests (Satariano, 2023). If a large segment of social media users decides not to share their data, this will be detrimental to Meta's advertising business, especially since the European Union is one of its largest markets.

Before this latest case, Meta was already experiencing a drop in advertising revenue due to a change introduced by Apple. In 2021, Apple gave iPhone users the ability to decide if they wanted to block advertisers from tracking their data. Surveys estimate that the majority of users have declined tracking permissions, costing Meta "about $10 billion in 2022" (Satariano, 2023). It can be assumed that the same decision will be made if users are able to deny the collection of their data for personalized ads. This judgment by the European Union "puts 5 to 7 percent of Meta's overall advertising revenue at risk" and has serious implications for other companies of the same nature operating out of the EU (Satariano, 2023).

This ruling will likely be applied to companies like Google, Apple, and X/The former Twitter since their European headquarters are also in Dublin.

These companies will likely align their privacy policies with the GDPR because it's easier to implement global rules rather than enforce them on a country-by-country basis. Meta stated that it plans to appeal this decision which would test "the power of the G.D.P.R. and how aggressively regulators use the law to force companies to change their business practices" (Satariano, 2023). This case represents a monumental step in consumer privacy policy because social media companies have no other option but to adjust their practices or risk losing substantial amounts of revenue from advertising losses and/or regulatory fines.

The battle between Meta and the E.U. is far from over. In May of 2023, Ireland's DPC announced that Meta would have to cease transferring data from European Facebook users to the United States after failing to comply with a 2020 ruling by the European Court of Justice (Satariano, 2023). Meta had failed to ensure that Facebook data sent across the Atlantic was "sufficiently protected from American spy agencies" (Satariano, 2023). As a result, Meta was fined a record $1.3 billion with a five-month grace period before it had to comply. Although this ruling only applies to Facebook, and not Instagram or WhatsApp, Meta believes that restricting the data flow will leave users in some countries without access to some of the shared services they're accustomed to (Satariano, 2023). This ruling takes a specific hit to Meta's ability to practice targeted advertising in European countries. As of now, the United States and the European Union are negotiating a new data agreement, however, there is little information on the progress. If an agreement is not made, Meta might be forced to "delete vast amounts of data about Facebook users in the European Union" which might present unintended technical difficulties (Satariano, 2023). This ruling is the latest in the ongoing struggle for social media companies to adequately protect users' data and represents the potential for data privacy laws, such as the GDPR, to prove very effective.

Case Study Conclusion

The last few years have demonstrated that Meta has taken inadequate measures to protect their user's private data. As a result, consumers are demanding to have control over their data collection, a request that is being supported by legislation, such as the GDPR. The most important takeaway from this case study is that other government entities consider these social media privacy concerns legitimate and have taken action to create and implement legislation, which provides an example of how the United States could react. Although laws such as the GDPR are proving to be an effective means to push Meta and other social media companies to re-engineer their data protection practices for the average adult user, children need to be at the forefront of these discussions and potential regulation and legislation.

Recommended Solutions

In conclusion, the issues of social media, children, and privacy are very complex. Children are vulnerable consumers and are increasingly spending more time on social media platforms engaging in a variety of content. Social media puts children in a vulnerable position to have their personal data collected without their permission, resulting in the potential for great privacy violations. Although the topic of social media and privacy concerns has increased in recent years, children are oftentimes left out of these conversations. This chapter discusses the potential harms of social media and children, and it provides an overview of current regulatory agencies that aim to protect children, as well as current and forthcoming legislation. We also provide a case study and suggest that the United States can look to the GDPR as a model for a data privacy law that holds social media companies accountable for the well-being of their users—although children need to be included.

Moving forward, there are a variety of ways to go about protecting children's data from exploitation via social media. A primary recommendation is for the United States to implement laws and regulations to protect children's privacy on social media platforms. The laws and regulations issued by the FTC and state legislators are insufficient at protecting users' private data because they often fail to place blame on social media companies when rules have been violated. For instance, Section 230 made it so that internet service providers, like Meta, cannot be sued for the content found on their platforms (Ortutay, 2023). Likewise, Facebook was not required to admit any wrongdoing in the Cambridge Analytica scandal if they paid a monetary fine to each of the Facebook users participating in the United States' class action lawsuit (Zialcita, 2019). The precedent that these examples set does not require social media companies to be held accountable for the harm their users experience on their platforms. Thus, since the function and operation of these platforms are controlled by social media companies, the United States should specifically hold them liable for violations of the law.

On a smaller scale, we encourage parents to educate themselves on privacy implications and data use on social media platforms. Additionally, school districts should invest in social media literacy training for their adolescent students to become aware of online dangers. However, to make a greater impact, solutions will need to be sought from those who can create change on a national scale. For instance, age specification plays a crucial role when examining issues related to social media, children, and privacy. Due to the influence of the COPPA, most social media platforms have an age restriction of at least 13 years old to use their services. Nevertheless, when considering most legal jargon, the word "children" is almost always synonymous with the word "minor," such as in Section 230 of the Communications Decency Act. In the United States, the word "minor" refers to anyone under the age of 18. Since these individuals are not considered legal adults, and therefore cannot explicitly consent to have their data collected, advertisers can view children ages 13 to 18 as a loophole in regulations since there isn't a law that directly relates to this age group. Therefore, to resolve this matter, lawmakers should ensure that language regarding age specifications is consistent throughout all advertising regulations related to children.

References

American Bar Association. (2017, March). Advertising in social media. *American Bar Association*. Retrieved April 22, 2023, from https://www.americanbar.org/news/abanews/publications/youraba/2017/march-2017/advertising-in-social-media/

Berry, K., Libin, N., & Seiver, J. D. (2022, March 31). Utah passes consumer privacy law. *Davis Wright Tremaine*. Retrieved April 29, 2023, from https://www.dwt.com/blogs/privacy-security-law-blog/2022/03/utah-consumer-privacy-act

Bloomberg Law. (n.d.). What is the VCDPA and when does it take effect. *Bloomberg Law*. Retrieved April 28, 2023, from https://pro.bloomberglaw.com/brief/what-is-the-vcdpa/

Browne, R. (2023, January 4). Meta fined more than $400 million in Ireland over EU privacy breaches. *CNBC*. Retrieved May 2, 2023, from https://www.cnbc.com/2023/01/04/meta-fined-more-than-400-million-in-ireland-over-eu-privacy-breaches.html

Chen, B. X. (2021, September 21). The battle for digital privacy is reshaping the internet (published 2021). *The New York Times*. Retrieved March 5, 2023, from https://www.nytimes.com/2021/09/16/technology/digital-privacy.html?auth=login-google1tap&login=google1tap

Cornell Law School Legal Information Institute. (n.d.). *Child*. https://www.law.cornell.edu/wex/child

De Veirman, M., Hudders, L., & Nelson, M. R. (2019). What is influencer marketing and how does it target children? A review and direction for future research. *Frontiers in Psychology*, *10*, 498106. https://doi.org/10.3389/fpsyg.2019.02685

Duffy, C. (2022, December 23). Meta agrees to pay $725 million to settle lawsuit over Cambridge Analytica data leak. *CNN*. Retrieved April 30, 2023, from https://www.cnn.com/2022/12/23/tech/meta-cambridge-analytica-settlement/index.html

FindLaw. (2018, August 21). Social media privacy laws. *FindLaw*. Retrieved April 22, 2023, from https://www.findlaw.com/consumer/online-scams/social-media-privacy-laws.html

Fraser, A. (2023, September 17). Congress, it's time to put kids before big tech profits. Pass KOSA. *The Hill*. Retrieved September 20, 2023, from https://thehill.com/opinion/congress-blog/4208638-congress-its-time-to-put-kids-before-big-tech-profits-pass-kosa/

Frenkel, S., & Kang, C. (2018, April 4). Facebook says Cambridge Analytica harvested data of up to 87 million users (published 2018). *The New York Times*. Retrieved April 30, 2023, from https://www.nytimes.com/2018/04/04/technology/mark-zuckerberg-testify-congress.html?auth=login-google1tap&login=google1tap

Frenkel, S., & Rosenberg, M. (2018, March 18). Facebook's role in data misuse sets off storms on two continents (published 2018). *The New York Times*. Retrieved April 29, 2023, from https://www.nytimes.com/2018/03/18/us/cambridge-analytica-facebook-privacy-data.html?smid=url-share

Fung, B. (2019, July 25). Facebook will pay an unprecedented $5 billion penalty over privacy breaches. *CNN*. Retrieved April 30, 2023, from https://www.cnn.com/2019/07/24/tech/facebook-ftc-settlement/index.html

Fung, B. (2023). Senators unveil bipartisan legislation to ban kids under 13 from joining social media platforms, *CNN*, https://www.cnn.com/2023/04/26/tech/senators-social-media-kids-wellness/index.html

Graber, D. (2023, January 18). FOSI | Three reasons social media age restrictions matter. *Family Online Safety Institute*. Retrieved October 1, 2023, from https://www.fosi.org/good-digital-parenting/three-reasons-social-media-age-restrictions-matter

Graff, S., Kunkel, D., & Mermin, S. E. (2012, February). Government can regulate food advertising to children because cognitive research shows that it is inherently misleading. *Health Affairs*, *31*(2), 392–398. ProQuest. https://doi.org/10.1377/hlthaff.2011.0609

Hayes, J. L., Brinson, N. H., Bott, G. J., & Moeller, C. M. (2021, August 1). The influence of consumer–brand relationship on the personalized advertising privacy calculus in social media. *Journal of Interactive Marketing*, *55*(1), 16–30. Science Direct. https://doi.org/10.1016/j.intmar.2021.01.001

Holiday, S., & Brinson, N. H. (2022, April 4). The influence of perceived personalization in TV advertising targeting children on parental advertising mediation: Implications for addressable TV advertising. *Journal of Interactive Advertising*, *22*(1), 75–94. Taylor and Francis Online. https://doi.org/10.1080/15252019.2022.2037029

Jaeger, J. (2023, January 20). A recap of U.S. data privacy laws taking effect in 2023. *JD Supra*. Retrieved April 29, 2023, from https://www.jdsupra.com/legalnews/a-recap-of-u-s-data-privacy-laws-taking-4269754/

Jennings, C. J., & Engel, M. K. (2004, March 2). *Advertising to kids and the FTC: A regulatory retrospective that advises the present* (pp. 1–23). https://www.ftc.gov/sites/default/files/documents/public_statements/advertising-kids-and-ftc-regulatory-retrospective-advises-present/040802adstokids.pdf

Knighton, C. (2022, January 18). Did you know that sometimes it's illegal when marketing to children? *ENX2 Marketing*. Retrieved April 22, 2023, from https://enx2marketing.com/marketing-to-children/

LoMonte, F. (2018, April 15). The law that made Facebook what it is today. *PBS*. Retrieved April 27, 2023, from https://www.pbs.org/newshour/nation/the-law-that-made-facebook-what-it-is-today

Meyer, M., Adkins, V., Yuan, N., Weeks, H. M., Chang, Y. J., & Radesky, J. (2019). Advertising in young children's apps: A content analysis. *Journal of Developmental and Behavioral Pediatrics: JDBP*, *40*(1), 32–39. https://doi.org/10.1097/DBP.0000000000000622

Minc, A. (n.d.). Section 230 of the Communications Decency Act—Minc Law. *Minc Law*. Retrieved April 27, 2023, from https://www.minclaw.com/legal-resource-center/what-is-section-230-of-the-communication-decency-act-cda/

Montgomery, K. C., Chester, J., & Milosevic, T. (2017, November 1). Children's privacy in the big data era: Research opportunities. *Pediatrics*, *140*(2), 1–5. American Academy of Pediatrics. https://doi.org/10.1542/peds.2016-1758O

Moyer, M. W. (2022, March 24). Kids as young as 8 are using social media more than ever, study finds (published 2022). *The New York Times*. Retrieved May 24, 2023, from https://www.nytimes.com/2022/03/24/well/family/child-social-media-use.html

National Archives. (2023, September). 16 CFR part 255—guides concerning use of endorsements and testimonials in advertising. *eCFR*. Retrieved October 1, 2023, from https://www.ecfr.gov/current/title-16/chapter-I/subchapter-B/part-255

Naydonov, A. B., Rodgers, P. J., Margaret, A., & Esquenet, M. A. (2022, January 11). Children's advertising standards for marketers. *The National Law Review*, *13*(116). Retrieved April 26, 2023, from https://www.natlawreview.com/article/caru-s-revised-guidelines-children-s-advertising-what-they-mean-marketers

Ortutay, B. (2023, February 21). What you should know about Section 230, the rule that shaped today's internet. *PBS*. Retrieved April 27, 2023, from https://www.pbs.org/newshour/politics/what-you-should-know-about-section-230-the-rule-that-shaped-todays-internet

Owens, L., Lewis, C., Auty, S., & Buijzen, M. (2013, Fall). Is children's understanding of nontraditional advertising comparable to their understanding of television advertising? *Journal of Public Policy & Marketing*, *32*(2), 195–206. JSTOR. Retrieved May 10, 2023, from https://login.ezproxy.lib.utexas.edu/login?qurl=https://www.jstor.org/stable/43305783

Pew Research Center. (2019, November 15). *Americans and privacy: Concerned, confused and feeling lack of control over their personal information*. Pew Research Center.

Pop, C. (2022, September 27). EU vs US: What are the differences between their data privacy laws? *Endpoint Protector*. Retrieved May 2, 2023, from https://www.endpointprotector.com/blog/eu-vs-us-what-are-the-differences-between-their—data-privacy-laws/

Radesky, J., Reid Chassiakos, Y., Ameenuddin, N., & Navsaria, D. (2020, July). Digital advertising to children. *Pediatrics*, *146*(1), 8. The American Academy of Pediatrics. https://doi.org/10.1542/peds.2020-1681

Rampton, J. (2016, June 1). What rules must advertisers follow when it comes to mobile marketing for kids. *Forbes.com*. Retrieved April 22, 2023, from https://www.forbes.com/sites/johnrampton/2016/06/01/what-rules-must-advertisers-follow-when-it-comes-to-mobile-marketing-for-kids/?sh=5ca1c71b4a29

Satariano, A. (2023a, January 4). Meta's ad practices ruled illegal under E.U. law. *The New York Times*. Retrieved May 2, 2023, from https://www.nytimes.com/2023/01/04/technology/meta-facebook-eu-gdpr.html

Satariano, A. (2023b, May 22). Meta fined $1.3 billion for violating E.U. data privacy rules. *The New York Times*. Retrieved May 25, 2023, from https://www.nytimes.com/2023/05/22/business/meta-facebook-eu-privacy-fine.html

Savage, C. (2023, August 12). Starting next year, child influencers can sue if earnings aren't set aside, says new Illinois law. *AP News*. Retrieved October 17, 2023, from https://apnews.com/article/tiktok-child-influencer-illinois-social-media-f784b4bc52cb75ad1e0d28785993b1c5

Schechner, S. (2021, May 14). Facebook loses bid to block ruling on EU-U.S. data flows. *The Wall Street Journal*. Retrieved May 2, 2023, from https://www.wsj.com/articles/facebook-faces-irish-ruling-on-suspension-of-eu-u-s-data-flows-11620983614

Secure Privacy. (2022, December 15). Comprehensive guide to the colorado privacy act. *Secure Privacy*. Retrieved April 28, 2023, from https://secureprivacy.ai/blog/comprehensive-guide-to-the-colorado-privacy-act

The Securities and Exchange Commission. (2019, July 24). Facebook to pay $100 million for misleading investors about the risks it faced from misuse of user data. *SEC.gov*. Retrieved April 30, 2023, from https://www.sec.gov/news/press-release/2019-140

Snyder, W. (2016). *Ethics in Advertising: Making the case for doing the right thing* (1st ed.). Routledge. https://doi.org/10.4324/9781315641942

State of California Office of the Attorney General. (n.d.). California Consumer Privacy Act (CCPA) | State of California—department of justice—office of the attorney general. *California Department of Justice*. Retrieved April 27, 2023, from https://oag.ca.gov/privacy/ccpa

Stransky, S. G., Zych, T. F., & Knight, T. (2022, December 5). Privacy & cybersecurity update, Connecticut enacts new consumer data privacy law. *Thompson Hine LLP*. Retrieved April 29, 2023, from https://www.thompsonhine.com/insights/connecticut-enacts-new-consumer-data-privacy-law/

US Influencer Marketing Spend (2019–2024) [Updated December 2022]. (n.d.). *Oberlo*. Retrieved October 1, 2023, from https://www.oberlo.com/statistics/influencer-marketing-spend

Vedova, H. (n.d.). Children's online privacy protection rule ("COPPA"). *Federal Trade Commission*. Retrieved April 26, 2023, from https://www.ftc.gov/legal-library/browse/rules/childrens-online-privacy-protection-rule-coppa

Vedova, H. (2013, July 1). Children's online privacy protection rule: A six-step compliance plan for your business. *Federal Trade Commission*. Retrieved April 26, 2023, from https://www.ftc.gov/business-guidance/resources/childrens-online-privacy-protection-rule-six-step-compliance-plan-your-business

Watson, C. (2018, April 11). The key moments from Mark Zuckerberg's testimony to Congress. *The Guardian*. Retrieved May 24, 2023, from https://www.theguardian.com/technology/2018/apr/11/mark-zuckerbergs-testimony-to-congress-the-key-moments

Winston & Strawn LLP. (n.d.). What is social media law? | Winston & Strawn Law Glossary. *Winston & Strawn LLP*. Retrieved April 22, 2023, from https://www.winston.com/en/legal-glossary/social-media-law.html

Wong, J. C. (2019, March 18). The Cambridge Analytica scandal changed the world—but it didn't change Facebook. *The Guardian*. Retrieved April

30, 2023, from https://www.theguardian.com/technology/2019/mar/17/the-cambridge-analytica-scandal-changed-the-world-but-it-didnt-change-facebook

Xie, W., & Karan, K. (2019). Consumers' privacy concern and privacy protection on social network sites in the era of big data: Empirical evidence from college students. *Journal of Interactive Advertising*, *19*(3), 1–15. Taylor & Francis Group. https://doi.org/10.1080/15252019.2019.1651681

Zialcita, P. (2019, October 30). Facebook pays $643000 fine for role in Cambridge Analytica scandal. *NPR*. Retrieved April 30, 2023, from https://www.npr.org/2019/10/30/774749376/facebook-pays-643-000-fine-for-role-in-cambridge-analytica-scandal

INDEX

Note: Page numbers in *italics* indicate a figure and page numbers in **bold** indicate a table on the corresponding page.

Printed and bound by CPI Group (UK) Ltd, Croydon, CR0 4YY
10/07/2024
01017552-0009